PRAISE FOR MARTIN DUGARD AND
KNOCKDOWN

"[A] white-knuckle account of the 1998 Sydney to Hobart yacht race, in which more than one hundred yachts encountered a freak hurricane."
—*Newsweek*

"Suspenseful and compelling. . . . In the tradition of the bestsellers *Into Thin Air* and *A Perfect Storm*."
—*Chattanooga Free Press* (TN)

"Recommended. . . . Dugard is a great storyteller."
—*Library Journal*

"A spell of a tale."
—*Kirkus Reviews*

"Full of its share of action. . . . Dugard probes the nature of adventure and the Australian men and women who seek it."
—*Publishers Weekly*

"All the elements of a great modern adventure tale are here."
—*American Way* (American Airlines magazine)

Also by Martin Dugard

Surviving the Toughest Race on Earth

KNOCKDOWN

THE HARROWING TRUE ACCOUNT OF A YACHT RACE TURNED DEADLY

MARTIN DUGARD

POCKET BOOKS

New York   London   Toronto   Sydney   Singapore

To Calene, who believes

 POCKET BOOKS, a division of Simon & Schuster, Inc.
1230 Avenue of the Americas, New York, NY 10020

ISBN: 0-671-03879-6

First Pocket Books trade paperback printing August 2000

10 9 8 7 6 5 4 3 2 1

POCKET and colophon are registered trademarks of
Simon & Schuster, Inc.

Cover design by Joseph Perez, front cover photo by Ian Mainsbridge/
PPL; back cover photo credits, left to right: Delly Carr/PPL,
Ian Mainsbridge/PPL, Ian Mainsbridge/PPL

Printed in the U.S.A.

ACKNOWLEDGMENTS

There are two men without whom this book could not have been written, Graem Sims and Adrian von Friedberg. Special thanks for all their help.

Also in Australia, thanks to the staff of Inside Sport—Australia, the Royal Australian Navy, the Royal Australian Air Force, Ed Psaltis, the Cruising Yacht Club of Australia, Hugo van Kretschmar, Phil Livingstone, Shane Pashley, Pat Sullivan, Peter Campbell, David Gray, Peter Gearin and family, and Shirley and Heath Sims, for the cricket balls.

In England, thanks to the Royal Ocean Racing Club, Margaret Charles, Anne Goodman.

In Park City, thanks to Sean and Al Railton, for the perspective.

In San Francisco, thanks to Mark Rudiger.

In Orange County, thanks to Mach Two and the Rose, Tom and Norene Danley, Craig Stutzman, Eric and Lynne Nachtrieb, Forrest Ropp, Gary Gosper and Chuck Wright, Brian Myers, Bill and Brigitte Otto, Groover Bentley, Rich and Laura Caruso. A special thanks to Ted Newland for words of motivation and focus.

In Texas, to Cal Johnson.

To Kay Yerkovich, you have a great gift.

In Los Angeles, thanks to Dick Shepherd at the Artists Agency, the man who knows everyone. And to Bill Baker, who is a true friend.

In New York, thanks to Jason Kaufman for the edit, Scott Waxman for the representation, and Tris Coburn for being on the same wavelength.

And, as always, to Calene, Devin, Connor, and Liam, thanks for enduring the writing process with such love and understanding.

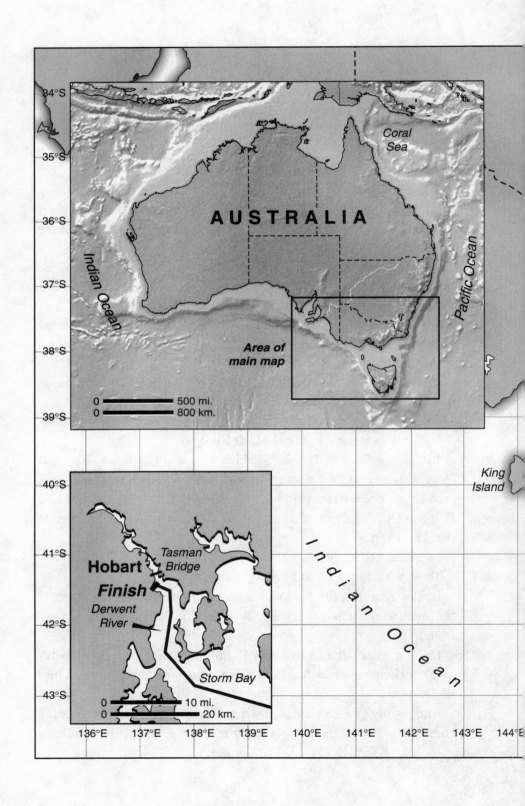

34°S
35°S
36°S
37°S
38°S
39°S
40°S
41°S
42°S
43°S

Coral
Sea

AUSTRALIA

Indian Ocean

Pacific Ocean

Area of
main map

0 ——— 500 mi.
0 ——— 800 km.

King
Island

Indian Ocean

Hobart
Tasman
Bridge
Finish
Derwent
River

Storm Bay

0 ——— 10 mi.
0 ——— 20 km.

136°E   137°E   138°E   139°E   140°E   141°E   142°E   143°E   144°E

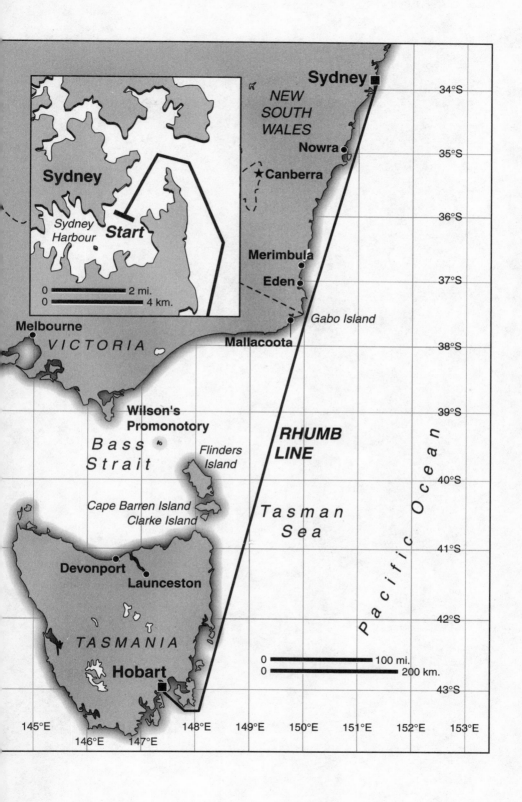

Sydney

NEW
SOUTH
WALES

★ Canberra

Nowra

Merimbula

Eden

Gabo Island

Mallacoota

Sydney

Sydney
Harbour

Start

0   2 mi.

0   4 km.

Melbourne

V I C T O R I A

Wilson's
Promonotory

B a s s
S t r a i t

Flinders
Island

RHUMB
LINE

Cape Barren Island
Clarke Island

T a s m a n
S e a

P a c i f i c   O c e a n

Devonport

Launceston

T A S M A N I A

Hobart

0   100 mi.

0   200 km.

34°S

35°S

36°S

37°S

38°S

39°S

40°S

41°S

42°S

43°S

145°E   146°E   147°E   148°E   149°E   150°E   151°E   152°E   153°E

"—and men go forth, and admire lofty mountains and broad seas, and roaring torrents, and the course of the stars, and forget their own selves in doing so."

—Petrarch, 1336

KNOCKDOWN

PORTSMOUTH

"The Hell on High Water" is what sailors call the Bass Strait. It's a siren, they add. Unpredictable. Demanding. Withholding. Bitchy. Every year men finish the Sydney to Hobart Yacht Race and state emphatically they'll never challenge the Bass Strait again. It's a rare admission of weakness for an Australian sailor, and the act is usually accomplished with eyes lowered, staring into a beer during that postrace celebration in Hobart known as A Quiet Little Drink—which is anything but quiet. They justify the fear with harrowing stories of rogue waves and monster winds, of being scared like they've never known possible.

But every year the siren calls them back. Some men put off telling their wives they'll be racing, swearing until Christmas Eve that this is the year they stay home. Most likely, they mean it. But every year they cave. Come Boxing Day (the day after Christmas), they're tacking out of Sydney Harbor and barreling south to Hobart.

Most years the Bass Strait lies dormant, allowing the fleet a calm passage—*calm* being a relative term describing winds of

1

forty knots—almost fifty miles per hour. These are the years that make men forget the time in the 1950s when a blizzard struck the fleet and sailors struggled to find something—anything—on board resembling a snow shovel to dig out their cockpits. Or even 1993, when a storm front dropped in from nowhere blowing Force 10— that is, with winds of fifty-five miles per hour. The calm years are why the novice sailors tell their loved ones nothing can go wrong during Sydney to Hobart. Why, they'll say, only a few people have been killed—and none because their boat sank. And even that guy who fell overboard in 1993 and spent five hours in the water was rescued. Everything'll be okay. It's just sailing.

"Everyone gets to Hobart and comments how they beat the Bass Strait," notes three-time Sydney to Hobart vet Adrian von Friedberg. "But deep inside they know the Strait allowed them to win."

One look at a world map shows the deceptively simple race course. Sydney sits on the southeast corner of the huge island nation. Directly south of the Australian mainland, separated by a two-hundred-mile sea known as the Bass Strait, is another section of Australia's Commonwealth, a smaller island called Tasmania. Hobart is the capital of Tasmania.

Sydney to Hobart is a 735-mile dose of nonstop punishment down Australia's east coast, across the treacherous miles of the Bass Strait, then down the length of Tasmania. The combination of wind and waves and currents and freak weather is unparalleled in sailing competition around the world. And unlike other races, such as Whitbread or Around Alone, Syd-Hob sailors don't have the option of steering away from bad weather. It's a race. An Australian race. The winning sailor stays the rhumb line from Sydney straight to Hobart, atrocious weather or no. "This has the reputation of being the toughest race in the world," George Snow, owner of the maxi *Brindabella*, states flatly, "and it is."

The worldwide sailing community refer to "The Hobart" as their Everest and agree no race is more difficult on men and boats. The race starts Boxing Day, with boats in the fleet ranging in length from eighty feet (the maxis) on down to thirty. Unlike in other major competitions, Syd-Hob's roster is loaded with individuals in rather innocuous occupations. Engineers, plumbers, insurance agents, and factory foremen are as likely to compete as professional sailors. This diversity gives the event an everyman feel. And while prerace conversations are usually filled with backslapping and well wishings, the subtext is apprehension to the point of horror. Every man in the fleet fears that moment when the mainland is left behind and his sailboat plunges into the Bass Strait breach.

But fears will be hidden and the challenge attacked with zest. This Australian bent toward the extreme owes its origins to history. When Captain Arthur Phillip of the Royal Navy set sail with the First Fleet on May 13, 1787, from Portsmouth, England, his charter was not to discover a new world, but to establish a convict settlement. He was bound for an unexplored island long familiar to Malay and Chinese sailors for its incredibly strong wind systems. The island was called Australia and had been claimed for England by Captain James Cook in 1770. His ship, HMS *Endeavour*, anchored first in a place known as Botany Bay, a sandy locale unprotected from the wind. Searching for fresh water and better shelter, Cook sailed north, finding by accident the greatest natural harbor in the world. "This is a place," Cook wrote in his journal upon discovering what would later be known as Sydney Harbor, "where a thousand ships can anchor in peace."

The refuge was shaped roughly like a compressed horseshoe. The entrance was a mile wide, with basalt cliffs on either side rising several hundred awesome feet straight out of the Pacific. These harbor vanguards were dubbed the North Head and South Head. Swells marching westward without landfall for thousands of miles smacked headlong into the Heads, bouncing off with a force that made for massive waves on the outside of the harbor, but leaving smooth seas inside.

The deepest reaches of the horseshoe, on the harbor's southern shores, were the most tranquil of all. Rivers, like tentacles, squiggled inland. Large coves formed harbors within the harbor. The water was clear, no waves lapped the sandy beaches, and rolling hills just inland provided another barrier from coastal winds. The tranquillity of these coves—eventually given such names as Rushcutter's Bay, Double Bay, Rose Bay—would one day make them Sydney's prime real estate. Forests of trees would be planted, stately brick homes wedged onto the hills, cricket pitches laid out in public parks, and a road from Rushcutter's Bay to the South Head paved.

It would be the most beautiful road in all Sydney, affording a glimpse of the harbor and its countless sailboats as the well-traveled route slowly rose from water level to the South Head's peak high above the sea. Drivers would feel the wind get stronger with every passing mile, so that when they stepped from their cars and gingerly hiked to the edge of the South Head and peered so very far down into the Pacific, their hair would be plastered back on their heads and their cheeks would flush. And they would comment to themselves, or to the person they might be alongside, how strong the wind was compared with docile Rushcutter's Bay that they had left just moments before. But the sightseers would stand atop the South Head and stare into the sea for minutes and sometimes hours, becoming oblivious to the wind. The roil of the sea would fascinate and mesmerize and even hypnotize. When they finally walked back to their cars, they would feel strangely full of life, as mankind is wont to do when encountering the ocean.

But all that was two centuries off. When Phillip landed on January 27, 1788, his fleet included eleven ships carrying 759 convicts. These would be the forebears of today's Australian population. Through a policy known as transportation, thousands more convicts were banished there between 1788 and 1849.

Transportation left a permanent mark on Australia. It is a nation with an underdog's mentality—Britain's naughty stepchild—and a decidedly egalitarian societal spin. "Australia's a place where a plumber and a thoracic surgeon are comfortable spending a day sailing," notes one Sydney resident. For sailing is not just a rich man's sport in Australia. With the exception of the aborigines, the entire nation's ancestry came by ship, and Australians share an infatuation with the sea. It is one of the few places on the globe where blue-collar workers unwind from a hectic week by hoisting a spinnaker and running downwind.

The modern Australian sailor is a hybrid seen nowhere else on the planet, a combination of that oceangoing bent with the underdog mentality. Australian seamen are competitive to a fault, unwilling to back down in the face of danger, inclined constantly to prove personal worthiness, and bonded to their crew—their mates—by an overwhelming sense of loyalty. The *Sydney Daily Mirror*, reporting on a 1948 race in Sydney Harbor, spoke of this phenomenon. After two eighteen-foot skiffs collided at the finish of a race "with a bone-jarring thud . . . fifteen men battled it out with fists in shallow water and neither crew asked for nor gave quarter while a single man remained on his feet to continue the brawl."

The words are without irony or titillation, as if competition must always be taken to its logical extreme. That's the Australian way. It goes for women as well as men.

It's no surprise that Sydney is known now as the City of Sails. The moniker is embodied in the profile of the city's famous white-shelled opera house—a fleet of spinnakers up, running downwind. It's also no surprise that Australians are arguably the best sailors in the world today, having swiped bragging rights from the United States in 1983 by winning the America's Cup.

● ● ●

Portsmouth, England, the bustling port that saw the first British ships set sail for Australia, is from where, in 1998, top British sailor Glyn Charles sets out to spend December sailing in Sydney. He is a man on the verge of greatness. In 1985, penniless and sleeping in his yellow Ford van, sailing bum Charles shocked the staid British racing establishment by winning the Laser-class national championships. Since, Charles's career has been pocked with crushing defeats to rival Lawrie Smith at the 1988 and 1992 Olympic Trials (adding insult to injury, Smith poached Charles's crew just before the Trials), but has otherwise been meteoric. He has skippered everything from the one-man Laser to open-ocean Admiral's Cup yachts.

After the near misses, Charles defeated Smith to make the British team for the Atlanta Games in 1996. He was eleventh there. Experts predict he will win the gold medal in 2000, at Sydney.

Glyn is flying to Australia to prepare. Practice makes perfect. Before he sees Portsmouth again, Glyn wants to know every current, every wind variable, in Sydney Harbor. He will know how the water gets choppy under the Harbor Bridge and how Shark Island can be a precarious spot if the tide is running out. Glyn will fill his head with local knowledge until he is as good as the Aussies—no, better—on their home course. Glyn will do this because he dreams of winning an Olympic gold medal. Has dreamed of it, in fact, since he was eight. He used to pen the dream on his school satchel, just to let everyone know who he was and where he was going. The strange thing is that Glyn wasn't even a sailor then. Just a boy born in Wales who dreamed of racing the seas. He'd find a way to fill in the blanks.

Now thirty-three, Glyn Charles has seen his childhood dream manifest itself into more adult ambitions and emotions—arrival, success, status. A handsome, confident man with a quick wit and thick black hair hinting at recession, Glyn enjoys the enigmatic comment people use to describe him, that he's hard to like, but harder to dislike. Glyn views himself as the perpetual underdog. Maybe that comes from losing his father twice, at a young age. First, at sixteen, through divorce. Then, after his father had moved away to live in Andorra, through death. A fall off a ladder killed the elder Charles when Glyn was just nineteen.

Glyn ignores long odds, preferring to trust skill and perseverance to ultimately triumph in any situation. In the 1996 Olympic Trials, he sailed miserably in his first heat. To unseat Lawrie Smith and make the Olympic squad, Charles would have to win every remaining heat. And so he did.

Some call him a perfectionist. "An exciting man to share a boat with—enthusiastic, focused, committed—but unlikely to have endless patience," John Derbyshire, British Olympic manager, notes of Glyn. That impatience, Derbyshire quickly adds, is "always offset by his charm and integrity."

Glyn's Olympic coach, Rod Carr, is even more effusive, calling Glyn "one of the outstanding yachtsmen of his generation."

The plan is to fly to Sydney with his girlfriend, Annie. He'll spend time sailing, help coach an Olympic developmental group, then they'll fly home for Christmas. Glyn doesn't know yet that a friend in Australia, Steve Kulmar, will ask him to join the crew of a boat named *Sword of Orion* for the Sydney to Hobart race. It will be Glyn's first Syd-Hob, and an opportunity to establish a new level of personal credibility within the sailing world.

Glyn doesn't know that he will call his mother two days before Christmas, asking if she'd mind terribly celebrating alone, with the proviso he'd be home just after New Year's.

And Glyn Charles will set sail for Hobart aboard *Sword of Orion*, wholly unaware of a speech given in 1982. Boat designer Alan Payne, addressing the Royal Ocean Racing Club of Australia, had warned of the day a hurricane would hit the Sydney to Hobart. His concern was that modern racing boats, built of lightweight composite materials to insure greater speed, lacked the structural integrity to withstand such a big blow. And a storm of one hundred knots or more, Payne guaranteed, would most definitely strike someday. "It might take a hundred years, but it's going to happen."

Glyn Charles doesn't know it, but Payne's prediction will come true in 1998. A storm of biblical proportions will rock the fleet. It will be the worst sailing disaster in history, topping England's 1979

Fastnet race (in an eerie coincidence, both the 1979 Fastnet and 1998 Syd-Hob were celebrating their fifty-fourth anniversary), with winds and seas of a magnitude almost twice what Fastnet endured. "It only blew there for five hours," says Andrew Buckland, who raced the 1979 Fastnet and 1998 Syd-Hob. "During Sydney to Hobart, it blew for two straight days."

Scores of boats will be destroyed or abandoned to the sea, tossed about like so many toys in a bathtub by mind-boggling conditions: hundred-plus mile per hour winds and waves cresting a hundred feet in the air. There will be moments of inconceivable heroism and courage and cowardice. Grown men will weep, among them billionaire Larry Ellison, owner of Oracle Corporation and skipper of *Sayonara*. The man once described as having a "godlike" charismatic presence will face reporters after the storm. His trademark bluster will be replaced by the persona of a man who has confronted someone or something far greater than himself—and been badly beaten. "Racing is meant to be difficult, yes. Dangerous, no. Life-threatening, definitely not. I wouldn't go out there again if I lived to be a thousand years."

Above all, it will be a disaster like all disasters involving men who chase adventure—a brutal confirmation that the elements can flick mankind off the map, giving no measure for expertise or size of bank account. Questions about motivation obviously follow.

Many men will die in the Bass Strait.

What Glyn Charles can't possibly know is that he will be one of them. His sailing dreams will be left in the Bass Strait. He will never return to Portsmouth.

ONE

BLUE CHRISTMAS

We're the ones who wear the notion, the notion deep inside,
that it ain't no sin to be glad you're alive.

—Bruce Springsteen, "Badlands"

Blue-water sailors are adventurers. Their opponent and lover is a fluid, ever-changing, conniving, aggressive sea, but they would rather be pushing themselves and their boats in wet and miserable situations on the high seas than be anywhere else. Veteran blue-water sailors will tell you in all humility that what they do is not dangerous, but they know in their heart of hearts that things can go terribly wrong in a matter of seconds—decks buckling and ropes cutting off fingers and men tossed overboard with a single wave's crash. Stepping on dry land again is intoxicating, however, and a passage's pains are quickly forgotten. And soon the blue-water sailor is sitting in his office again, staring out the window toward a squall line on an otherwise perfect day, dangerous notions percolating.

Ed Psaltis is such a man. Christmas, to Ed Psaltis, is not a day of celebration, but a time of stomach-cramping nerves and nonstop errand-running. He comes from a family of Australian blue-water sailors, and Sydney to Hobart starts the day after Christmas. The peripheral symbols—Santa, Rudolph, maids-a-milking—are heartwarming traditions to be endured, so that the true meaning of Christmas—Sydney to Hobart—can get under way. Christmas is a prelude to battle.

Christmas is when the crew gathers at the work yard next to the Cruising Yacht Club of Australia and lowers the boat back in the water. It's been up on slips to dry for a few days because a dry boat is lighter and faster than a boat whose laminated molecules are saturated.

Then it's a walk along the jammed CYCA patio, from where competitors will set out, eyeballing the competition and pretending not to be nervous. Pretending not to think that tomorrow they'll will kiss their spouses good-bye, try not to let their crying children tug too much at their heartstrings, and sail off for Hobart. With luck, they'll get there in about three days. With luck and skill, they'll get there first.

Getting there first is Ed's greatest dream.

Ed and Sue Psaltis remark to each other how someday things'll be different. How someday they'll relax on Christmas and maybe sing a few carols while picking up scraps of wrapping paper and discarded bows. But though Ed means all those sentiments as he mumbles them—even kisses Sue with open lips when she gazes straight at him and says he's the best thing that ever happened to her—Ed's spending a quiet Christmas at home is at least three decades away. They both know that. Racing the Sydney to Hobart is what he's about. It's how he has known Christmas since his father raced the first of his nineteen Hobarts thirty years ago. It's what, given the choice, Ed Psaltis will do until he retires from the sport at a ripe old age.

And Ed Psaltis, like his father before him, is not just a blue-water sailor, but a blue-water skipper. Principal helmsman. The man. The *Midnight Rambler* (official name: *Australian Financial*

Review—Midnight Rambler, after a sponsor) is Ed Psaltis's boat. He is thirty-eight, with sixteen Syd-Hobs to his credit, including the gale of 1993. He'd have an even twenty if it weren't for the occasional year off during college, and that time of personal crisis.

If Ed were a movie star he would be Kevin Costner, circa *Field of Dreams,* or a young Jimmy Stewart—square-shouldered, unimpressed with himself, given to describing something as "neat." His father devoted himself to sailing at a time when Australian sailing meant being a real man: hemp ropes, bare chests, knee-length khaki campaign shorts, deck shoes sometimes, and bare feet more often. Sailing was primal. Sailing was innate. A skipper—and Bill was the sort of decisive man of the sea lesser men dreamed of becoming—was king, mentor, lord, alpha male.

But Ed is one of the mates, a quiet man who doesn't like to pull rank on board, but will when necessary. His sailing prowess makes him a natural skipper, and his business prowess has made him a partner in a downtown Sydney accounting firm. As with Bill, a family cruise is Ed's idea of relaxation. Benjamin and Matthew, four and two, have already seen Sydney Harbor on Daddy's boat.

Another form of relaxation for Ed is reading books about men he considers "real" adventurers—mountain climbers, explorers, single-handed circumnavigators. One suspects Ed sits in his twenty-third-floor office in Sydney's MMI Centre and stares out the window toward the harbor, dreaming of the day he can quit accounting and chase adventure full-time. Maybe he would sail around the world, trade in the pinstripes for the helm of a Whitbread boat. What a notion . . . what an utterly dangerous notion . . .

But that's the nature of adventure. Dangerous notions. It's a gift to be born a natural adventurer. It's genetic, with one brother getting the adventure gene and another bestowed philately. Like any gift, the possessor has an obligation to use the gift to its fullest. In another time, Ed Psaltis might have been Bass or Flinders, the two men who charted the Bass Strait. Or even John Hanning Speke, the British explorer who discovered Lake Victoria and its connection to the Nile. But the gift of adventure sometimes means being perceived as selfish or silly, and perhaps it's no symbolic mistake that Speke's austere memorial in London's Hyde Park abuts a statue of Peter Pan. Often mistaken as a symbol of eternal youth, Pan is actually a symbol of adventure. A shadow motif in J. M. Barrie's story hints at the grounding effects of reality, mortality.

Blue-water sailors live with that shadow. Most are average guys with full-time jobs. The corporate side of their personalities dictates obedience forty hours or more per week. The sailing side of their personalities breaks loose, and their code is one of self-reliance: personal responsibility for all actions, as little centralized authority as possible.

Most people have a hard time understanding blue-water sailors. Such as a Sydney television personality who once asked CYCA commodore Hugo van Kretschmar to specify who makes decisions during the Sydney to Hobart. "Well . . . no one," he says as if she's daft.

"No one makes decisions? No one's in charge?"

"Of course, someone's in charge."

"Then who is it?"

The interviewer believes she has van Kretschmar cornered, but he sputters because the concept of self-determination is so foreign to this woman. How to tell the nonsailor that once a boat is at sea, no one on land can possibly exert control? Only the skipper has control at sea. And his control is more ponderous, contentious. He's playing chess with the gods out there, with his life and the lives of his men the tariff.

There was a moment—and though he was only ten years old, Ed describes it vividly still, using words like *freedom* and *excitement*—sailing island to island across the Mediterranean on a family vacation, where Ed first dreamed of winning Sydney to Hobart. His father had set the course, trimmed the sails, then gone below for a rest. Ed was at the helm, gliding with a following wind through waters azure and bottomless. Arthur, three years younger, sat on the rail. What would it be like, young Ed thought, to know this same excitement and freedom as you made the turn up the Derwent River to cross the finish line first for Syd-Hob?

The notion stuck, and like Glyn Charles writing the dream of Olympic gold on his book satchel, Ed Psaltis told every kid in school that he would someday win the Syd-Hob.

Six years later, Ed raced blue water for the first time. It was with his father, Bill, in the *Meltemi*, heading north up the coast of Australia. "It was blowing hard from the south and the forty-five-footer we were on had all her gear up, including bib spinnaker. The feeling of power as that big boat carved the sea at that impressive speed remains with me today," Ed will say in his calm, even voice. "It was magical."

But though Ed was a natural sailor, Bill wouldn't allow him to race Syd-Hob until he was eighteen. This frustrated Ed, infuriated him. Why, he would scream at Bill, can't I race? You let me do all those other races on *Meltemi*. I'm better than half your crew.

Bill would stand tall in that imposing way of his and listen until Ed was through. Not until you're eighteen, he'd repeat quietly. Then he'd walk off without another word, leaving Ed to fume about the injustice.

Not until much later did Ed learn that Bill was protecting him. The Syd-Hob weather could physically stun you. One time a crew member aboard a boat from Queensland was so overwhelmed that he slipped into catatonia, not speaking from the moment the boat entered the Bass Strait until it docked in Hobart two days later. Subject a boy to that too soon, and he might become too scared to try ever again. Worse, what if a pressure situation came up? An immature sailor was more likely to make the wrong—potentially fatal—choice. No, Syd-Hob was no place for a young sailor—especially one's own son.

That cautious notion has been proven again and again since the first time the race was contested. It was 1945 when a loose group of sailors hit upon the idea of racing across the Bass Strait to Hobart. World War II had just ended. The Cruising Yacht Club of Australia, the workingman's answer (the CYCA's charter was to bring sailing to the masses) to the Royal Yachting Squadron and Royal Ocean Racing Club, had just opened in Rushcutter's Bay. Nine sailors sat in the wood-paneled bar one July afternoon, drinking tap beer and relating stories about where each planned to sail for the Christmas holiday. The subject soon shifted from leisurely vacation planning to a discussion of who had the fastest boat. Things got heated. Challenges were issued. It was resolved that a race was in order.

A race to Hobart.

The following paragraph ran in an Australian yachting magazine in October 1945: "Yacht race to Tasmania: It is expected that an ocean yacht race may take place from Sydney to Hobart, probably starting on December 26, 1945. Yachtsmen desirous of competing should contact Vice-President Mr. P Luke, 62 Castlereagh Street, Sydney, for information. Entries close December 1, 1945."

Their boats were heavy cruising yachts with deep keels instead of true ocean racers, but nine skippers sailed that first Syd-Hob. One of the nine starters was a fifty-two-footer named, in a moment of midwar patriotism, the *Winston Churchill*. Huon-pine planking, copper nails, cloth sails. Hauled up from the water two days before to let the hull dry, then a hull polish of Johnson's floor wax to help her slip through the water faster. Built in 1942 by Tasman shipwright Percy Coverdale, *Winston Churchill* was considered the finest yacht in all Australia. Legend has it that her namesake even gave his blessing to her moniker on a postwar trip to Australia.

Overlooked in the prerace hoopla was *Rani*, a thirty-four-footer skippered by John Illingworth of the Royal Navy. *Rani* was also made of Huon-pine planks, pounded into the frame with copper nails. Her sails were hand-stitched cotton. All ropes were Indian hemp. The mast was Oregon pine, the rigging was cast iron, and the bilge pump was a pair of sailors clutching a tin bucket and frying pan. The crew wore Royal Australian Navy gear, mostly cotton impregnated with wax.

Illingworth was taking the Syd-Hob challenge seriously, having spent the months beforehand visiting Australia's south coast and speaking with fishermen about the winds and currents of the Bass Strait. He also developed friendships at Sydney's local weather bureau to learn more about weather patterns over Eastern Australia and Tasmania.

But all that knowledge went missing. The Bass Strait didn't take kindly to the event, heaving a gale at the fleet. Boats were scattered. *Rani* went missing. In an era before radios were aboard racing boats, there was no way to inquire about her location or the condition of the crew. All that was clear was that she had left Sydney with the standard issue of navigational aids: paper charts, coastal guides, a compass for steering, and a sextant for determining position. The CYCA gave her up as lost. It had been a major blunder allowing such a small boat to race across the Bass Strait.

But five days after the storm began, *Rani* suddenly sailed up the Derwent River into Hobart. This greatly amazed the CYCA welcoming committee at the dock for two reasons: first, *Rani* had been given up; and second, no one else had yet finished. Little *Rani* had won the first Syd-Hob in six days, fourteen hours, and twenty-two minutes. It's still the slowest winning finish in race history, but henceforth, the first boat across the finish line would receive the Illingworth Trophy. *Rani* also won on handicap that year, the first of only four boats in Syd-Hob history to do so. *Winston Churchill* finished third.

As with all events clouded in near-death and calamity, a public fascination mushroomed. Casual sailors were initially petrified of the event, and the number of entrants grew slowly over the next ten years. But this proved a blessing, as the men racing Syd-Hob became seen as the elites of Sydney sailing. This gave the race a certain macho heft. Sydney to Hobart in 1940s Australia was as big and adventurous as the moon shots of 1960s astronauts in America.

The sailors were heroes, off to tempt fate and prove themselves. And like astronauts, once their craft was launched, there was no way off. "The Race That's Too Tough," banner headlines would scream. Or "Test of Yachts and Men."

Over time, Sydney to Hobart became a tradition in Australia, one so beloved the start is broadcast on national television. And thus it became a rite of passage for Australian men. Nonsailors try to wiggle onto a crew at least once in their lifetime. Many pay. In Australia, it's important to say you've sailed Sydney to Hobart. Just once. Sure. But you did it. Definitely a feat worth bragging to your mates about. "It's a disease, not a yacht race," the *Sydney Daily Telegraph* once wrote.

For all the bravery and skill a Hobart requires, the race was perceived as nothing more than an Australian peculiarity until tragedy struck the 1979 Fastnet, halfway around the world. Named for Fastnet Rock, a lighthouse off Ireland's southern coast marking the British race's turnaround point, the Fastnet stood alone atop the blue-water sailing world at the time. No other race held more status. Winning Fastnet was to win sailing's Super Bowl. Starting from the Isle of Wight (off Portsmouth), the fleet sailed into the wind along the southern coast of England and across the tempestuous Irish Sea. After rounding the lighthouse, the race doubled back to finish in Portsmouth. As in many blue-water races the fleet ranged from twenty-eight-footers all the way to the seventy-nine-foot maxi (extremely long sailboats with oversize sails, capable of great speeds) *Kialoa.* Experience levels ran the gamut from defending America's Cup champions such as Ted Turner on down to London accountants with only a concept of how the human body responds to the rolling of the ocean; of how a man can puke until his nostrils sting of bile and his face is soaked from the splatter. And how the nausea of total seasickness is actually paralyzing.

At 1:30 P.M. on Saturday, August 11, a Royal Yacht Squadron cannon sent the Fastnet fleet on their way. Three hundred and three boats set off, the largest number in race history. Every competitor was aware that the Irish Sea was capable of boat-breaking wind and waves. They knew of the 1931 race, where a gale had swept one sailor overboard. The 1957 race saw only twelve of the forty-one starters finish. The waves, described one sailor, were "high-breaking mountains of water."

Bad as all that, the 1979 Fastnet got far worse. A Force 10 storm born in the Great Lakes region of North America spun its way across the Atlantic in just four days. Somehow it eluded the gaze of forecasters until descending upon and wrecking the fleet their third night out. The wind took on a banshee's keen that was a fright all to itself. Fifteen sailors died, whether by hypothermia after getting tossed into the frigid North Atlantic or by drowning. Boats were knocked flat (a "knockdown") by thirty-foot waves. Some were rolled all the way over and dismasted, crew trapped in the floating coffin waiting for another wave to roll them back over before the air pocket turned foul. Horror stories, such as men unclipping their lifelines by accident then getting washed overboard, or sons witnessing their fathers getting swept away, never to be seen again, came out in the postrace inquiry. "You'd just sit there on deck in the total darkness," one survivor said, "listening to that big freight-train sound of waves coming to get you. That is, without a doubt, the scariest thing I've ever heard."

The bulk of deaths were preventable. Many crews didn't have proper life rafts or survival gear. Amazingly, given the cold climate, many sailors didn't even wear thermal underwear, thus inviting hypothermia. Some wore cotton tracksuits under their foul-weather gear, mindless that cotton is infamous for sucking heat from the body when wet.

As some sort of absurd footnote, a competitive race-within-the-race occurred even as tragedy raged. Fastnet was the concluding race of the biannual Admiral's Cup Series, a proving ground for top sailing nations such as England, Ireland, the United States, Australia, and Italy. Australia had not won the Admiral's Cup since 1967, but was in contention as Fastnet got under way. The Australian syndicate was led by a hard-boiled former rugby star, Syd Fischer, on board his boat *Ragamuffin*. A second Australian entry was *Police Car*. While other boats were floundering, running away from the storm, or seeking a sheltering port, *Police Car* pressed on. The crew said it was a gravelly voice booming over the radio that inspired them. The voice was Fischer's, repeating a single refrain over and over and over: "Don't give up, Australia. Keep on going. Never give up."

Police Car, and Australia, won the Admiral's Cup that year. The America's Cup came to Australia four years later. And though no proclamation was ever issued, a sea change occurred at the 1979 Fastnet. No longer would the sons of transportation be second-best to England. That day was gone. And along with the acknowledgment that Australia's sailors were of a more rugged breed came the equally unspoken awareness that their blue-water race was tougher, as well. The conditions descending upon Fastnet were atrocious, yes, but seen regularly at Sydney to Hobart. And while both races were peopled with elite blue-water sailors and adventure-seeking locals, in 1979 storms like Fastnet's had yet to cause loss of life at Sydney to Hobart. The English sailor encountered such conditions because it was a fluke. Australian sailors encounter such conditions because they have no choice—their nation borders the Bass Strait. After 1979, Sydney to Hobart became the standard by which blue-water races were measured—the toughest race on earth.

• • •

Ed and Sue start Boxing Day with a cup of coffee. They sit on opposite sides of the kitchen table. Christmas wrappings and unwrapped presents still lie under the tree. With the boys asleep upstairs, it will be their last quiet moment for a week. Ed is having a hard time sitting still, what with all the tasks to perform—what if I forget something?—but calms himself. Plenty of time for action. Now is a time to relax, be in the moment.

They sip the coffee, make small talk, avoid the obvious. As frayed and disassembled as Ed feels, a warm jolt runs through his body as he glances over at Sue. How he loves her. What's not to love? Smart, athletic, blond, with a "bubbly"—that's the word Ed uses to describe Sue when she's not around—personality that complements his perpetually calm outlook. He's devoted to her, and she to him.

Sue was a nurse at a Sydney hospital when they met. A novice sailor from the CYCA named John Whitfeld, eager to try his hand at blue water, wangled a weekend sail on the boat Ed owned at the time, *Nuzulu*. Ed and John got talking during the sail, one thing led to another, and soon John was introducing Ed to his sister, Sue. When Ed and Sue got married in 1993, Arthur Psaltis, John Whitfeld, and Ed's childhood friend Michael Bencsik were the groomsmen. When Benjamin was born a year later, the godfather was Ed's sailing buddy and *Nuzulu* co-owner, Bob Thomas.

All those men will be aboard *Midnight Rambler* when it sails from the CYCA dock at eleven this morning. If anyone has a reason to be worried, it's Sue, who stands to lose a husband, brother, brother-in-law, and the godfather of her first son if bad things happen.

There was a time when Sue allayed her worries by flying to Hobart to meet Ed and the guys at the finish. That way she was surrounded by the wives of other sailors in an impromptu support group that made the wait more bearable. But the trip isn't really practical with young children. Sue knows what many wives don't—that Hobart on New Year's Eve is drunken sailors braying about their Bass Strait crossing. The scene at the airport the next morning is even more comical, with sailors still wearing the same clothes from the night before, apologizing to other sailors or other crews for a slight on the water during the race, or in a bar the night before. "I was drunk," they'll say, which explains away almost any indiscretion in beer-loving Australia.

So Sue stays home and quietly prays that Ed returns in one

piece. She won't tell the boys her fears, though Ben is in tune with her moods and will sense it anyway. She'll calm herself twice a day by calling Bill or the CYCA to make sure Ed's checked in during the two daily mandatory radio skeds—or "scheduled" location checks. In alphabetical order, boats report their precise latitude and longitude at 3:05 A.M. and 2:05 P.M. It's illegal, but a skipper will sometimes remain quiet during a sked if he's attempting some aggressive racing maneuver. This keeps other boats from knowing his location. If a boat misses two skeds, however, it's presumed lost. A search party is sent out. Ed has never missed one sked, let alone two, though there's always a first time with the Bass Strait.

Ed and Sue chat about the ship's gear list—has anything been left off? This evolves into a discussion on how the boys will react with Ed gone. It's a tender subject, one they're just learning to deal with. Little Matthew doesn't mind so much; he's too young to know what's going on. But Benjamin is at the age where he needs Ed. He mopes when Ed leaves for even a routine business trip. Daddy going off for a week on his boat will be really tough.

Don't worry about it, Sue tells Ed. Ben will be fine. Just make sure you come back in one piece.

Ed studies Sue as she prattles on about what she and the boys will do while he's gone. He's not a worrying man, but at the prerace skippers' briefing, race meteorologists warned crews that a low-pressure system might be developing in the Bass Strait, meaning bad weather was possible.

Ed doesn't think about dying—even if he did, he wouldn't share those ruminations with Sue—but anytime there's a chance that the weather will get big, he wonders if his passion is worth all the worry it causes her. Whether or not *Midnight Rambler* sails is Ed's choice. Fundamental Rule 4 of the International Rules of Sailing states: "A boat is solely responsible for deciding whether or not to start or to continue racing . . ." *Boat* here is synonymous with *skipper*.

Ed glances at his watch. It's fifteen minutes from his Lane Cove

The crew is assembled by Winning and his friend John "Steamer" Stanley, fifty-one, who is also the shipwright responsible for *Winston Churchill*'s overhaul. The crew are all mostly old friends. All but two know the sea with a sixth sense of lifelong sailors. Bruce Gould has thirty-one Syd-Hobs under his belt. Jim Lawler has fifteen. John Dean was a former commodore of the Vaucluse Amateur Sailing Club. Mike Bannister, a self-employed truck driver, is a well-known local sailor. John Gibson is a lawyer.

But life is not about sailing, and so the crew's bonds run much deeper. Winning, Dean, and Bannister grew up together, went to college together. In the 1960s they were the top sailors on Sydney Harbor, regularly winning joint and individual sailing titles.

Only nineteen-year-old family friend Michael Rynan and thirty-two-year-old Winning Company accountant and former stuntman Paul Lumtin are relatively novice blue-water sailors (the risk-taking Lumtin, who lists "shark diving" as a favorite hobby, sailed the 1997 Hobart on *W-C*). The crew uniform is blue sailing trunks and a short-sleeved polo shirt with thick vertical blue and white stripes. *Winston Churchill*'s mainsail number is 27. The boat lacks the on-board tension of a more competitive craft, but has a far more wondrous air about it: friendship. The men of *Winston Churchill* know each other, care for each other. The older men know each other's wife and children and adopt Rynan as a surrogate son. They can discuss the occasional personal matter without fear of crossing some invisible male boundary. Their time at sea will be a celebration of sailing—the antithesis of every time they have sailed with strangers or egotistical skippers with half their knowledge. This is the way, the crew silently acknowledges, sailing should always be.

On Christmas Day, *Winston Churchill* is rubbed down, then slipped back in the water. The grande dame of Australian sailing is now just one of 115 boats bobbing near the CYCA. "She has lasted a long time," Winning tells all who ask why he would consider sailing a fifty-six-year-old wooden boat through some of the most treacherous water on earth, "and will be here long after we're gone." Later, when the Bass Strait has proven him wrong, that quote will be splashed in newspapers worldwide.

• • •

Midnight Rambler is docked on the far side of the CYCA Boxing Day fracas. Ed arrives at 8 A.M., long before the rest of the crew. Five hours before the start, he moves through the crowd of sailors and media, saying hellos and waving across the deck at old friends. Most of the prerace press attention is centered around *Sayonara* and *Brindabella*. Other boats attracting a crowd include the *Winston Churchill*. *Nokia* has three company executives aboard, all nonsailors. *Team Jaguar* attracts attention because she's a maxi and because of Melissa McCabe, the plucky eighteen-year-old high school student from Eden who won an essay contest that asked the question "Why would you want to sail the Sydney-Hobart?" Telstra has stocked *Team Jaguar* with satellite phones so that the crew can communicate a blow-by-blow account of the race.

A host of other boats attract crowds—*Atara, Quest, Sword of Orion.* So as Ed walks down the dock to *AFR-Midnight Rambler,* no one seems to be paying much attention. Before stepping aboard, he takes a loving moment to size her up. She is thirty-five feet from bow to transom, ten and a half feet wide. Her mast rises forty-five feet up from the deck, with a wind gauge and radio antenna on top. She has a shallow cockpit with a traditional tiller. Six winches. The transom is open in back, so any water washing up onto the deck will drain straight back into the sea. Her two Fraser D4 sails are new and bulletproof Kevlar, a five-figure gift from the fine people at the *Australian Financial Review. MR*'s sail number is 8338. The hull is all white, save for the red stripe at the waterline and the Syd-Hob sticker on the bow. Her keel is a fin, with no lead bulb on the bottom because Ed thinks they make for unpredictable steering. She carries four spinnakers—one for light wind, one for medium wind, one for heavy wind, and a "bulletproof" model for those moments when the wind is really blowing, and the boat is barely surviving downwind but still racing. The spinnakers are all-black, save for the words *Australian Financial Review* in light blue.

The crew numbers seven, four of whom are on deck at any given time. Navigator Bob Thomas stays below. *Midnight Rambler* carries the latest in communications and navigation gear. There's a long-distance high-frequency (HF) radio for checking in during the skeds and VHF radio for coastal communication. An autohelm package provides data on navigation, current, speed, wind direction, and water depth and temperature. There's a chart plotter. And a built-in global positioning system, with a handheld backup in case the primary system fails or gets waterlogged. Many boats also carry a laptop and fax for receiving midrace weather updates, but Ed feels that's too much clutter and weight for a small boat.

Ed doesn't really know *Midnight Rambler* that well. Or, this version of the *Midnight Rambler*. Ed and Bob Thomas, the San Francisco native who's his longtime racing partner and navigator, have owned several boats together. The most successful was *Nuzulu*, in which they placed fifth in the 1991 Syd-Hob. The first *Midnight Rambler* was purchased soon after, but was never able to equal *Nuzulu*'s success. One chief rival over the years was a boat named *Chutzpah*. Designed and built by Melbourne naval architect Robert Hick, *Chutzpah* was raced by orthodontist Bruce Taylor. Though the boat once led the Syd-Hob and even won its division, it never crossed the line first.

Still, when *Chutzpah* was put up for sale just four weeks before the 1998 race, Ed and Bob bought her immediately. Though some consider it bad luck for a boat to change names, *Chutzpah* was renamed *Midnight Rambler*. This was partly because Taylor had commissioned a new and improved *Chutzpah* and wanted to retain the moniker.

So Ed stands on the dock, sizing up the boat that will soon become synonymous with his name. She's different from the first

MR, shorter by five feet and narrower across the beam. But the hull design is cleaner, meaning the new *MR* is as fast upwind, and faster downwind.

There are other, more subtle differences to the *MR*. The sort of thing only the skipper can know. She's more stable, for instance, more forgiving to the poor tack or sail choice. When nonsailors ask the difference, Ed just shrugs and says she's easier to sail.

What gives Ed pause is that shallow cockpit. There's little protection from wind and waves. Steering will be a very physical experience, with Ed sitting at the tiller like a forsaken Hemingway character, using his upper body to steer the boat while his torso and legs struggle to provide balance and leverage.

Knowing this, Ed's trained like a prizefighter for the 1998 Syd-Hob. Every day for the past six weeks has been a regimen of running, weights, rowing, and swimming. He endures the jokes about how it's bad luck for a sailor to get preoccupied with swimming. The weight sessions—forearm curls, bench press, lat pulldowns, and stomach routine—build the upper-body strength necessary to manhandle the tiller, or a sopping-wet mainsail in a gale. When sails are changed, they must be taken down, slipped into a sailbag, then stowed belowdecks. Meanwhile, the new sail is brought up from below and hoisted. This is accomplished with the speed of a NASCAR pit stop, as every second without a sail means missed wind and lost speed. With sails weighing upward of eighty pounds dry, changing sails isn't a procedure for the weak.

The bulk of Ed's training, however, is geared toward endurance. A seldom-discussed condition in blue-water racing—from the horrible chop of the Bass Strait in particular—is exhaustion. The bumping and banging of a boat cutting through big waves makes regular sleep impossible.

Hence, Ed's preparation is an essential weapon. "It's like this," says Don Buckley, a veteran sailor nicknamed the Admiral who would sail the 1998 Syd-Hob aboard *B-52*. "You get up at four A.M. Christmas morning because one of your kids is sick. Then you stay up because the other kids wake up and it's time to open presents. Pretty soon some of your mates come over and you celebrate with a little Christmas cheer. Then you notice you've got the same cold as your child, but you don't feel it so much because you've had a few. You might get to bed by midnight, if you're lucky, what with the big Christmas dinner and all, and going to the marina to work on the boat. Then you've got to get up before dawn to go down to Rushcutter's Bay and get the boat prepared to race. You leave the dock at eleven A.M. for the one P.M. start—this just as the hangover and flu are at their worst. Then the pandemonium from the start picks you up for a bit. But by the time it's dark on that first day, all the crew can think about is sleep. Everyone's exhausted. The absolute worst time for a storm to hit would be about midnight or one A.M. that first night out. No one's ready for anything."

Being ready for anything, however, is an Ed Psaltis trademark. Not only did he prepare himself, but he drove his crew as well. They spent four days a week sailing in December, most of it outside the Heads.

For all the trouble—the physical training, the sailing training, taking *MR* from the water to let her dry—Ed knows there's little chance she'll be remotely competitive, let alone win. The *Midnight Rambler* is only thirty-five feet long. Next to maxis like *Sayonara* and *Brindabella* and even *Team Jaguar*, which was dismasted in a freak accident during the 1997 Syd-Hob, *Midnight Rambler* looks humble. A maxi typically runs eighty feet in length and carries twenty-five tons in weight. Such heft irons out waves as the hull bashes through.

A boat like the *Midnight Rambler* weighs just five tons, making it much more susceptible to the whims of the sea. Wave-bashing would be suicide. Waves are more able to flick the craft around, inducing nausea and seasickness—and more than occasional fear—among the crew. The big wave must be approached at an angle, delicately.

That such different boats compete side by side can be attributed to a handicap system known as IMS (International Measurement System). IMS was designed so that racing is about being a great sailor, as opposed to being the sailor with the most money and able to buy the biggest boat. This great equalizer involves taking a boat's measurements (front to back, side to side, top to bottom), sail area, and tonnage, then feeding them into a computer. The IMS handicap ranking is arcane and few understand it entirely, except to say that it favors big boats in heavy wind and small boats in light wind. The race, then, isn't to be first to Hobart—known as line honors—but to be first on handicap. Among sailors, this is considered the truest test of sailing ability. Which is why the boat winning on handicap, not line honors, is immortalized by having a scale model of her hull hung on the boardroom wall at the CYCA.

Having said that, it's the big boats that generally win.

So though Ed and his crew have won other ocean races on handicap—most recently the Sydney to Mooloolaba over Easter vacation in April 1998—no one gives *Midnight Rambler* a chance of ever winning Syd-Hob. Too many top boats. Too much time downwind. Too many top skippers—guys who've won America's Cups and Olympic gold medals. Compared with a guy like Larry Ellison, whose $360,000 carbon-fiber masts cost more than two *Midnight Rambler*s, Ed Psaltis is nothing more than a weekend warrior with a quaint pedigree.

When the Sydney papers selected their prerace favorites for 1998, the Mooloolaba victory was written off as a fluke. Ed and *Midnight Rambler* made none of the expert's top-ten lists. Sydney betting houses place *Midnight Rambler's* odds at 18–1.

Ed doesn't care. Take the bet, he tells friends and family. He has confidence in the new boat. Given the choice between *Midnight Rambler* and a maxi, he'll take *Midnight Rambler* any day. *Midnight Rambler* is an individual's boat. A maxi carries a crew of twenty-two. In a tight spot, *Midnight Rambler* can be crewed efficiently by a lone man with a world of talent. The romance, the self-determination of the notion, appeals to Ed Psaltis. He and Bob

Thomas can't afford anything much bigger than *Midnight Rambler*, but it doesn't really matter. The point is to be competitive in a smaller boat.

As Ed sizes up *Midnight Rambler*, his father appears quietly at his side. Bill's been over visiting his old mate Jim Lawler on the *Winston Churchill*. Jim's done fifteen Hobarts and works full-time as an Australian representative for the American Bureau of Shipping. "In my day," Bill tells Ed sternly, sizing up *MR*, "we sailed real boats."

"Very funny, Dad."

They laugh. It's an old joke. Bill is above all a competitive man. Quiet most times, even distant, but always competitive. Bill's boat was *Meltemi*, a solid chunk of pine and fiberglass that made the Syd-Hob passage a dozen times. It was always Bill's dream to win the thing—as commodore of the Cruising Yacht Club, the race organizer, it would have been quite appropriate—but though he was a good sailor, *Meltemi* was a slow boat.

As the years went by and space-age composite materials replaced Huon pine and fiberglass as the standard of boat construction, Bill felt the Syd-Hob dream slipping away. The new light boats, he told anyone who would listen, weren't safe in the big water. (Like all Australians, Bill vividly remembers the moment of national embarrassment when *Australia II* folded in half during the America's Cup trials off San Diego in 1992. She sank within seconds, the surprised crew diving overboard to await rescue. The debacle is discussed in Australian sailing circles with the somber tones Americans reserve for the Kennedy assassination.) Their decks were vulnerable to destruction from big waves, their masts were too easily toppled, and boats turned over in those high seas. All the while, Bill knew the lightweight boats were the only way a man could be competitive at Syd-Hob. When men choose between safety and speed, speed wins every time.

Bill gave up *Meltemi* in 1986, selling her. She's been turned from a racing yacht into a cruising yacht. More comfort, less speed.

She's moored in Pittwater, twenty miles north of Sydney Harbor. Ed still sees her from time to time when he sails up that way.

Bill gave up on the Syd-Hob dream next, sometime in the early 1990s. He doesn't remember the date or the cause of the epiphany. Bill just knows he woke up one day and realized the quest was done. The pursuit of a Syd-Hob championship became Ed's goal. Sometimes a man takes up his father's passion out of duty, never really owning it as he blindly pursues. The attainment—if it comes—is hollow, and the son is left with the realization that he has squandered his life for another man's grail. Nothing could be further from the truth with Ed.

As Ed and Bill share a private moment before the start, Ed thinks for the millionth time that it would be sublime to race one last Syd-Hob with his dad. But he doesn't ask. Bill only sails inside the harbor. Besides, no boat is big enough for two skippers.

Bill, now seventy-one and retired, doesn't dwell on failing to win Syd-Hob. Now his focus is on making sure his boys come back in one piece. Bill doesn't ever share sentiments like that with Ed and Arthur, though they course though his heart with greater deliberation every passing day.

How does an old man tell his boys that the tranquillity he found on a boat—unquestioned, alone with his thoughts, tingling with the slap of wind on the face and the sun's burn on the nose and back of ears and neck—once dominated him because it was the only way he knew peace? And that older, more content to sit still and listen to a grandchild's babble, he finally values his sons more than time aboard a boat. Some things you just have to learn the hard way.

"You've heard about the storm, then?"

"Yeah. Roger Badham's been spreading rumors about a deep low."

"And?"

"If we can't sail through a fifty-knot blow, then we don't belong in the race."

"Good on you, Son."

Finally, it's time to say good-bye. Bill puts an arm around Ed's shoulders. Bill isn't much for sentiment, nor lavishing praise, so he keeps the last-minute advice brief.

"Relax, Ed. Enjoy your race, and get as much rest as you can before the gale hits."

"I will, Dad."

They part with their usual handshake. No real emotion. No admissions of worry or fear.

"And Ed . . ."

"Yeah, Dad?"

"Be careful."

"That's my plan, Dad."

• • •

Just about the time Ed and the boys ease *Midnight Rambler* away from the CYCA dock toward the starting line, sportswriter Peter Gearin eases into his favorite easy chair in a beach town called Manly, north of Sydney. In one hand is a cold bottle of ale. In the other, a bag of salt-and-vinegar potato chips. Gearin has waited for this day—this very moment—for weeks. He is an avid cricket fan, and today he will do nothing but watch one of Australia's biggest cricket matches of the year, the annual Boxing Day Test Match. For 1998 it's Australia versus the Pommies—the British.

But there's more. Per cricket tradition, the teams will take a lunch break after the first two hours of play. The action will then shift from the cricket match in Melbourne to live coverage of the Syd-Hob start in Sydney.

In the first years of Sydney to Hobart, the start was sometimes eleven, sometimes noon. But as the race became more of an annual national rite—ask any Australian and he can tell you where he watches the start of Syd-Hob each year, just as Americans note where they watch the Super Bowl—the time was moved to one in the afternoon. It became possible for the rabid Aussie sports fan to turn on his television at eleven, watch the first two hours of cricket, watch the start of Syd-Hob, then segue right back into cricket for the remainder of the afternoon.

But as Gearin clicks on the television, something's wrong. The picture shows buckets of rain dropping onto the pitch. The cricket match is most obviously rained out. Melbourne, Gearin notes, is on the Bass Strait. Flipping to another station, a weather channel shows a solid wall of clouds marching east through the Strait. Curiously, at the exact same time, a cold front is pushing southwest across the Australian mainland, dumping a summer snowstorm onto the Australian Alps highlands of Victoria and New South Wales—both regions contiguous to the Strait.

On top of those two storm systems, massive winds from the northeast are pushing down Australia's east coast. Gearin's not much of a weather buff, but one look at the screen makes it perfectly obvious that all three weather systems are on a collision course. Rough estimation shows they'll smack into each other at the eastern side of the Bass Strait.

The snow's good news for skiers, Gearin thinks, flipping again in hopes of finding something—anything—resembling a sporting event. Wonder how all that bad weather's going to affect the Sydney to Hobart.

• • •

The start. All of Sydney seems to be on or around the harbor. Later the crowd will be estimated at over a million. The ocean is a brilliant turquoise, riven by wakes from a thousand sailboats, skiffs, outboard racing boats, dinghies, and Zodiac rafts pressed close for the grand moment. Women in chic dresses nibbling finger food aboard luxury yachts such as the *Olympic Spirit* ($110 a head, drinks included), and bare-chested youth in canoes drinking Foster's. Helicopters are overhead in the perfect blue sky. Television crews can be seen on the press boat, in the sky, and even aboard a racing boat.

In the harbor, big boats swamp little boats, sailboats collide with powerboats, and every one of the 115 skippers in the Syd-Hob fleet looks anxiously at his watch, awaiting the 1 P.M. start. On *Sayonara*, Larry Ellison fumes. Syd-Hob, in keeping with Australia's classless nature, starts all boats together. Other races worldwide stagger the start, with big boats racing out first, followed by waves of smaller craft. With the northeast wind blowing in hard through the Heads, a series of strategic back and forth motions—or tacks—will be necessary to race out of the harbor. Ellison has flown seven thousand miles in his Gulfstream V jet with the hope of shattering the course record held by his chief rival, German software billionaire Hasso Plattner and *Morning Glory*. There is a good chance that the armada of smaller craft will obstruct him, delay him.

Just as chaotic is the scene on land. The South Head is covered with spectators. Traffic lines New South Head Road from Rushcutter's Bay to Watson's Bay and the South Head, and parking is at a premium. Some try to picnic amid the craziness, spreading a blanket on the small patches of grass and pretending it's just a normal summer's day. The rest just party. The *Sydney Morning Herald* has described the Syd-Hob start as a "must watch" event, and it appears their entire readership has taken the advice.

Amped on adrenaline, Ed Psaltis warms up the *Midnight Rambler* and crew by taking a spinnaker run down the bay. With all the media, he figures it's a good chance to show *Australian Financial Review* that he's making an honest effort to give them publicity. The billowing black sail looms above the bow like a fighting cock puffing out its chest.

All of the crew is on deck—Bob Thomas, Arthur Psaltis, Michael Bencsik, John Whitfeld, Gordon Livingstone, and Chris Rockell. All wear the blue and white *MR* sailing uniform of shorts, polo shirt, and deck shoes. In time, Bob and Arthur will take the helm when Ed is tired. But he's primary helmsman, and he alone will pilot the boat out the Heads.

The start is a mythical line in the water between Nielsen Park and Taylors Bay. The commercial-use catamaran with starter SuSie O'Neill, CYCA director Peter Bush, and local dignitaries aboard bobs to one side. The city's famous Harbour Bridge and Sydney Opera House are well behind the fleet. A northeast wind is blowing in the Heads, so boats will be aiming into the wind when the starting cannon sounds.

The ten-minute warning crackles over radios. Those sailboats cruising under power turn the outboard engines off and hoist the mainsail. Spectator boats that have crept into the off-limits area are shooed away. Ed orders the spinnaker lowered and turns into the wind. At Shark Island he tacks north, toward the Taylors Bay side of the harbor. The logic is clear: with the entire fleet (and their party-boat escorts) looking to make a right-hand turn at the South Head, Ed wants *MR* as far to the left as possible. Those on the inside will get caught in traffic. Ed wants nothing but open seas. This habit of sailing his own path is an Ed Psaltis trademark. Sometimes it works, sometimes it causes big trouble.

Ed sails in lazy circles just behind the starting line, trying to time the start just right. The penalty for breaking the starting line before the cannon means turning around and doing it again. But since bobbing in place at the line means a slow start, skippers hove just behind the line, hoping to time the cannon so they'll be running at full speed when it booms. It's a dance, really. A nerve-racking dance. Though Syd-Hob is a multiday race, it is often decided by mere minutes. There's no time to waste, even with the finish over seven hundred miles distant.

Five minutes. Ed feels a knot in his stomach. Nerves. This is the moment. No time to think of Sue or the boys. Time to focus. Sing out the orders in a high, sure voice. Take command. Set aside fears and indecision. This is it. This is what all the training's been for.

SuSie O'Neill lights the cannon. The roar echoes from the starter's catamaran like a punctuation mark to the bedlam on the bay. Ed times the start perfectly. He's at the top end of the line, bearing toward the Heads in an unobstructed angle. He's clear of other boats, meaning *Midnight Rambler* can tack without worry of colliding with another competitor. He swings the boat to starboard until her decks lean over at a forty-five-degree angle. The crew sits on the high side of the boat, feet dangling over the edge. The boom is dipped so low to the right that it almost trails in the water.

A presence looms on either side of *Midnight Rambler*, then steeple-shaped shadows cross her deck. It's the maxi fleet, right on schedule, with about a million men aboard each—*Sayonara, Brind-abella, Marchioness, Wild Thing*, and where's *Nokia*?—and enough sail run up to swaddle *Midnight Rambler*'s hull twice over.

Ed's heart skips a beat. He's doing it. This is just where Ed wants to be. Maxis mean the fast boats. Maxis mean Ed Psaltis and *Midnight Rambler* are among the lead boats in the Syd-Hob. For an instant—this instant, which means nothing overall but feels so good right now—he's winning the Syd-Hob. The thrill is sublime and electric at once.

A whoop goes up from the crew. They're thinking the same thing. This is our year. Blue skies above, front of the fleet, about to turn right at the South Head and put the wind behind them for a sled ride down the coast with spinnaker up. Champagne sailing. Ed smiles, but doesn't speak. Too many boats too close together. Too much to focus on. Traffic is closing around *Midnight Rambler*. Ed's fears of getting stuck are coming true.

Then, just before the South Head, calamity. *Nokia*, the eighty-two-footer, appears directly before *Midnight Rambler*. Ed cries out, but there's nothing he can do but watch as *Nokia* barely misses his hull. Then *Nokia* makes a sharp left turn toward another boat running alongside. The second boat, half the size of *Nokia*, doesn't have time to get out of the way. The two boats collide. Rigging tangles. Shouts and profanities launch from boat to boat, each clearly believing it has the right of way. *Nokia*, though clearly in the wrong, bases her argument on size. She's a maxi. Smaller boats sail among her fleet at their peril. The sailors from the second boat tell the *Nokia*'s crew where to shove their maxi.

No lines are tangled, no sails torn. In a few seconds, the two boats push off to follow separate paths to Hobart. *Nokia*, like a fat, drunken sailor, wobbles right and immediately rams another boat, *Bright Morning Star*.

Those few seconds are all Ed needs. *Nokia*'s tack to port opened a gap in the fleet big enough for Ed to steer *Midnight Rambler* through. And while *Nokia* and the other boat are dead in the water, hulls pressed together, then finally pushing away and saying things like no harm done, see you in Hobart, Ed and *MR* punch past. His little *Midnight Rambler* sails out the Heads alongside *Sayonara* and *Brindabella*. The cheers of the spectators lining the cliffs above are carried his way on the northeast breeze now at his back. Nothing between *MR* and Hobart but blue water. With that northeast wind blowing twenty-five knots, *Midnight Rambler* will hit the Bass Strait in less than twenty-four hours. Ed's never even come close to racing that fast before.

Sayonara raises her spinnaker. The signature white sail with red rising sun is impossible to miss. Rounding a mark, though, *Sayonara*'s spinnaker rips—blows outs, sailors say—and it flaps in the wind like a big white bedsheet drying on a clothesline. The crew immediately hustles to replace it as *Brindabella* pulls alongside, then takes the lead. Hundreds of spectator powerboats have followed the fleet outside the harbor. They cheer as the *Sayonara* crew haul down the ripped spinnaker and replace it in just a matter of moments. They cheer even harder when *Brindabella* asserts herself. The battle is on.

Alright then, lads, Ed barks, raise the kite. A sudden shadow covers the deck, then the words *Australian Financial Review* block out all but the horizon, and the little *Midnight Rambler* begins galloping toward Hobart with a speed Ed had never known before. A chill runs down his spine—this could be the year. Arthur walks back to the cockpit and the two high-five.

They're finally racing. Just like when they sailed the Mediterranean as kids. And for the first time all day, Ed Psaltis goes below. He suddenly feels hungry. What, he wonders, are Sue and the boys doing right now?

■ ■ ■

My parents live about fifty miles south of Sydney in Austinmer, a seaside suburb wedged between a towering rain-forest escarpment and a series of classic beaches in Wollongong's scenic north. Boxing Day is always a family get-together, and it's something of a tradition to watch the Syd-Hob race start live on TV at 1 P.M. (during the lunch break of the Test cricket) as we prepare for lunch—always Christmas Day leftovers (ham, turkey, etc.) and salad. It's always one of those days where you spend more time outside than in, down on the beach or playing backyard cricket. But you come inside for the race start and intermittently to check cricket scores. Australia might have the highest skin-cancer rate in the world, but who cares on Boxing Day? And this year the weather was out of the box. Stunning. Boxing Day also means the start of the Boxing Day cricket Test, a Melbourne perennial. A huge crowd turns out—but this year the first day was washed out. Relentless wind and rain. In fact it was the weather front that the yachts were heading into, but up our way the weather was absolutely perfect. Frankly, I hardly made the connection with what was to come for the race.

Later in the afternoon, toward dusk, tradition dictates that a swim is usually in the cards, or at least a walk down to the headland at Bell's Point with the binoculars to see if we can spot any boats. We've been doing it all my life. You always see other small groups of folks down there with the same idea. In southerly winds, the smaller boats can come in quite close, to half a mile or so, as they tack south. But this year it was a nor'easter (following winds) for the start, so we knew we'd be lucky to get a glimpse. Their kite runs normally take them well out to sea. It would have been around 6 P.M. that my nephew Luke spotted the first of about half a dozen sails on the horizon as we headed back home after a surf. Just tiny white triangles, but still a thrill. As always. Mum got a new set of her own binoculars from Pa this Christmas, so we decided to put them to the test and took our customary walk down to the headland (my folks only live a few hundred yards from the point). I helped my six-year-old line up the boats through the binocs, and I remember the kick he got when he finally held the things still enough to sight one and yelled to us all that he could see it. I remember doing the same thing when I was his age. The yachts were way too far out to identify them, but it's still special. It's our connection to the race.

—Graem Sims, Deputy Editor,
Inside Sport–Australia

THREE

SWORD

The boat colliding with *Nokia* first is *Sword of Orion*. *Sword* pushes off from *Nokia*, swearing hard while straining to be polite—
there's a TV camera on board *Nokia,* and no one wants to be
remembered on national television for their four-letter words—but
clearly agitated that the fleet is slipping out the Heads without
them. Both sides think the other's at fault, but aerial views show
that *Nokia* has gotten herself surrounded by smaller boats.

Nokia's action can be blamed on her constitution—her crew is
equal parts professional sailors and novices, with three corporate
representatives of the title sponsor on board to stay below when
conditions get rough or sit up top in good weather with their feet
dangling over the side. In polite terms, they're human ballast, also
known to sailors as rail meat.

That *Sword of Orion* allow themselves to get fouled is more em-
barrassing.

Blue-water racing crews are formed for a number of reasons.
Sometimes, it's because a bunch of talented sailors want to spend
time together, with competition being a sideline. They're mates.

Success has long come their way. The need to validate themselves through racing is past. *Winston Churchill* is such a crew.

Sometimes, the crew has a weak link or two, but that's forgiven as long as the man's a good mate. Family ties and an uncomplaining work ethic gloss over lack of sailing experience. *Midnight Rambler* is like that.

Sometimes, however, the skipper's competitive. Really competitive. Making friends isn't as important as winning, because everyone becomes friends when you win, anyway. A skipper like that selects a battery of free agents with particular skills. He might select one man because he's a crack navigator. Another is a top helmsman. And so on, until the crew's depth shouts to the world that this boat is a contender. The crew, in turn, is attracted to the boat despite the crusty skipper because her hull and rigging are first-class. Maybe the designer is world famous. Maybe the skipper throws money at his boat, outfitting her with every pricey gewgaw under the sun. All this describes *Sword of Orion*.

Not mates, not buddies, but a collection of top professional and amateur sailors banding together with a hypercompetitive skipper and his speedy new boat for one glorious run to Hobart. In centuries past these Machiavellian rogues would have been pirates. Their loot is the fame and the higher peer standing of a Syd-Hob win instead of plundered treasure, but they are pirates nonetheless.

The individual crewmen of *Sword of Orion* march to the beat of a different drummer, but skipper Rob Kothe and his mavericks—among them Portsmouth's Glyn Charles—have collided with brawny *Nokia* (Glyn was offered a slot on *Nokia* but turned it down for the more competitive boat). *Sword*'s stanchions, or vertical supporting braces above decks, are seriously damaged. They will take an hour to fix under sail. If *Nokia*'s actions prevent *Sword* from winning, Kothe wants the world to know it was clearly not his crew's fault. He decides to race under a protest flag. It seems the only rational thing to do, as *Sword* clearly had the right of way, and that the behemoth with the yellow mainsails and crew containing several nonsailing rookies inadvertently rammed his crew of top blue-water men.

Then there was the controversy of a name change. Sailors are a superstitious lot, and renaming a boat is considered bad luck. It happens more often in modern times, which may be why a new sailor such as Kothe ignored this when purchasing the *Brighton Star* (sixth on handicap in the 1997 Syd-Hob and finisher of four Syd-Hobs altogether). Or maybe he was just trying to correct a wrong—when the San Diego–based design team of John Pugh and Jim Reichle launched the forty-three-footer in 1993, the descendant of America's Cup challenger *America3* was christened *Sword of Orion*. Kothe was merely changing it back.

In Greek mythology, Orion was the hunter. Son of sea king Poseidon, he was a volatile character, an outcast. Orion lived on Crete and was in love with Aurora, goddess of the dawn. Another goddess, Artemis, was jealous that Orion loved Aurora. She had him killed, then placed in the heavens as a constellation.

The constellation's most well-know features are the three diagonal stars constituting Orion's belt. The sword is a faint row of stars pointed straight down from the belt. If Orion were a living man—and the constellation has four stars indicating his two shoulders and two feet, with the belt at the very center—the sword would be dangling to just above the knees. While mythology holds this line of stars to be nothing other than a sword's outline, some sailors and astronomers joke that the dangling stars represent Orion's penis—his manhood, his essence. At fifteen light-years long (and glowing bright red because of a surrounding nebula) Orion's is the largest phallus on record. There's a certain swagger to naming a boat so brazenly, a swagger befitting a band of mavericks. Sons of the sea god, but walking a different path.

Finally, there is the perceived threat of Kothe. The Sydney businessman who owns a company known as Tetra Systems, specializing in marine safety gear, is new to sailing. He learned just four years prior at the CYCA sailing school.

Already one of the world's top glider-airplane racing pilots, sailing was a new challenge to Kothe. The attraction was based on Kothe's existing technical knowledge—the angle into the wind to produce optimal speed, hull composition, the geometry of rigging. In gliding, pilots ply the sea breezes off coastal mountain ranges. Sailing uses the same winds, but offshore. In gliding, a four-man ground crew completes a crew, while a sailing team is within arm's reach, looking to help if someone is in trouble. Kothe considers sailing easier in that respect.

This is Kothe's second Syd-Hob. In 1997 he placed second in his division aboard *Witchcraft II*.

For the 1998 race, he aims to build the most competitive crew possible. An astute businessman aware of personal limitation, Kothe settles on two-time Syd-Hob winner Steve Kulmar as principal helmsman. Kothe will navigate and serve as skipper, but Kulmar is in charge. For an owner and skipper to hand over control of his boat during a race is not uncommon. The postrace glory still goes to the skipper, no matter who does the actual steering. In his late forties, with sixteen Syd-Hobs to his credit, the affable, clean-cut Kulmar is also well-known on the international racing circuit, having steered Australia's *Sea* in the Admiral's Cup competition. Good friends of Kulmar's from past Admiral's Cup competitions are Fraser sails retailer Andrew Parkes, thirty-four, with eight Syd-Hobs and four America's Cup campaigns; and twenty-four-year-old bowman Darren Senogles, an up-and-coming sailor with Admiral's Cup experience despite his youth.

All three joined *Sword*'s crew.

Glyn Charles found his way onto *Sword* through Kulmar. The international bent of sailing makes for hybrid crew, with sailors jumping from boat to boat wherever a crew is needed. In the end, the logic goes, they're all citizens of the sea anyway. Which is how Englishman Glyn came to sail the 1997 Admiral's Cup aboard Australia's *Sea*. The older Kulmar took Glyn under his wing, seeing in him the same spitfire mentality Kulmar once employed. Both possess the same direct manner of speaking. Both live and breathe sailing. By the time Kulmar and Glyn met, the Englishman was no longer the angry young man—glimpses still remain, but that scathing self-righteousness is five years past. Instead, Glyn channels rage into successful sailing. Kulmar likes Glyn very much, considers him a dear friend. Glyn, though he won't admit as much, considers Kulmar a father figure. He's gone half his life without one.

When Steve Kulmar asks his young friend on December 23 if he'd like to join *Sword*'s crew, Glyn first gets the blessing of his girlfriend, Anne Goodman. Annie is a pivotal presence in Glyn's life, an attractive, self-assured marketing executive for Price Waterhouse Coopers. She is independent enough to endure, and support, his long sailing absences, but is secure in the knowledge he will always come back. Sydney to Hobart is something, Glyn pleads with Annie, he's always wanted to tackle. Though their plans originally saw them flying home on Christmas Eve, Annie says yes. While he sails, she'll fly down to Melbourne and see the old city. It's supposed to feel quite European.

Then Glyn gets his mother's blessing by phone. I'm fine with it as long as you're doing what makes you happy, Margaret Charles tells Glyn.

Then Glyn gives the good word to Kulmar, who passes it along to Kothe. He immediately accepts Glyn as a crew member. Glyn will assist Kulmar at the helm. In all, *Sword* will have four helmsmen on board, all with proven international experience. *Sword*'s crew now has a combined eighty Hobarts, twelve Fastnets, ten Admiral's Cup, and four America's Cup campaigns. On paper, she is looking more and more unbeatable.

But that's on paper. Never mind that crew compatibility and empathy is paramount in ocean racing. Even with a band of mavericks, bad chemistry can detract from performance. When a crew is forced to spend every moment of every day under extremely stressful conditions, even the way a man chews his food or brushes his teeth can become irritating. The crew of a racing sailboat is many cogs working together effortlessly, like a Swiss watch. When cooperation breaks down—and it does when petty animosities develop—those cogs cease functioning efficiently.

There's no personal space once the race gets under way—no secret hideaway where a man can stroll for a moment's peace. Even going to the toilet is a public function, with most boats fulfilling the mandatory privy rule by carrying a tiny chair used for potty-training infants. For this reason, most sailors do their business over the side. Reading the sports page and contemplating life is impossible.

Glyn Charles joined *Sword of Orion*'s crew not for the camaraderie, not for a peaceful outing, but for the competition. *Sword*, he knows, will be a contender. It is the reason why Glyn is now sailing down the eastern coast of Australia under full spinnaker on a gorgeous Boxing Day afternoon. Though spectators in Wollongong, an hour south of Sydney, stand along the ocean and spot distant specks offshore, none of them can possibly glimpse *Sword of Orion*. Those specks they see are more likely Ed Psaltis and *Midnight Rambler*, just eight miles out, riding the two-knot current above the continental shelf. It's safe, it's fast, it's close to shore in case trouble blows in.

They can't see *Sword* because Kulmar's got the heart of a gambler. He's not following the rhumb line, or the straightest line from Sydney to Hobart. He's angled *Sword* twenty miles off the coast to take advantage of a monster southerly current. The eight-knot river combined with a tailwind of thirty-five to forty knots moves *Sword* down the coast at close to twenty-five knots. There is risk in straying so far off the coast—going twenty miles out will mean having to come twenty miles back in at some point—but Kulmar thinks the additional speed from the current is worth it. With *Brindabella* and *Sayonara* making the same decision, Kulmar's logic seems sound.

• • •

Seventy-five minutes into the race, forecasters are facing weather concerns with growing trepidation. The Bureau of Meteorology issues a gale warning for the Bass Strait. Race meteorologist Kenn Batt radios the fleet that a southerly change with near gale-force winds will hit the leaders around midnight. The winds will reach forty-five to fifty-five knots, with seas rising two to three meters. The southerly wind hitting the south-flowing current, Batt tells all boats monitoring their radios, means sailors can expect "atrocious" seas.

Sword hears the radio warning as she surfs under spinnaker. Two-meter swells run with the boat, and she rides the knife's edge atop them, the very tip of the bow peeking over the face. It's the most heady, carefree sort of sailing there is. Other than for Parkes making the occasional trim to the spinnaker, there's no need to touch a sail. The crew stay up top, savoring the day. When they tell stories at the CYCA bar twenty years hence, ticking off a list of their most perfect sailing afternoons, this will be at the top.

Steve Kulmar controls the wheel with just one finger. Darren Senogles and Andrew Parkes perch out on the bow, smearing on extra sunscreen. Glyn sits on the rail near the cockpit, staying close to pal Kulmar. As the new guy on the boat, Glyn really has no one else to talk to. Kulmar coaches him on the upcoming Bass Strait currents and how best to sail the waves in the Strait.

There's a different character to the Bass Strait waves, Kulmar tells Glyn. With their white-water crest and tendency to break when they get big, they're more like waves you see at a surf beach than out in the open ocean.

They talk about what waves like that can do to a boat. Glyn figures the worst that can happen to *Sword* is a knockdown. As long as they can see the waves coming, he and Kulmar have the expertise to change course quickly to avoid getting hit broadside or having a wave break atop them.

They chat like that until 4:05 P.M., and the first sked. Today's the only day for a 4:05 sked. Every day from here on out, the daytime sked will be at 2:05 and nighttime sked at 3:05. As boats report in alphabetically—*ABN Amro Challenge . . . Adagio . . . Adrenalin*—it becomes clear the maxis are well past Nowra, where the Aussie coast juts jaggedly inward. The current's so strong and wind so brisk that *Sayonara, Brindabella, Nokia, Marchioness,* and *Team Jaguar,* with their larger sail area, are already four hours ahead of *Morning Glory's* course record. They should be in the Bass Strait by dawn. No boat has ever reached the Strait that quickly. Sometimes it's a two-day sail all by itself. Crews throughout the fleet buzz with excitement about the speeds.

Sword reports in, twenty miles out to sea, roughly even with Nowra. There's a Royal Australian Naval Aviation Base at Nowra, HMAS *Albatross.* Two squadrons of crack helicopter rescue crewman such as pilot Tanzi Lea and the legendary Petty Officer Shane Pashley are stationed at Nowra when they're not flying off the HMAS *Newcastle.* The *Sword* crew knows of Pashley through his Autissier rescue in the Southern Ocean. Made the front page of all the papers. They know of Lea only through reputation and the sailing rumor mill. An old-timer once stationed with Britain's Royal Air Force, Lea flew helicopter rescue during the 1979 Fastnet. Since coming to Australia he's made several dangerous rescues. Word about a man like that gets around. The Australian blue-water sailor respects, for very good reason, the capability of Australia's complex search-and-rescue system. Australia has the best SAR force in the world, bar none. Myths have sprung around these men and women, such as a belief that rescue swimmers are trained to swim one hundred miles at a time. Or that low-flying military Orion radar aircraft have a hidden towline for dragging boats to safety. There's even quiet grumbling in the Australian search-and-rescue community that blue-water sailors take this exceptional skill for granted. The sailors, say SAR professionals, take too many risks they shouldn't, knowing that someone's always going to bail their asses out.

Pashley, the star of search and rescue, and Lea are on Christmas leave as the fleet sails past Nowra. Each carries a beeper in event of emergency. They've also given the base a list of phone numbers where they can be reached. Sailors in the Sydney to Hobart fleet might be surprised to know that the navy isn't on standby with the bad weather forecast. In fact, the primary mission of their surf rescue swimmers isn't lifting yachtsmen, or even downed military aviators, from the water. It's antisubmarine warfare. Thus the attitude of Naval Maritime Headquarters in Sydney when first apprised Saturday morning of potentially gruesome weather: the Sydney to Hobart yacht race is a private event. In the eyes of the Royal Australian Navy, Sydney to Hobart is a national treasure, but definitely a private event. The navy will be called in as a last resort should things go very wrong. Until then, the yachties are on their own.

• • •

As the sked winds down, the Bureau of Meteorology issues another weather warning. The gale warning has been upgraded to a storm warning. Winds should reach forty-five to fifty-five knots, with six-meter seas.

Kulmar and Glyn had sat through a detailed prerace weather briefing from Clouds Badham, and oceanographic briefings from Dr. Mark Gibbs, as a supplement to the weather data passed by Kenn Batt in the Christmas Eve fleet weather briefing. But they need only look at the horizon ahead for confirmation the weather's changing. A line of fat, black thunderclouds crosses the sky. Experience tells them it's the edge of a cold front—a squall line. With the excitement of the start fading and the grind of a long ocean race just setting in, Kulmar decides that conditions will indeed change for the worst within hours. Now it's time to rest. Both Kothe and Glyn duck below to get some sleep.

The Sydney to Hobart is lost at night, when sailors are tired after the first day's sail and festivities. Mentally, they let down. Inexperienced crews tend to go below and sleep, or to sail less aggressively. But experienced crews pick this time to press harder. Darkness hides their movements between skeds.

Rob Kothe isn't as experienced as his crew is. They'll push on through the night. After a few hours' nap Glyn Charles will skipper *Sword* through the thunderstorm. Conditions like these are what make blue-water sailing so exciting. As he ducks below, Glyn is almost too excited to sleep. He grabs an open bunk and turns to face the hull.

Kothe doesn't turn in quite yet. He first sends an E-mail back to the CYCA. It's a precautionary measure, so if *Sword* loses, his formal protest will have teeth. "The damage to the starboard stanchions has been repaired," he writes, choosing each word carefully. "However, delamination occurred in a meter-long section at the starboard stern quarter.

"Of major concerns, however, is the damage sustained by the mast. There's a compression crease about two meters above the deck."

The makings of a hole in the hull and a mast on the verge of toppling . . . that should get their attention. Kothe signs off and slips into a bunk, sure that his offensive has raised eyebrows back in Sydney. Or maybe it's just pissed someone off. Who knows? It's hard to tell, especially when things turn political. Kothe hates judgment calls. Give him a clear-cut winner any day. Take all that subjective nonsense out of the equation.

What's worse is that *Nokia*'s big-dollar sponsors have a ton of pull with the CYCA. No one wants to piss them off. If Rob Kothe's going to win this protest, he'll have to get his facts in a row and continue the E-mails detailing any woes—all woes, real or suspected—caused by the collision.

FOUR

THE WEATHER BOMB

Saturday, December 26, 4:30 P.M.

There are now 115 boats sailing due south with the wind at their
backs. Extremely bad weather has been forecast, though until now
the fleet has ignored predictions. The horizon dead ahead is nothing but black thunderclouds. The east coast of Australia lies to
their right, with only *Midnight Rambler* close enough to see it. To
their left is the Tasman Sea, and New Zealand two thousand miles
away. Their chief adversary is the Bass Strait, roughly one hundred miles straight ahead. Their goal is Hobart, Tasmania, at least
six hundred miles and three days' sailing distant. All around them
are the other boats of the Sydney to Hobart fleet, spread out over
a thirty-mile radius.

Moments ago, the Bureau of Meteorology issued a new weather
warning. The waters in the Bass Strait, the report said, would be
"atrocious." Towering seas, obnoxious winds, blowing spume. The
fleet does not take the storm warning lightly. The BOM has issued

only one other storm warning in 1998, and that was on August 7—in the dead of winter.

Several boats turn back. *Midnight Rambler, Sword of Orion,* and *Winston Churchill* do not. All three are crewed by capable men who have chosen to press on, regardless.

The storm that will nibble at the fleet is eight hours off. The storm that will wreck it is a day away. So the first bolts of lightning sizzling from sky into sea aren't really a part of all that. This light show is just the warm-up act. All three boats know that. Only the two novices on *Winston Churchill*—the boy, Michael Rynan, and the accountant, Paul Lumtin—show fear. The veterans on board *W-C* calm them by recalling their first Bass Strait crossings and how scared they felt. They say the words with the quaint chuckle of nostalgia.

But Richard Winning, like Ed Psaltis and Glyn Charles, isn't worried. The BOM report spoke of "atrocious" seas, but atrocious isn't deadly. The sailors are all thinking that they'll tough out the thunderstorm, then slog through the next day's storm. No big deal. They've done it before: reduce the size of sails, minimize the number of men on deck, steer up waves at an angle to avoid being broached or pitchpoled, and ignore the inevitable seasickness. The storm will last four or five hours.

But this storm will be much worse than all that. Every small boat should be turning back for Sydney, and big boats should be reducing their sail size or heading due east to circumvent the storm. In fact, the entire Sydney to Hobart race should be scrubbed until the weather passes, and maybe altogether. The entire fleet should be instructed to seek shelter at a port along the coast. A heretical notion, to be sure, and one the folks at the CYCA are reluctant to invoke. "It's not like calling cars into the pits at an auto race," says CYCA spokesman Peter Bush. "These people are far out to sea."

In the history of the Sydney to Hobart, the CYCA has never instructed the fleet to run for safe harbor—Rule 4 designates that the skipper's duty—and "atrocious" seas aren't reason for starting now. The seas are always atrocious in the Bass Strait. It's all a matter of how a crew deals with the adversity. In one memorable instance from the 1957 race, the crew of the sloop *Renene* roped themselves to her decks to avoid being swept overboard during a seventy-knot gale in 1957. Just thirty-three feet long, *Renene* was blown a whopping two hundred miles off course. The ship's instruments were broken, and the crew had no idea which direction they were being abducted. They lost their sea anchor and several sails. When *Renene* finally made her way to Hobart, the seven men on board were too exhausted to stand. They staggered on the dock until friends forced them to sit down.

"Terrific waves hammered us nonstop," skipper Tom Proctor gasped. "Eight times every hour, a forty-footer broke right over us. We were shooting the seas like a surfboard. One time a wave knocked us flat, and we thought we'd never come up again." Then, the ultimate admission from an Aussie sailor: "I was pretty scared."

The history of Syd-Hob is about storms as much as sailing. That's what makes the Syd-Hob so special, and that's why the CYCA does not direct the fleet to safe harbor as the storm of 1998 takes shape. Later, backpedaling, the CYCA will say they might have considered such an action if only they'd known how bad the weather was going to get.

As afternoon turns to dusk on Boxing Day, one group of people know exactly how bad things will get—or at least suspect. They have the power to warn the CYCA of these suspicions. They even have the authority to make such a pronouncement publicly (even if it means being incorrect, with all the ensuing public furor), thereby exerting pressure on the CYCA to recall the fleet.

This group is Australia's Bureau of Meteorology. Every bit of data pouring from satellite photos and computer screens confirms to the eight-man skeleton crew in the Sydney office that fifty-five-knot winds are likely. A closer look suggests, however, that fifty-five knots is likely a jumping off point—winds could get as high as one hundred miles per hour. That's Force 12 on the Beaufort wind scale. As defined by the National Oceanic and Atmospheric Administration (NOAA). Force 12 means any time winds reach over 72 miles per hour. The impact of a Force 12 is defined as "effects on land: severe damage and destruction; effects on water: exceptionally high waves, sea filled with foam and spray, sea [surface] completely white."

To put a Force 12's power in perspective, consider that small craft advisories, the government warnings commanding sailboats to flee for safe harbor, are issued when the Beaufort scale reads just Force 6. The fifty-five-knot winds already forecastd by the Sydney Bureau of Meteorology are Force 10, the 1979 Fastnet strength. Most alarming of all, even if the possibility of Force 12 is setting off alarm bells inside the BOM, they're not telling anyone. Professional decorum prevents the BOM from making a Force 12 pronouncement without hard data—and in their eyes, that data does not exist. As they have no wind sensors in the Bass Strait, it's unlikely the BOM will ever have this data.

What's taking place is a standoff: few Australian skippers are willing to invoke Rule 4, even with Fastnet conditions being forecast. Rule 4 is tinged by cowardice. If the Poms could sail through Force 10 in 1979, the Aussies can certainly do likewise. The CYCA is reluctant to assert their will on the fleet, instead adhering to the notion that each skipper is in control of his ship. And the BOM's professionalism prevents them from insisting publicly, and in the most specific terms, that winds will almost double Fastnet speed. "Any sailor out there was forewarned," the BOM's Pat Sullivan says, wiping his hands with a clinical logic. "Even before the race started there was a warning of gales."

Because the three factions will not take action, people will die. Boats will be crushed. Children will lose their fathers.

Weather forecasting, despite the casual way nightly news presents it, is a bona fide science. This is the BOM's position. Weather falls under the banner of meteorology, or the study of the atmosphere. Predictions are based on objective data and established weather patterns. Data is collected from radiosondes (weather balloons), which measure air temperature, air pressure, and humidity from ground level up to one hundred thousand feet; Doppler radar (uses microwave transmissions to judge how far off precipitation is; can peer into thunderstorms and find approaching tornadoes); and satellites (orbiting observation platforms to scrutinize cloud movements from space). Low-resolution visible and infrared imagery is collected daily from the NOAA sun-synchronous, polar-orbiting satellites.

Information is sent to meteorological centers to be analyzed. Results are transmitted electronically to forecast offices in regional centers. On Australia's east coast, this means Sydney's regional Bureau of Meteorology. The man in charge is Pat Sullivan. Kenn Batt works for Sullivan. Batt's official long-range forecast, issued December 23 and repeated to skippers and navigators at a CYCA prerace briefing Christmas Eve morning where Batt wore a Santa hat, spoke of a "thirty-knot southerly wind . . . the southerly is expected to ease to fifteen to twenty knots over Sunday before swinging back to the north on Monday as the majority of the fleet make their way across Bass Strait under spinnaker."

But Batt is also a sailor, a veteran of six Syd-Hobs as navigator, including a winning effort aboard *Solbourne Wild Oats* in 1993. He suspects the fleet wouldn't touch their spinnakers once the southerly hit, let alone make their way across the Bass Strait with these big-daddy sails flying. The kind of winds he privately fears use a spinnaker to drive the bow of a boat downward into the sea, violently enough that the ship would sink.

Many skippers picked up on Batt's confusion and complained after the Christmas Eve briefing that the BOM was sending mixed messages about the weather. The forecasts weren't specific, but meandering, alluding to low-pressure systems without pinpointing their location.

The BOM's first hard evidence of severe weather came Boxing

Day morning, before the fleet had left the docks. Meteorologist Peter Dunda, working in the Sydney office, glanced at a download of satellite photos, then at computer models of the weekend's anticipated weather. The models were generated in the BOM's Melbourne headquarters, hard along the Bass Strait. Using a LAPS (Meso Limited Area Prediction System) model, Dunda noticed a mass of clouds four hundred miles off Tasmania's east coast. This low-pressure system wouldn't bother the fleet, other than for winds. Dunda assumed thirty-to-forty-knot winds off Gabo Island—just off the Australian coastline where the Bass Strait begins—by nightfall and issued a gale warning.

Batt was down at the CYCA dispensing last-minute weather advice. Dunda faxed him the gale forecast. Batt photocopied the information and passed it out to racers. This bit of weather data was the last most of the fleet would receive until Hobart, except by radio.

But even before the fleet was out the Heads, Dunda was looking at new—more ominous—computer models. The latest satellite photos showed a massive low-pressure system some nine hundred miles across. Only it wasn't off Tasmania, but off Gabo Island. LAPS suggested winds as high as fifty-five knots by Sunday afternoon. That figure had a plus/minus accuracy of 30 percent.

The low-pressure system had the potential to become hurricane strength. When Batt returned from his morning watching the fleet off, Dunda showed him the new photos. Batt stared at them, exhaled sharply. "Those people are sailing into a massacre," he said softly, then stepped into another room and wept.

• • •

Science, however, prevented Batt or Dunda from repeating all but the known facts. Their science, meteorologists will tell you—as they have told friends and family at cocktail parties ever since they made the atmosphere's study their lifelong occupation—is about a whole lot more than sticking a wet forefinger in the air and trusting their gut. Which is why weather forecasters are forbidden to make official pronouncements based on hunch. So while Kenn Batt privately fears the fleet is sailing into a monster storm, official radio broadcasts are limited to pronouncements based on hard and fast data: steep seas and winds of forty-five to fifty-five knots.

Batt thinks the weather will be far worse. Sixty-to-eighty-knot winds, with waves in the thirty-to-sixty-foot range. His hunches are based on his own experiences in the Bass Strait. Given the Antarctic wind ripping across the Southern Ocean, a northeast wind system shoving down the coast of Australia, and a low-pressure system developing over the Bass Strait, forty-five to fifty-five knots would be a mild convergence. Each of the three weather conditions is a catalyst for disaster. On their own, each can destroy the fleet. Put them all together and the results will be incendiary.

Long-range forecaster Roger "Clouds" Badham, not employed by the BOM and thus not constrained by science, feels freer to discuss his hunches. Badham, a balding man with a thick black beard, runs a weather-forecasting company known as Marine Weather Services. He was hired as a consultant by twenty boats prior to the race, and his warnings of the fleet's getting hammered started the dockside rumors of fifty-knot winds and big seas. Top sailors in such events as the America's Cup, Whitbread Around the World, and Newport-Bermuda listen closely to the BOM reports, but they often bet their lives on Badham's.

Seven or eight days prior to Syd-Hob, Badham's global computer weather forecasts predicted a strong low-pressure system far off the southeast coast of Australia. It appeared unlikely to bother the fleet. Peripheral big winds would whip the seas, nothing more. But Badham's intuition—based on a little science, years of experience, and a sixth sense about weather off Australia—told him a monster storm would sweep through the Strait. Forget thirty-five-knot winds. Look for something more like seventy.

And, unlike Kenn Batt, Clouds Badham was free to tell the world.

After walking the CYCA docks in the morning before the start, giving the forecast briefing clients had paid for, Clouds made another surreptitious run from slip to slip. This time, Clouds, so sure something bad would strike the race, visited good friends and doled out advice for free. "You're in for a big blow," he warned Roger Hickman of the *Atara,* a director of the CYCA and Australian Ocean Racer of the Year. "Half the boats in the fleet should think about staying home."

Hickman, shaken, considered it. "When Roger Badham makes a statement like that, you'd better listen." In the end, *Atara* sailed.

Badham foresaw the potential for an East Coast low, also known as a weather bomb. These unforeseeable episodes are raging winds at high altitudes (often ripping along at close to four hundred miles per hour) rushing toward the earth's surface. Due to the Coriolis force, a gravitational pull resulting from the earth's rotation, winds don't simply hammer straight down. They spiral, sucking clouds down with them. While wind is an invisible force, clouds are not. The weather bomb—once it descends—suddenly appears on satellite transmissions as a swirl of clouds.

Like any bomb, Australia's East Coast low needs several ingredients. The first is raging winds. Wind is nothing more than moving air, and horizontal layers of air stack from the earth's surface to the stratosphere. Air has weight. When one layer is heavier than another—a high-pressure system—gravity sucks it toward the earth to fill an area containing cooler air—a low-pressure system. This near-vertical mass of downward air is known as a current. Again, the Coriolis force drags the air down in a spiral. The tighter the spiral, the greater the wind's force.

An East Coast low would start at the south pole. The air there is cold and dense. This wind gradually rises and moves toward the equator, blowing from west to east due to the spin of the earth. Above thirty thousand feet, these east-blowing winds are sucked into a narrow belt known as the jet stream. Winds in the jet stream have been measured at up to 340 mph. The jet stream is why a flight from Los Angeles to Sydney—against the jet stream—takes sixteen hours, but the return flight takes as little as twelve.

The breath of wind that begins at the south pole rises to thirty-thousand feet above the earth, whizzing along at half the speed of sound. Nature abhors a vacuum, so every now and then a current rushes down to fill a low-pressure system, equalizing pressure in the atmosphere. The presence of a huge low-pressure system, such as the one taking shape off Australia, causes the full brunt of these high-force winds to rocket down to ground—or sea—level, generating horrific conditions.

This is why Badham had his premonitions. What he foresaw was an unholy convergence: first, extremely strong winds from the northeast moving down the Australian coast; second, more extremely strong winds, but moving through the Bass Strait from west to east, preparing to collide with the northeast winds.

Sailors are used to hitting this "southerly change" at the mouth of the Bass Strait. But a third and more dangerous factor is the cold front moving across the Australian mainland. Cold air from Victoria is pushing aside the subtropical air hovering over Sydney and the east coast, producing summer snowstorms in the coastal mountains. A powerful cold front creating a low-pressure system over the Bass Strait is the weather equivalent of gasoline being poured into a Molotov cocktail. The convergence of all three may possibly create a weather bomb right on top of the unsuspecting boats.

Badham feared two more intangibles. First, the relative difference between the high-pressure and low-pressure systems. If the wind speed aloft was great, and the low-pressure system at the ocean's surface incredibly low, that high-altitude air would rush down to the surface almost instantaneously. The already fierce southerly winds in the Bass Strait would double, even triple, in speed.

The final variable was most subjective of all: timing. Everything—wind speed, low pressure, exact proximity—had to happen at once for an East Coast low to become reality. The BOM probably figured there was no point in scaring everyone over a long shot, and something historically unlikely.

The only news sailors had of all this were Badham's dockside rumors. But rumors and speculation aren't enough cause to pull out of a Syd-Hob. Skippers and their crews spend months preparing a boat for the big race. Their friends and neighbors and coworkers know they're going and have held parties or even rented a boat to be out on the harbor to see them off. A skipper would be either downright silly or incredibly brave to pull out of Syd-Hob based on waterfront rumor and the gut reaction of a freelance weather forecaster.

• • •

Based on the BOM warning seventy-four minutes into the race, a few boats turn back, including Ian Kiernan on the thirty-four-foot *Canon Maris*. The "hollow log" is almost forty years old, and her crew includes seventy-year-old Richard "Sightie" Hammond, competing in his fortieth Syd-Hob—the most for anyone ever. Even as she surfs down waves with spinnaker flying, Kiernan concludes *Canon Maris* is better off not risking big seas. Never mind that Kiernan won his division in the previous Syd-Hob with *Canon Maris*, and that archrival *Southerly* is still racing. It's time to go home. *Canon Maris*, just a foot shorter than *MR*, is too small for thirty-foot seas.

Just as *Canon Maris* turns around, Clouds Badham is back at his office in Sydney, checking his computers again. He hopes to pinpoint the storm more exactly, take it beyond hunch into the realm of fact. With facts he can go public in a big way, maybe even appear on national television (Channel 10 has signed Badham on as their

Syd-Hob weather forecaster) with his predictions. But without the facts Badham's reputation will be ruined. Making dire predictions based on hunches, then having no storm develop, will make Clouds Badham the laughingstock of Australian meteorology. No sailing event with any credibility would touch him.

As he stares at the latest information from weather balloons and satellite passes, Badham—a man who's forecasted thousands of storms—is horrified to discover his predictions are wrong. There's still going to be a storm. But the storm is going to be exponentially worse than he originally foresaw. What Badham sees on the screen is what Dunda and Batt's computers showed at noon. "Oh, shit," Badham moans, rechecking the data for the tenth time. "This is going to be Armageddon."

Badham then takes the unprecedented step of radioing all twenty of his clients at sea to give warning. This sort of assistance is illegal in blue-water racing. For a professional such as Badham to endanger his very business by placing such radio calls speaks for his urgency. Reduce sail, he tells some skippers. Still others are urged to drop their spinnakers and flee back to Sydney. Now.

While the BOM is sticking only with the facts, understating the severity of the storm, an anguished Badham spells out specifics to his clients. As he is not an official race forecaster, these warnings are not broadcast to every boat.

That night Badham will go one step further, appearing on the Channel 10 news to tell the country what's about to happen. The fleet is far out to sea, beyond reach, in the line of a killer storm. This is the first time the general public is aware of the problem, as the BOM has not made such a forecast. Media outlets go on alert for storm developments. Updates will be broadcast regularly through the next two days. Viewers will clog the CYCA phone lines and Telstra Web site, seeking information on loved ones.

Sue Psaltis will ignore the media hype for a time. But she will succumb to worry, trying to hide it from the boys, especially Ben. A phone call from Ed's oldest brother, Charles, will make her feel better, but only slightly.

"*Midnight Rambler*'s crew has lots of hard ocean miles of experience. They'll come through okay," Charles tells Sue in a late-night phone call on Boxing Day. That night, lying in bed and wrestling with her fears, she wishes she could believe him.

INTO THE LOOKING GLASS

Saturday, December 26, Dusk–Midnight

All of that's in the future. Right now, the Syd-Hob fleet sails into the squall line (a row of black thunderclouds indicating the collision of a warm front and a cold front), like Alice stepping into the looking glass. They are on the edge of the cold front—the edge of reality—about to sail from the perfect conditions of Saturday afternoon into a world like none they have known before.

Lightning is the visual cue that things are changing. Then comes rain. The sun goes down a bit before nine, so that the sky, between lightning bolts, is opaque.

Then seas climb to ten feet. The rolling swells of the afternoon have transformed into steep pitches. Sailors throughout the fleet wiggle into wet-weather gear. Novice sailors get tense, try not to show their fear. Navigators read weather information, try to plot a way around the storm. Short of running due east toward New

Zealand, there isn't a way, but it takes them all an agonizing hour of checking and rechecking maps and weather reports to be certain.

Midnight Rambler is running sixth on handicap—the real race. *Midnight Rambler* has no satellite modem laptop, has not paid Clouds Badham. They know nothing of the weather bomb beyond the BOM fifty-five-knot warning and rumors Ed heard before the race. As Ed watches the lightning storm, he feels engrossed instead of endangered. It's entertainment with an edge. He still has the spinnaker up, even though he's surfing waves and sudden gusts have twice led to near-capsize. Ed likes the speed—twenty-two knots is fast for a thirty-five-footer—and decides to keep the spinnaker flying. Then he orders the crew to stay toward the back of the boat so their weight will force the nose up when *MR* encounters bigger seas.

A pair of conflicting emotions charge through Ed. The first is an epic adrenaline rush. In the back of his mind he remembers his father's warning to get as much sleep as possible before the storm. But this is no time to be down below. This is what it's all about. This is a time to stand at the helm and experience life and the sea to the fullest.

The other emotion, equally strong, is a sense of foreboding. The fleet is sailing into a storm, for crying out loud. The need to be watchful is paramount. The decks are getting so wet and the waves so steep that the crew are having a hard time standing— any movement toward the bow is done sliding on their bottoms, or on hands and knees. Stray wave peaks flit into the cockpit, making Ed's shallow domain feel even more precarious.

Ed's thoughts turn to family. They always do when the going looks rough. He likes to say that the *Midnight Rambler* has no pre-race superstitious ritual or prayer because the act of leaving is hard enough by itself. But the busy distractions of the start are long behind. Now it's just Ed, skipper and principal helmsman, surrounded by a growing sea. Being out here makes Ed feel helpless sometimes. Not so much for himself, but for his family. If something happens to him, then that's the way it's supposed to be. Things happen for a reason. But he hates the thought of Ben and Matt growing up without a father. Or worse, the agony Sue will go through if he's lost, and maybe that she'd remarry. Ed can't imagine Sue with another man.

The obvious solution is giving up blue-water sailing. That way nothing bad would ever happen and life would go on as normal. But Ed figures you can just as easily get hit by a bus as you can fall off the side of a blue-water boat.

But sailing is so much a part of Ed. After a childhood spent on and around Sydney Harbor, it was natural for him to stay in Sydney for university. He went to Newington College, where his physical size and natural speed and strength led him into athletics. He rowed senior eights crew and played rugby on the first team. From rugby, Ed would say later in life, he learned tenacity. The important thing, especially after the bitter disappointment of a loss, was to never give up. Pick yourself up off the ground and come back harder next time.

That philosophy carried Ed through school, into marriage and career. Life was fragmented, difficult. There was the importance of job advancement, and the long hours required of a junior accountant. Balance that with learning the marital ropes, and sailing fell down on the scale of importance. Being on the water was a part of him, but he couldn't always find the time. His wife didn't share his fascination with sailing, either. The Syd-Hob dream grew hollow and distant, something that would have to wait until later in life, if it was going to happen at all.

When the first marriage didn't last, Ed began questioning every aspect of his personality. What was he about? What mattered to him? Where, exactly, was he headed? True love was fleeting. Childhood dreams—so vast and limitless—were replaced by basic desires such as feeling comfortable in your own skin.

At twenty-nine, Ed found himself climbing a rocky ridge twenty miles north of Sydney, Barrenjoey Head. It was a hot summer day.

"I just sat looking over the Pacific Ocean, trying to work out the hell of a mess my life was then in," he remembers. "A beautiful sea breeze was blowing in, cooling the land as it gained in strength. I decided on that day, that even though it may prove very painful for me, my life would be devoted to ocean yacht racing."

Right now Ed would be thrilled to be knocked to solid ground. With the crew growing scared—no one's said anything, but Ed can tell because they've all stopped talking—and the worst of the storm to come, Ed would give just about anything to be back on land.

He forces himself to stop thinking of family. Instead, he plots ways to beat the weather. The only solution is to sail straight through the storm. Get to Hobart in one piece, then suck down a few Cascade lagers and laugh with the mates. Winning doesn't seem so important when your life is on the line. Ed keeps pushing *MR* hard—might as well, the quicker she faces the storm head-on and sails through, the quicker they can laugh about the danger behind—but he knows the Syd-Hob might soon turn from race to survival effort. It all depends on how that low continues developing in the Bass Strait.

Ed considers sailing east toward New Zealand to go around the storm, then chooses to stay where he is. The current over the continental shelf is less than half what boats farther out are riding, but Ed's convinced the rhumb line from Sydney to Hobart is the only way to win. There's no dodging the storm on the rhumb line, but— if the blow doesn't break the boat—that's the path to glory.

Arthur comes up on deck. He's appointed himself in charge of crew rest. The *MR* crew is such a team that their tendency is to work too much, instead of finding ways to shirk. When a man has been on deck too long, Arthur appears at his elbow and softly encourages him to find a bunk. Now it's Ed's turn.

Go below, he tells Ed. You'd better rest now. While you can.

Ed remembers his father's parting words and nods to Arthur. No telling how bad the storm could be.

KNOCKDOWN

No matter that *Ragamuffin* passed them long ago, hoisting her spinnaker and vanishing into the distance. On an even playing field, for a short time, *Winston Churchill* had won. Life's little victories are what make it sweet.

That'll be all the racing for Winning and the men of *W-C*. From now to Hobart it's a pleasure cruise. Caution is the order of the day. Gentlemen's racing, after all, is their game. And gentlemen's racing does not involve taking undue chances.

WAITING FOR THE SKED

December 27, Midnight–3:30 A.M.

The lightning lasts until midnight. The fleet is still largely intact, but as the weather worsens, skippers are reaching a point of no return. The 3:05 A.M. sked will be the time of decision—if the weather continues to worsen, and other friends report they're turning back, they'll head for shore, too. But if the BOM is still forecasting no more than fifty-five knots, they'll soldier on.

The 3:05 sked is the critical time because waiting eleven hours for the afternoon sked puts the fleet squarely in the Bass Strait.

At this point, the fleet is so strung out that boats are in the three different weather systems running down the length of the Australian coast. The slower boats are nowhere near the Bass Strait. They still run with the northeasterly at their backs, though at the edges of the squall line. The waves are rolling swells, and a man can stand on deck without bracing himself. It's raining hard, but the lightning show is so spectacular that many crew stay up top just to watch. *Winston Churchill* is with this group. Winning is pleased to note how lightly she's handling. Clearly, Steamer Stanley did a fine job with that quarter-million-dollar revamp. The two huddle near the doghouse, watching the fireworks display.

Lightning is not some distant fireworks for those in the middle of the pack. The air crackles with static electricity, and each bolt seems sure to strike the mast. Thunder punctuates—a mild word to describe an otherworldly roar booming down from the heavens—each jagged spark. To a man, sailors remind themselves that atmospheric goings-on are more ominous at sea than back home. The stars are not pinpricks of light, but white splatters in the sky as big as dinner plates. The wind is not a gentle tickle on the cheek, but a brooding schizophrenic that can instantaneously destroy. The rain is not something to dodge, but an omnipresent, insidious assemblage of pellets that wet everything. Sailors think of two sensations when they think of rain: wet undergarments, because sooner or later the rain and wind act in symphony to push water inside wet-weather gear; and mildew—after the first rain of a voyage, the area belowdecks is a moist assemblage of men and their clothing. They will not dry until the boat kisses the dock, and man and clothing find a Laundromat. The term *foul* weather gear takes on a whole new meaning after a week at sea.

Boats in the middle of the fleet are reintroducing themselves to these sensations. They run well north of the Bass Strait. As a boat races from Sydney to Hobart, parallel milestones on land give sailors a sense of location. In order, there's Sydney, Wollongong, and Nowra, all bunched within a hundred miles. Then there's a long stretch before Eden, a fishing village. From Eden it's about twenty-five miles to Gabo Island and the Bass Strait. Once a boat enters the Bass Strait, it's two hundred miles to Tasmania. A whole new set of landmarks note the passage of boats down that coast.

The middle of the fleet is currently between Nowra and Eden. They straddle weather systems, with the easy run of the northeast winds behind them, and the sure blow of the Bass Strait southerly ahead. The wind is changing. Mildly, but it's changing. Some even say that it's swirling a bit, or "clocking around." But the difference is so slight that it's only manifestation is in the ocean. The seas are steeper, a tad more hostile. Andrew Buckland, the veteran of two decades of Syd-Hob and Fastnet aboard *Assassin*, comments to crewmates that these are the worst forty-knot seas he's ever seen. The forecasted fifty-five knots, he adds, is going to be very uncomfortable.

The scale for wind goes like this: forty knots is an aquatic nightmare, but boats are definitely still racing; fifty knots is hold on to your hats, and still barely racing; 60 knots is frightening, with survival replacing racing; and over sixty knots, there's so much noise from the wind, so much water in the air, that a pulsing jag of adrenaline and heightened sense of reality pervades crews. Sailors unafraid in weather over sixty knots can be deemed mentally unbalanced.

On a simpler scale, fifty-five knots is twice as bad as forty. And somewhere about sixty-five begins a whole other dimension. Sailors who have survived sixty-five-plus winds say they can't imagine sailing through anything greater and living.

The reason is that wind alone would be a handful. But wind is what riles waves. For the fleet to hear of winds officially climbing from thirty-five knots to fifty-five knots is confirmation that they're sailing into truly powerful seas. The waves have already gone from rolling swells ("Isn't this fun!" one sailor on *Assassin* exulted as they ran downwind atop the gentle giants) to steep seas to showing flecks of white water atop their peaks. That means breaking waves are soon to follow. Sailors will tell you that a wave is not dangerous until it becomes a breaking wave—and then it is deadly. Breaking waves knock boats down or roll them over and shove them under.

In this middle pack are the leaders of the handicap race. *Midnight Rambler* and *Sword of Orion* are in this group. Others: *Stand Aside, Business Post Naiad, Chutzpah, B-52*. They have stepped through the looking glass, but only slightly. The world is still a relatively normal place. Will Oxley, the hulking marine biologist navigating *B-52*, actually takes pleasure in the storm. Prerace, he'd spent considerable time with Clouds Badham plotting weather movements. Both agreed *B-52* would move past the lightning and into the front at midnight. And here they are.

The third group, at the front of the fleet, are the maxis. Starting at 11 P.M., everyone aboard the maxis gets a glimpse of things to come. They are not to Gabo Island, the recognized delineation between the Australian coastline and the Bass Strait. That moment won't come until dawn. But the southerly wind races across the decks of *Sayonara* and *Brindabella*. *Wild Thing* and *Marchioness* sled close behind. *Nokia* has ripped a spinnaker and mizzen sail in the early moments of the electrical storm and has fallen off the pace.

All the maxis are several hours ahead of *Morning Glory*'s pace when setting the course record in 1996.

The vastness of blue-water sailing is such that boats can race neck and neck without seeing each other. *Sayonara* and *Brindabella* are three miles apart. In daylight their sails would be obvious to each other—*Sayonara*'s bright white spinnaker with the red rising sun is hard to miss—but the storm's total darkness makes this impossible and the boats don't carry radar.

Marchioness, if nothing else, is the culinary favorite. Chef Peter Mcadam's planned menus for the twenty-four-man crew disdain the "three days of wet sandwiches" philosophy. Instead, it's entrées featuring avocado vinaigrette, lamb curry, sirloin steak with green salad and baby potatoes. Dessert includes flambéed strawberries and pecan pie. One menu heading is "Midnight Snacks on the Rail": banana pancakes, maple syrup, toasted cheese sandwiches.

So they sail side by side—*Sayonara, Brindabella, Marchioness,* and *Wild Thing*—unaware of each other's position. All four maxis are making tactical maneuvers under cover of darkness. Just before midnight, *Sayonara*'s crew thinks lightning has illuminated

Brindabella off their starboard bow. But the flash is all too brief, and with the seas rising, perhaps the image of sails in the distance is just a mirage. No matter. The position of both boats will be revealed by the 3:05 A.M. sked.

The sked is a highlight for competitive as well as psychological reasons. Crews gather around the radio to hear the sked. As each boat checks in, navigators plot their latitude and longitude. The competitive reason is that it's nice to know where the opponent lurks. In long-distance, multiday racing, winning means more than being a good sailor. It's that bold strategic move no one can see that often makes the difference, whether that's an aggressive change in direction or a risky sail change. The cover of darkness means the opponent can't counter. Meanwhile, because the opponent is plotting similar aggressiveness, a good skipper anticipates the move. Few sports offer day and night strategizing. A better comparison would be chess. Or war.

Psychologically—and counter to competitive emotion—crews crave the voices over the sked because it makes them feel good to know where everyone else is. It's easy for a crew to feel it's just their tiny boat against the big bad sea. But the sked makes everyone feel that they're in it together—part of something much bigger than the tensions and smells of their floating community. Knowing that others are close, even if they can't be seen, is comforting.

The sked, though, is still four hours off when the maxis meet the southerly. It's not *the* storm—not the apocalyptic low Roger Badham has predicted—but it's pretty awful. Waves go haywire as the current and forty-knot wind collide. (Currents are named for the direction they're headed, winds for the direction they've come from. This is how a southerly current can collide with a southerly wind.) The wind clocks around, so the maxis go from having forty knots at their back to sailing into the same wind. Spinnakers come down (*Sayonara* has already blown out three; they carry only four). Headsails and jibs slide up their tracks into position.

On board *Sayonara*, the mainsail rips at midnight. Crew slide forward to examine the damage and find that the rip is actually the minor problem. The main's track—the small rails upon which it raises and lowers—is detaching from the mast. If not fixed, *Sayonara* could lose the main altogether.

While the track is under repair, *Sayonara* takes the extreme measure of hoisting her storm trisail. Below, as the weather continues to deteriorate, experienced Whitbread and America's Cup sailors get seasick. The sounds and smells of almost two dozen men retching fills the hold.

Ellison, who steered *Sayonara* out of the harbor without getting hit, is taking the midnight helm. At three he hands it over to Brad Butterworth, a New Zealander. When Ellison slides below, he consults with navigator Mark Rudiger, trying to figure if the weather will get better or worse. Their computers show the front swirling toward the mouth of the Strait, almost in position to hammer the fleet. An incredulous Ellison recalls the last time he saw such a picture. "It was on the Weather Channel," he tells the unflappable Rudiger, one of the world's premier navigators. "And it was called a hurricane. What the fuck is that doing out here?"

• • •

The first people to cross the Bass Strait walked. Australia and Tasmania were once part of the same island, with a line of mountains known as the Great Dividing Range running from the tropical jungles at the northern tip of Australia's east coast, clear down to the southern tip of Tasmania. On the Australian mainland the peaks are known as the Australian Alps, but the mountains are almost as tall in Tasmania, laced with white-water rivers and alpine lakes. Between the Australian Alps and Tasmania's peaks is an inexplicable gap, a low plateau almost two hundred miles wide.

The plateau would one day be dubbed the Bass Plains, named for a man who would never walk on it by cartographers who would never see it. This land bridge connected Tasmania and Australia. The Bass Plains are how aborigines crossed into Tasmania 35,000 years ago. When the most recent ice age ended between 13,500 and 8,000 years back, the waters of the Southern Ocean and the Tasman Sea rose. The Bass Plains flooded. When the ice was done melting, water one hundred meters deep in some spots covered the land bridge, never to recede. The Bass Plains became the Bass Strait. A sailing "black hole" was born.

Black holes are freaks of the ocean, danger zones where the worst possible wind and wave and currents come together with remarkable—and unpredictable—force. Sailors will tell you that Cape of Good Hope, at the southern tip of Africa, is one such black hole. The Indian and Atlantic Oceans meet there, each bringing their quiver of currents, weather systems, wave patterns, and winds. When the maelstrom collides far out to sea, there's plenty of space to smash headlong, then smooth things out. But on landfall—the Cape of Good Hope—the conflicting forces meet an immovable mass. Winds swirl, swells abruptly crest and crash onto beaches, and the waters just offshore don't move north nor south nor east nor west, but in all those directions at once.

Ships navigating black holes must be on constant watch for the sudden wind change or blindsiding wave. Being mischievous in nature, waves like to work in pairs: the first comes out of nowhere to knock a ship over with a blinding jab. The following wave—coming right behind the first, so the hapless ship is without recovery time—pile-drives a hundred tons of water onto the craft's deck. The ship is typically rolled over, with those on deck washed away. If it's a sailboat, the mast is snapped. The radio antenna, which rides at the tiptop of the mast, is deep underwater, meaning the crew—the living crew, those trapped inside—can't radio for help. They can only stand helplessly inside their turtled hull, hoping another wave rolls them over before their air supply runs out.

Swimming away is out of the question for two reasons. First, swimming out the hatches means opening them, which means the air supply and the boat's watertight seal disappear immediately.

The instant a crew member opens a hatch to swim out, seawater will rush in with such force that swimming out is impossible. Drowning is a gulp of salt water and two minutes without oxygen away, and the boat will sink.

But let's say a lucky crewman swims out. He holds his breath until the water pressure equalizes, then swims past his mates out the hatch. Let's say he's even lucky enough to be wearing a life vest. Most sailors aren't, but let's just say he's lucky.

When he reaches the surface and gulps in his first lungful of air, the giant swells will try to shove salt water down his lungs instead. Blowing spume flecks so much moisture through the air in a gale that a man doesn't need to put his head underwater to take a drink.

Then this lost sailor will bob like a cork as swell after swell pushes him across the ocean surface. Within hours he'll be miles from his sunken boat, which is where search-and-rescue helicopters will be looking for him. If hypothermia or sharks don't get him, despair most surely will. This is the reason many open-ocean sailors don't wear life jackets. If washed overboard, without rescue in sight, they fold their arms across their chest, stop the eggbeater kick that keeps their legs treading water, say a final prayer, and surrender their bodies to the sea.

Even the lucky ones.

An accident like that can happen on any ocean in the world, but with more regularity in the treachery of a black hole. Other black holes can be found at the tip of South America, Cape Horn; the Maui Channel in the Hawaiian Islands; and the North Atlantic off Ireland's southern coast.

The Bass Strait owes its black hole status to an odd variety of factors. The most glaring is the "Roaring Forties" wind belt, circling the world between latitudes forty and fifty south. The Roaring Forties blow with the force of myth, and in the Patagonia region of Argentina, pilots have claimed the Roaring Forties blew so strong that jet fighter aircraft were forced backward. These same winds are funneled through the Bass Strait at sea level with even greater force.

Wind, sailors can handle. It's what they know. But the waves of the Bass Strait are a type unlikely to be encountered anywhere else. The Bass Strait is as deep as three hundred feet and as shallow as just one hundred. Swells coming eastward from the Antarctic (Southern) Ocean travel over waters several thousand meters deep. No landmass impedes their journey. Currents in the Southern Ocean rip at an average of thirteen miles per hour. Building seas from successive Southern Ocean storms ride along on that raging current (the typical white-water river runs at half that speed). At this point—unless a fierce wind is blowing—the ocean resembles a series of benevolent giants known as swells. Sloping shoulders, mushy heads. The swells range in size from one meter tall to thirty. They undulate slowly, often a half mile apart. Their summit is not the oververtical white-water pitch of a breaking wave, but the broad plateau of a mesa. As long as a sailboat doesn't turn sideways to a swell, the chances of rolling or sinking are minimal.

When these deep-water swells suddenly hit the shallow, wind-whipped Bass Strait, however, they react as all waves do when confronted by land and wind: they rear up, crest, and break. The swells—now waves—are squeezed through the Bass Strait's funnel by the sudden appearance of land on both sides. The current's force is intensified. The waves aren't a half mile apart anymore, but staggered atop one another.

So a sailor crossing the Bass Strait in rough weather can expect the winds to be abominable and the waves to be omnipresent and tall. There's a messy quality to the waves—rising, then folding and crumbling and collapsing when the wind from behind shoves the white-water crest off before it can tube symmetrically like a banzai-pipeline surf wave.

That's one-half of the Bass Strait black hole.

On the other end of the Strait, the churning water of the Southern Ocean merges with the Tasman Sea, an adjunct of the Pacific Ocean with a mass of powerful wave and wind patterns just as screwy as the Strait's.

Merge is a subtle word describing the collision of two great oceans. Water from the Pacific flows toward the Bass Strait from east to west. Like the Southern Ocean swells they're about to smack into headlong, swells from the Pacific have traveled over water several thousand feet deep, wholly undisturbed by landfall.

The meeting takes place near Gabo Island, just off the southeast coast of Australia. Sailors traveling from Sydney to Hobart feel a sea change well before then, but the waters off Gabo Island are the black hole's ground zero. The collision makes for the same unpredictable wave patterns as in other black holes, only larger. Satellite imagery done by the United States' National Oceanic and Atmospheric Administration (NOAA), the world's foremost authority on weather forecasting and meteorology, has shown the waves off Australia to be the biggest on earth.

In bad weather, a sailor never knows from which direction these waves will rise. Many boats stick one brave man on the bow with the sole function of wave-watching. He sees a wave, emphatically signals with his arms to point it out (the roaring wind makes vocal communications impossible), and the skipper steers away from, or into, the wave appropriately.

It was 1966 before a man died racing Syd-Hob. The tone of the race had begun to change. The cachet of finishing Syd-Hob and technological advances making sailing less physically strenuous meant an influx of average citizens racing alongside the elite Sydney sailors. So the first death wasn't from the ocean, but a heart attack. Barry Vallance, navigator on the Sydney yacht *Zilvergeest*, was stricken when the boat hit a reef at the entrance to the Derwent River, just eleven miles from the finish.

In 1973, John Varney, a young crew member on the New Zealand yacht *Inca*, died mysteriously the Syd-Hob's first night at sea. His body was transferred to a fishing boat, and citing "national obligation," the crew raced on.

In 1984, the first storm-related death occurred when Wal Russell, a seventy-two-year-old Syd-Hob vet, was washed overboard from *Yahoo* just after coming off watch. Efforts to rescue him failed, and he was last seen floating facedown.

More misadventure followed in 1989, when John Taylor, a Melbourne yachtsman, was fatally injured when struck in the head by a broken backstay block. A paramedic was lowered by helicopter to his boat, *Flying Colours*, but Taylor was already dead.

The only other fatality associated with Syd-Hob was the loss overboard of David Graham. His yacht was cruising back to Sydney after the fiftieth race in 1994. The senior crew member was washed overboard by a wave just as he unclipped his safety harness. His body was never found.

• • •

Sword of Orion meets the southerly just after one. The spinnaker comes down. Kothe, monitoring the weather from below, doesn't need a computer screen to tell him conditions have changed. The boat pitches, rolls. The wind is audible. Glyn Charles is on deck, calmly keeping *Sword* on course. When Kothe pokes his head above a hatch to note conditions on deck, he is struck by how serene Glyn is. His figure is loose, easy. Instead of focusing eyes straight forward, Glyn peers right and left from under his wet-weather hood, constantly sizing up wind conditions and wave direction. And while both seem pretty hairy to Kothe—bigger than he's ever seen—Glyn doesn't appear bothered. Kothe drops below, locks the hatch.

Glyn, meanwhile, isn't sure what to make of the conditions. As a first-timer to Syd-Hob, he feels like a visitor to a weather museum. They've got everything on display here: waves from all directions, winds that don't know which way to blow, and spray ripping off the ocean to sting his eyes.

The start, under clear skies in Sydney Harbor. Twenty-four hours later, a hurricane-force weather system will await the fleet in the Bass Strait (below). *(Delly Carr/PPL)* *(Ian Mainsbridge/PPL)*

BELOW: *AFR Midnight Rambler*, skippered by Ed Psaltis, leaving the dock on race day. *(Ed Psaltis)*

Sayonara, the Larry Ellison–owned maxi, blazes down Australia's east coast (just outside South Head) under spinnaker. *(Delly Carr/PPL)*

The crew of *Winston Churchill*, Australia's pride, sailing out of Sydney Harbor at the start. Note the doghouse just fore of the wheel. *(News Ltd./PPL)*

Brindabella, the George Snow–owned maxi, launching off a small wave on December 27, before the weather bomb. *(Ian Mainsbridge/PPL)*

Glyn Charles (left) sailing for England at the 1996 Olympics in Savannah, Georgia. Star Class; 10th place. *(Peter Bentley/PPL)*

Nokia, mid-storm. Note the bare mast and waves washing aboard (above). Below, *Nokia* gets pummeled by a breaking wave. Photo is taken from cockpit (note the bow underwater and severe angle of the deck). *(Ian Mainsbridge/PPL)*

Stand Aside crew readies life raft and awaits rescue, after being tossed and broken by violent waves. Notice the exposed fiberglass and foam core where the cabin has been ripped off. *(Rod Hunter)*

View of *Stand Aside* from life raft (notice the swell to the right); a rescue helicopter hovers overhead. *(Rod Hunter)*

Business Post Naiad, dismasted. The destroyed sails and rigging float to the left, the boom is bent. The rest of the crew has been rescued, but the bodies of Phil Skeggs and Bruce Guy are still strapped in bunks below. *(Ian Mainsbridge/PPL)*

Chopper view of *Stand Aside*, rolled and dismasted. December 27 between 4 and 5 P.M., before rescue began. Note life raft tied to stern. *(Ian Mainsbridge/PPL)*

Richard Winning, owner-skipper of *Winston Churchill*, stepping off helicopter after being rescued. *(News Ltd./PPL)*

The body of a dead crewman being loaded aboard an Australian navy plane. *(News Ltd./PPL)*

Business Post Naiad
after being abandoned
at sea and later towed
into Eden.
(John Ford)

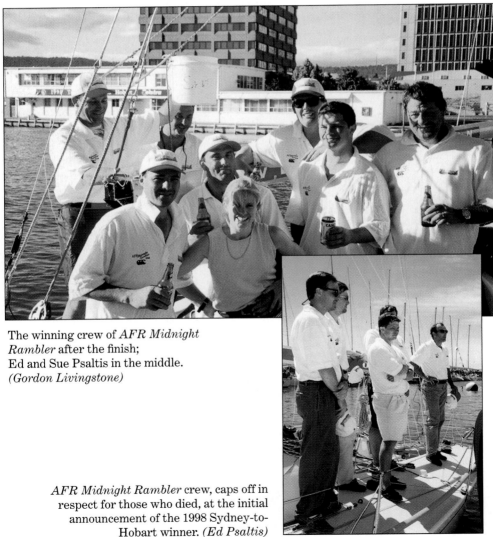

The winning crew of *AFR Midnight
Rambler* after the finish;
Ed and Sue Psaltis in the middle.
(Gordon Livingstone)

AFR Midnight Rambler crew, caps off in
respect for those who died, at the initial
announcement of the 1998 Sydney-to-
Hobart winner. *(Ed Psaltis)*

Some men might think the conditions miserable. Glyn Charles finds them educational—one more experience to make him a better all-around sailor.

And since the year his father moved out, Glyn has focused exclusively on that goal. He was just sixteen, showing up at the Olympic Trials for Finn-class dinghies with a boat so old and heavy he needed help just getting it off the beach. It didn't help that Glyn was slight, making his struggle to control the boat on the water just as daunting. British Olympic coach Rod Carr, impressed by Glyn's pluck, pulled him aside and suggested he sail the lighter Laser instead of a dinghy. This suggestion would prove Glyn's ticket to sailing success.

Glyn's first foray into blue-water racing was when he sailed the 1987 Fastnet aboard the thirty-three-footer *Decosol Car Care*. Fellow crewmen Andrew Preece noted at the time how tactically astute and focused Glyn was. Glyn Charles, he said, was the most focused sailor he had ever seen. Even at twenty-one.

Preece, racing with Charles again in 1994, noted that Charles's wondrous focus had matured into an aura of control.

Now, an Olympics under his belt and in demand worldwide as helmsman and tactician, Charles is coming into his own. Margaret Charles attributes her son's success to a new maturity. The temper problems, she notes, that had caused Glyn to lash out at less-driven sailors during a race, are a thing of the past. "He's no saint," she says of Glyn. "I know that. But he's much more together sailing-wise and in temperament, too."

Annie has a great deal to do with the change. She knows the same focus and bent toward success as Glyn. She can parry his wit with an equally quick tongue and possesses the resources to jet off to far-flung ports, which means Glyn's travels don't crimp the relationship too severely. And Annie loves Glyn enough to purchase a home with him in Emsworth, overlooking a marina, and adjacent Portsmouth. This despite the fifty-mile commute from Portsmouth to London.

She is party to his rage when he tells her about his battles to succeed as a professional sailor and helped him overcome his disillusionment with the Royal Yachting Association after the two failed Olympic campaigns. She knows how all that disappointment drained him mentally and physically. And how even now, the constant hustling to find a boat or a sponsor can make a man lose his way.

There's a saying about sailors and their dual nature: they make love offshore. Meaning, as creatures of land equally comfortable on water, they never know where they fit in best—on a boat all they talk about is women, but on land all they talk about is sailing.

But Glyn Charles is a professional sailor. He doesn't make love offshore, he sails. That means Glyn isn't thinking of Annie right now, much as he'd like to. Every fiber of his being is devoted to processing tactics, analyzing winds, shouting orders in crisp fashion. Sailing is life. If Glyn is going to be *the* top sailor in a market-driven world where professional positions are few, he needs to make up for his lack of political savvy with sheer professionalism (after sailing with Charles, Royal Yachting Association Olympic manager John Derbyshire was miffed by Glyn's confrontational style: "According to Glyn, I had failed to call a single layline correctly," Derbyshire sniffed), physical fitness (Glyn takes a two-mile swim several days a week), and experience in all conditions.

The southerly change is a unique problem to Glyn, and he enjoys the challenge. As the wind grows more fierce, he calls for the sails to be reduced to a double-reefed main and small jib. He pushes his hood back off his eyes, even though the blowing sea rakes his face.

It's dark out there, he thinks, looking into the night. Not the kind of night to make mistakes.

• • •

At the same time, on *Assassin*, which also sailed into the southerly at 1 A.M., four bunks on the right side break from the pressure of waves lifting and dropping the hull. Skipper Hugo van

Kretschmar has the crew poke around for more structural damage. The danger for a wooden boat like *Winston Churchill* is springing a plank. On modern boats, the hull is likely a "foam sandwich," in the terms of top designer Scott Jutson. The black art of hull building means several different substances are used, but most have foam on the inside with Kevlar skins, and some sort of laminate on either side.

The problem for these hulls is delamination caused by pounding, then a corrosion of the Kevlar and foam until a hole develops. The process can take hours, or—if the right wave strikes—seconds. "Sydney to Hobart cannot be seen as a typical race," Jutson notes. "And events occur in Sydney to Hobart that cannot be seen as typical. There's a ferocity to that sea. Boats break out there. A boat that can survive Sydney to Hobart can survive anywhere."

Seemingly impervious to such worries, Ed Psaltis guides *Midnight Rambler* into the southerly at two. He boldly surfs waves, spinnaker up. The entire hull rides the knife's edge, bow poised precariously atop swell's crest. A trough lies fifteen feet below the bow, meaning the front section of *MR*'s hull isn't even in the water. Ed uses the term *surfing*, but from where he stands—sea far below, sky so low it feels as if the blackness is sitting on his shoulders, wind pushing his face—it's more like flying. Touching immortality. He's Peter Pan at the helm of Hook's flying pirate ship, on his way to Neverland. Or maybe just ten-year-old Ed Psaltis at the helm of his parents' boat on a Mediterranean summer's day.

The display of sailing skill ends violently. First one staggering gust, then a second, whips into the spinnaker, pouring sharp downward pressure on the bow. The first jolt baptizes the bow, knocking her from her perch but not shoving her far into the trough. The second jolt tries to bury *Midnight Rambler*, pushing the spinnaker downward into the trough with so much force it feels as if the world's heaviest anchor is chained to the bow. Ed is no longer surfing nor flying nor really even sailing—but making like a submarine. If the wave were bigger, Ed would find himself and *MR* shoved even farther underwater, perhaps buried by the following sea. But the wave is small by Sydney to Hobart specifications, just ten feet. Ed recovers and guides *Midnight Rambler* back on top of the knife's edge.

Lying on his back in the navigator's compartment, Bob feels the boat lurch when the first gust hits. He slides forward the second time, glad he wasn't on deck to know how close they came to capsizing. Bob sidles up to the cockpit and diplomatically suggests that if Ed doesn't take down the kite immediately, they won't have a kite—or a boat—in a few minutes.

Ed, shamed by his own hubris—what was he thinking? This is no time for foolishness—agrees immediately. He calls all hands on deck to get the spinnaker down.

One by one the crew charges up through the hatch, buttoning and zipping wet-weather gear, flopping feet into boots. Profanity and dark humor stumble from the lips of those roused from sleep.

But the crew is ready, Ed having put them through countless storm drills in Sydney Harbor in the months leading up to the race. In the old days of sailing, boats suspended racing during a storm. They took all their sails down and "hove to," or floated under bare poles until a storm passed.

Ocean-racing theory now holds that boats continue forward progress. As the mainsail—the boat's largest sail—catches too much wind during a storm, the racing sailor has three options. First, reduce the size of the mainsail through reefing.

To facilitate reefing, the mainsail has two or three lines of eyelets parallel to the boom, that appendage of the mast that controls the base of a sail and moves laterally across the deck (*boom*, one sailing joke goes, is the sound it makes when it hits your skull). When the wind is excessive for a full mainsail, the sail size is reduced by lowering the sail to one row of the eyelets. A mainsail reefed to its smallest size is known as triple-reefed. If this is still too much sail—and Ed will know because the boat will be going too fast to control, and the bow will nose too deeply into swells—the second option is taking the mainsail off and replacing it with a much smaller sail known as a storm trisail.

The trisail allows the boat rapid forward movement, but with more control. This is hoisted up the mainmast. Raising the storm trisail is something of an emergency maneuver and invariably means chaos reigns. The boat is overpowered and heeling to one side, with waves crashing across the decks. Men are screaming to be heard above the roar of the storm, yet can barely hear each other. Each wave pushes them sideways, and they cling to winches and ropes and mast and stanchions so they don't fly overboard. The boom, when the wind shifts, swings impulsively across the deck at head level, threatening all. On top of that, hoisting a storm trisail doesn't happen often, meaning the crew members lack the muscle memory that comes with performing a task over and over. So a simple procedure becomes a complicated mess.

A final, desperate option for the sailor who wants to continue racing in the most awful conditions is removing the trisail so that mainmast is bare. Then a triangular sail known as a storm jib is raised from the diagonal wire running from the front of the boat to the top of the mainmast. The problem with a storm jib is that it shifts all steering power from the back of the boat to the front. This makes the rudder useless. The skipper has to fight the wheel extrahard to pilot the boat. Still, it beats hoving to in a competitive situation.

Even on sunny days leading up to Boxing Day—"people must have thought we were idiots"—*Midnight Rambler*'s crew rehearsed for a Bass Strait storm again and again and again. "Once more," Ed would yell to the crew after they had reefed the main, taken off the main, set the trisail, taken down the trisail, set the storm jib, removed the storm jib, then taken all the survival sails off and hoisted the main again. He put the crew through the process until they were sick of it . . . then did it a few more times. The crew grouses—that's what crews do, even ones containing brothers and childhood friends, even ones with over fifty Syd-Hobs between them—but they perform the ritual until Ed asks no more.

Now, the time for drills is past, and *Midnight Rambler*'s crew take down the spinnaker in the teeth of some serious weather. Arthur is the last man to come on deck. He was sleeping. He wears only his bear suit. Though the wind clocks mightily—blowing first from the south, then the east, then west, not making up its mind—his choice not to wear wet-weather gear is sound. It doesn't take seven bodies to pull a spinnaker down. And besides, seas still follow the boat. No water's going to wash over the bow. And, hey, since Arthur's come up late, they've already begun taking the spinnaker down without him. In fact, the rest of the guys appear to be doing quite well without him. He stands in the main hatchway, poised to help if things get dicey, but actually hoping he can slip back into his warm bunk as soon as the spinnaker is safely lowered.

Ed is at the helm. Arthur stands a foot in front of him, in front of the main hatchway. On the bow, twenty feet in front of the brothers Psaltis, wrangling with a spinnaker that's twisting like a bad phone cord in the swirling wind, are five of the best sailors anywhere: Bob Thomas ("can fix anything, anywhere," describes Ed), Michael Bencsik ("huge determination, never gives up"), Chris Rockell ("a New Zealander, dependable in any conditions"), Gordon Livingstone ("great team man, a real doer"), and John Whitfeld ("tough as they come").

Ed surfs up a wave. *Midnight Rambler* handles differently now that the spinnaker isn't in place. Less steering power. He struggles to compensate. She races down the face of the wave, once again burying the nose in the trough. A wall of green water cascades over the decks, drenching everyone.

Especially Arthur.

The worst part is, for weight purposes the crew only carry one set of thermals apiece. Arthur is doomed to spend the rest of the race in the cold and damp bear suit. The crew thinks it's hilarious. Arthur's swearing. He'll continue for the next half hour. After a short break, he'll resume the swearing when Ed orders all hands to stay on deck through the night. With the front upon them, they have to be ready for anything.

Ed has the crew walk the deck, ensuring that *Midnight Rambler* is as prepared as can be. Winches tightened, hatches sealed, ropes coiled. Sailing a boat through rough seas is like driving a car down a bad road—the car can make the journey, but the constant pounding causes things to break and fall off.

Ed talks himself through his emergency preparedness checklist. It begins with the sailing-oriented and ends with survival: What smaller sails will he hoist? Are the crew all wearing safety harnesses? Where are the other items of safety gear—life rafts, flares, extra food and water? Ed chatters with the crew about strategic ways to handle all this.

It's like a washing machine, Chris says. The waves are becoming steeper, their direction unpredictable.

All the other boats, Ed hears himself replying in a voice that's much too stoic, are going through the same shit.

Is he trying to reassure the crew or himself?

After the boat has been checked and rechecked, Ed stations all of the crew except Bob along the windward rail (high side of the boat as she tilts to one side) as ballast. This allows him to sail *MR* at an extreme angle into the wind, making maximum speed. Bob heads below to listen for weather updates and to double-check their position by GPS.

The weather has turned sour, with the worst of the storm still to come. Ed knows he's gotten about all the rest he's going to get for a while. Now it's time to make a final decision about sailing across the Bass Strait. Bob comes back with weather reports stating that the low is deepening. The storm will continue moving from west to east. The question is whether to run east to go around the storm. Or head west—straight into the teeth of it—so that the storm passes over them immediately. That way—assuming *Midnight Rambler* doesn't delaminate into thousands of foam and Kevlar pieces—they'll be done with the worst of it right off.

While the rest of the fleet faces the storm, *Midnight Rambler* would be done with it, focusing on the business of racing (is this our year?). The remainder of the trip to Hobart would be on relatively smooth seas. And by staying west, they also stick close to the rhumb line.

Variables affect Ed's thinking: How long will the storm last? Which direction will it move? Will it really take place, or is this just another BOM false alarm?

Nothing the maxis are enduring four hours ahead is relayed to the rest of the fleet. Weather information—even horrendous weather warnings—are a closely guarded secret in sailing. It's tactical.

That sort of knowledge would make Ed's strategic choice easier.

By 3:05, Ed has made his decision. After he checks in, using the cover of darkness, he'll sail west. The storm will be tackled head-on.

The sked starts with a BOM weather report: forty-five-to-fifty-five-knot winds within twelve hours. Then, one by one, boats report position: *ABN Amro Challenge . . . Adagio . . . Adrenalin . . .*

Assassin doesn't report in. Highly unusual, as she's skippered by the CYCA commodore. That word gets around the fleet, with all agreeing that Hugo wouldn't miss a sked for tactical reasons. He's too responsible for that.

A minute later, a more glaring omission: *Brindabella*. Skippers throughout the fleet wonder how a maxi can disappear like that.

Chutzpah checks in, leading the handicap division, but angling east toward New Zealand.

Midnight Rambler is ten miles behind *Chutzpah*, still over the continental shelf.

When *Sayonara* checks in, she's four miles north of Green Cape and twenty miles out to sea. She'll be in the Bass Strait by sunrise. Assuming nothing has happened to *Brindabella*, she'll be alongside.

And so on . . .

The Aussies think nothing of it, however, because the Australian connection to the sea is greater than in any other modern society, hearkening back to the Polynesians when the South Pacific was an outrigger waterway. So it is that the Royal Australian Navy has a vast pool of experienced ocean swimmers to choose from when selecting rescue swimmers. But just six men are selected annually from hundreds of applicants. The training is harsh, and even those completing the entire 105-day course are never certain they'll work as part of a rescue crew. Tenacity, as RAN training supervisor Petty Officer Phil Livingstone sums up, is what makes a rescue swimmer. "They must never give up. There isn't a swimmer in the branch who won't jump when he has to. They all know their actions could mean the difference between life and death for a person in distress."

But a rescuer clipped to a lifeline is just the tip of the spear for Australian Search and Rescue (AusSAR). Their headquarters facility is in Canberra, 120 miles southwest of Sydney, and fifty miles from the nearest ocean. In a white, cement office building on Constitution Avenue, the Rescue Coordination Center is poised to respond to rescue requests around the clock.

The key to success, AusSAR's mission statement proclaims, is flexibility. As Australia has almost ten thousand miles of coastline and not enough financial assets to maintain dedicated search and rescue nationwide, a tiered strategy is undertaken. First, local resources. Second, defense resources, if requested. Finally, enlistment of peripheral resources such as private aircraft or fishing vessels.

Most sea rescues begin with either a radio distress signal or satellite distress signal. EPIRBs (emergency position indicating radio beacons), PLBs (personal locator beacons), and ELTs (emergency locator transmitters) bounce Maydays off the International COSPAS-SARSAT search-and-rescue satellite. Within seconds of transmitting by EPIRB, the emerceny shows up in Canberra as a target symbol on a computer screen.

A call is immediately placed to the entity responsible for a specific region. Whether it be the Victoria Police Airwing with their helicopters and rescue swimmers, or the Royal Volunteer Coastal Patrol (Australia's aquatic version of the volunteer fire department) and their thirty-foot rescue boats. Sometimes the military is called in, whether navy or air force, but only after civilian authorities have expended all resources.

In long-distance sea rescues, C-130 Hercules and PC-3 Orion fixed-wing aircraft coordinate grid searches—basically, flying back and forth over an area in an overlapping pattern. A flare is dropped when a boat is sighted. Often, if the victim's craft is going under, a life raft with survival gear inside will be dropped, too.

In cases of major calamity—say, a sinking ocean liner—an additional step is added: thirty of Australia's top aerial and nautical rescue experts gather immediately in the Rescue Coordination Center. Known as the Australian Search and Rescue Team, these thirty work from the War Room, a massive open area on the third floor of the AMSA headquarters. White boards line the walls. Maps, faxes, satellite reports, and the nonstop ringing of telephones describe the War Room in time of crisis. The white boards are covered with the names of ships and aircraft involved—location, last reports, status, number of hours the crew has flown. The AusSAR team works round the clock until the rescue is complete, coordinating civil, military, and other extraneous resources. As an example, in addition to launching Orions and Hercules, the AusSAR team might find a tanker to deliver an extra load of fuel from Sydney to some remote air base so search planes can fly a little longer. Or set up rescue charts to figure out the drift path of boats and life rafts. Or even order civilian mariners to join the search.

Take the John Quinn rescue in 1993. It was an horrific year for Syd-Hols racing, with a fifty-knot gale forcing 66 of 104 starters to turn back. Quinn's thirty-six-footer, *MEM*, was swamped by a forty-foot wave. Quinn, standing on deck at the time, was hit by such a powerful wall of water that his safety line broke. He was shoved into the sea while the boat sailed on without him.

Quinn would stay in the water five long hours. Even after his inflatable life jacket began to lose buoyancy, Quinn fought to stay alive. Day turned to night. Then, riding the crest of a wave, Quinn saw what looked like a wall of illumination chugging his way. It was the cargo ship *Ampol Sarel*, spotlights blazing. Training its lights on Quinn, the *Ampol Sarel* called in a rescue ship to lift him from the water. A half hour later, Quinn was safe. Amazingly, Quinn raced Syd-Hob the next year. Even more amazingly, he won.

• • •

Lit up like "a Christmas tree on water," in Murray's words, Patterson's crew pull alongside the stricken boat. After insuring there are no medical emergencies, a rope is thrown. It's a four-hour tow back to the Clyde River and a sheltered mooring off Snapper Island. *ABN Amro Challenge* is dragged by the nose like a prize bull. The harrowing, stressful journey sees Patterson and *Community Spirit* endure the same fierce waves as before, but while struggling to stay in the boat, they must also strain to keep tow ropes from breaking, their engine from being overtaxed, and the useless chunk of laminate off their stern from capsizing.

Back in Canberra, the skeleton holiday crew on duty at AusSAR see *Amro Challenge*'s problems as singular. Like all men working midnight to dawn over the holidays, few are senior in rank. None of them wants to damage a budding career—especially since Aus-SAR is a glorious fast track in the mundane world of government work—by making frantic predawn phone calls to supervisors. They are aware of the pending storm, but the rest of the fleet seems to be doing well. No sense in rousing people from a bed on Sunday morning during Christmas vacation unless absolutely necessary.

In addition to the short AusSAR staff, Royal Australian Navy (RAN) and Royal Australian Air Force (RAAF) personnel are on holiday leave. All RAN vessels assigned to coastal waters are in port. None of the half dozen men on duty at AusSAR in Canberra wants to be the guy sending ships to sea or planes in the air unnecessarily. Better, as in the case of *Amro Challenge*, to let those local volunteer zealots get their jollies and a little good press bouncing around at a time of night when they should be sleeping off a Saturday night in the pub. Everyone knows the Syd-Hob runs into bad weather. Happens every year. But it's a private race. Those idiot sailors are good at what they do, and they always pull through. Why should this year be any different?

The midnight crew's talk shifts to the cost of a carbon-fiber mast and who has that kind of money and I think it's covered by insurance and why in the world would you willingly climb inside a sailboat no bigger than the foredeck of a frigate (even an eighty-foot maxi like *Nokia* is toy-proportioned) and sail across Bass Strait? Might as well act like old Bass and Flinders themselves and make the journey in a rowboat.

Then the skeleton crew enjoys a burst of energy as sunlight streams in their office windows, kick-starting circadian rhythms. Not bad, they congratulate themselves over a last cup of stale coffee before stumbling home. A rescue in high seas, nobody hurt, Syd-Hob progressing into better conditions. Situation over. Not bad at all.

All this is good news to Shane Pashley. Now thirty-three, Pashley was just twenty-nine when he was lowered to Isabelle Autissier's boat on New Year's Day. The Autissier rescue was his first, and he considered it easy. The Australian and worldwide acclaim that followed was a nice sidelight. He was stationed in Adelaide then, halfway across the country and closer to the Southern Ocean. Now HMAS *Albatross*, 817th Squadron, in Nowra is home. The *Albatross* mission focuses on the Pacific Ocean and the Bass Strait.

Pashley and his wife like the Nowra posting. Their home is actually off base, in the quaint historic village of Berry. He's on holiday leave and would like nothing more than to continue his off-duty routine of a morning bike ride, an afternoon of fishing, then sinking into his favorite chair in front of the TV. All days off should be so serene.

Then he wakes up December 27 and hears on the news that a boat named *Challenge Again* lost a man over the side in the night. The man was quickly recovered by the crew, and the Mayday was probably a matter of protocol in case they couldn't fish him out. But it's a sign that the sailors are having trouble. Pashley's thoughts immediately turn to rescue's own dangers.

To actually be in the water, clipping a lifeline to a victim, that's a war unto itself. In really big seas, the wind whips so much moisture in the air that it's like taking a drink each time Pashley breathes. The water is more like rivers of foam atop a black madness. The combined force of the waves and current and wind push him back, making a twenty-yard swim to a boat the equivalent of a half mile in the pool.

Sometimes Pashley will be swimming the other way, with the current and waves pushing him into the boat—pilots try not to drop him upwind, but it often happens—and he actually has to swim backward or he'll be thrown against the hull. Once at the craft, he'll tread water, talking to the victims. Even the rational ones will be mildly frightened and incoherent. The irrational sorts will be flat-out panicked, not listening to anything, yammering hysterically.

Sailors are never big about jumping into the water. Most don't wear life jackets or even have them on board. Another problem is clothing. Rescues generally happen because of storms. Sailors are layered in wet-weather gear—waterproof overalls, Gore-Tex jacket with hood, rubber boots. Add that to the thermals and fleece they're already wearing and you've got a man in ten pounds of clothing. Now ask that sailor—who's not wearing a life jacket, and in some cases isn't in great physical shape or can barely swim—to leap from the secure platform of a boat into a heaving sea. It's the biggest leap of faith in his life. He'd just as soon jump off a cliff. Nine times out of ten, he stalls or balks.

Now multiply that coaxing times a dozen, which is the average-size sailing crew. And know that up in the chopper the pilot is growing increasingly agitated about diminishing fuel supply, which means the coaxing must be addressed with greater urgency, and you have the stress and strain of a normal rescue.

● ● ●

As of dawn on Sunday, December 27, those thirty top rescue authorities are not called in—pending weather bomb or no pending weather bomb—and the Australian Search and Rescue Team is not formed. The fleet is radioing that winds have died and the clouds are thinning. The weather bomb, it seems, will not drop.

Meanwhile, a pale red sun rises over Snapper Island as the rescue of *Amro Challenge* is accomplished. Patterson and his men talk to the press, clap each other on the back, and go home to bed.

■ ■ ■

Next morning, Sunday the twenty-seventh, we lived the whole thing as best we could through the news reports on radio and television. We woke up to radio reports of carnage. They'd had a hellish night. It was one of the few media events that you're completely gripped by. A bit like the Gulf War. Or 1997, when there was a landslide in the ski resort of Thredbo, and the painstaking search for days for survivors, with every media outlet in the country broadcasting from down there. We were due back up to Sydney to lunch with friends up at Palm Beach, on the northern beaches peninsula. So we were a few hours in the car. We listened to the radio on the way up each hour, following the news updates. Sailors overboard, missing, boats knocked down. The whole catastrophe. I'd actually paid little attention to the field prior to the race day, but suddenly we're all talking about these boats as if they're old friends or something. They became so familiar, so soon. Even Shirley, my wife, and not a particularly sporting type, was sharing her worries for the yachties out there, and dropping the yachts' names into conversation as if they were entities in themselves. "Have they found *Business Post Naiad?*" she'd ask. The news got worse and worse all day. By the time we got home that night, I was ravenous for information. It was a huge story, so I tuned into *Sports Tonight* at 11 P.M., because I knew Woodsy was broadcasting from Hobart and would be right on it. He sat there grimly and gave the news of three boats missing. Completely off the map. Huge search under way. I remember the disappointment when they went to other news items after an ad break. It didn't seem like any other news was relevant in the circumstances, let alone something as trivial as basketball scores. Hell, there were people dying. In fact, there didn't seem to be a lot of information for Woodsy to go on. He kept repeating himself. Three boats missing. Something like three sailors already gone. "Just reconfirming the latest news if you've just joined us," etc., etc.

Over the next week, the story completely dominated the news and conversations at work and home. As I said to my wife later, "I've knocked back three invitations to sail in the race in my journalistic career. This is why."

—Graem Sims, Deputy Editor,
Inside Sport–Australia

EIGHT

MORNING HAS BROKEN

December 27, Dawn–Noon

Australian Broadcast Corporation helicopter pilot Garry Ticehurst is the only helicopter in the sky Sunday morning. He's been up since before dawn, alerted that the *Amro Challenge* is in trouble and *Brindabella* didn't report in for the 3:05 A.M. sked. Part of Channel 10 and ABC's comprehensive race coverage means film of the fleet at sea, so Ticehurst's job is to cover the whole story, both the ongoing race and the hunt for troubled boats. Sort of search without the rescue. So with a camera crew riding backseat, Ticehurst follows the coast down from Sydney. At six-thirty he finds *Brindabella*, sailing dead even with *Sayonara*, but three miles farther inshore. They're both thirty miles past Gabo Island, deep in the Bass Strait. *Brindabella* offers no reason for missing the sked.

Then Ticehurst choppers back to record the serene moment when, backlit by the rising sun, *Amro Challenge* is towed up the Clyde by *Community Spirit*.

Skies are clear along the Australian coast. Swells are nonexistent, especially as the Snapper Island mooring nears. Crew from both boats stand on deck with not much to do, and although the

Amro Challenge has severe structural damage and no one on either boat got much sleep last night, the moment is unexceptional. Disappointment is sweeping over *Amro*'s crew already, replacing the previous night's fears of being rolled or knocked down. This close to shore, that water seeping into the hull seems more a nuisance than a threat to life.

Ticehurst refuels in Merimbula, then choppers back out to sea. His radio is picking up chatter from several damaged vessels. *Marchioness*, the gourmet's maxi that won line honors in Easter vacation's Sydney to Mooloolaba race, radios Ticehurst that they're turning around and heading for Eden with rig damage. The seas are getting nasty, comes the report. With the damaged rig, and the weather to come, things will only get worse. *Marchioness* is motoring, a sure sign the crew wants to get off the seas as quickly as possible.

Ticehurst sees their withdrawal as a startling act of prudence: the *Marchioness* crew have 150 Syd-Hobs between them. If any crew can limp a boat across the Bass Strait for appearance' sake, it's the *Marchioness* syndicate. Strange of them to sail into the Bass Strait, then turn around and run for cover.

Another report crackles over the radio, another startling casualty: *Wild Thing*, the dark-horse contender for line honors, has joined *Marchioness* in flight back to Eden. Like *Marchioness*, *Wild Thing* was in the Bass Strait. Wind and waves combined to stress her mast. The crew, used to the flexing and heaving of a mast under full sail, pretended it was business as usual. But when the mast emitted a loud cracking noise, like a thick oak about to topple, they lowered the main and turned *Wild Thing* around almost immediately. The worry was that another series of forces would break the mast entirely and leave them at the mercy of the growing storm.

Other reports trickle in: Philip Bennett's King 38, *King Billy*, is taking on water and heading back to Sydney. The sixty-footer *Sydney* has lost its rudder. So did *Sledgehammer*. Both are making their way to Eden with jury-rigged steering systems. Conditions are drastically different from onshore, with the sun nowhere in sight and waves climbing higher than ever.

Ticehurst flies over them all, performing the dual function of letting his camera crew shoot great footage and reassuring crews aboard the damaged vessels that the world knows where they are. With every discovery, Ticehurst speaks with the skipper or navigator, then radios position and status back to race headquarters. Ticehurst's chopper becomes a radio relay vessel, much like *Young Endeavour*.

Assassin is the only boat Ticehurst can't find. *Assassin* is the first knockdown of the race, suffering the blow at 2 A.M. Running sideways to a wave, water breaks over her decks. The wave is fifteen feet tall, owning just enough heft to force *Assassin* onto her side. The knockdown is slow, accomplished in conspiracy with ensuing waves—the first one shoves *Assassin* over just far enough to get the mast near horizontal. Following waves fill the flattened mainsail and jib with water, like a pair of massive Kevlar reservoirs. *Assassin*'s decks are soon perpendicular to the sea surface. The crew holds on to stanchions, boom, rigging—anything—as they dangle over the sea.

An anxious van Kretschmar hugs the tiller and scans to his left and right—just one more wave will roll *Assassin* upside down. He cautiously pries his left fist from the tiller and hand-checks his safety harness. Made of the same industrial webbing as parachute harnesses, it coils around his shoulders and chest. A metal clip brings all four points of the design together on his sternum. A mountaineer's carabiner connects the clip to a thin length of industrial webbing. That webbing, in turn, is clipped to a safety wire or solid section of deck—sailors call this a hard point. The rest of the crew wear one, too. Should they get washed overboard, the lifelines will still connect them to the boat. If *Assassin* rolls and they are trapped beneath, a quick-release mechanism on the carabiner will allow them to swim to the surface.

KNOCKDOWN

That wasn't always so. Before Fastnet, the chest portion of the safety harness was secured to a rope, but had no release point. The rope clipped into the safety wire on a boat's rail. Posttragedy inquiries showed that many sailors drowned when trapped under the hull when their boat rolled and they were unable to detach their harnesses and swim to the surface. Hence, all harnesses made since 1979 have a release point on the chest and a release point on the boat.

As van Kretschmar anxiously scans for that next killer wave, the keel's counterweight begins righting her. The water filling her sails drips off. First, just small drops, then rivulets, then great rivers of water pouring onto the decks. *Assassin* rights herself as slowly as she'd been knocked over—like a slow-motion replay on some late-night sports show. Kretschmar's wait for his boat to stand tall is agonizing. He never stops expecting the mighty wave that will bear down from nowhere—the waves are traveling across the surface at forty miles per hour—and knock the stuffing out of *Assassin* once and for all.

Van Kretschmar successfully steers away from the 2 A.M. calamity, but just before dawn, *Assassin* is knocked down again. Blindsided by a pair of cruel waves like a little old lady getting beaten senseless by convicted felons, she repeats the slow process of falling flat, her sails filling, then emptying, and once again standing upright, her crew knock-kneed with terror after a second glimpse of death.

The second knockdown is more horrific, more powerful, but the primary damage to boat and crew was done on the first knockdown. She misses the 3:05 A.M. sked because of a broken HF radio. All she has is VHF radio, which only works in line of sight. Well over the horizon from land and the HMS *Young Endeavour*, *Assassin* is effectively mute.

Below, all bunks are broken, save one. The only good bunk is occupied by a seasick crew member. While something like broken bunks sounds minor, it's actually a catastrophe. Skippers depend on the crew's weight to steer a sailboat. Sailors are instructed to sleep—and even to change bunks in the middle of the night—on the windward side of the boat. This serves the basic purpose of keeping a boat from tipping over. The crew are, in effect, mobile ballast.

With bunks broken, *Assassin*'s crew will no longer have the luxury of descending belowdecks to sleep. Every man will be forced to stay up on the rail, feet dangling over the water, catching forty winks clipped to a lifeline, all the way to Hobart. That's still two days away. Rain and wind will be their constant companions, along with total drenchings by every wave smacking the hull. "I'll tell you what it was like up there," skipper van Kretschmar said later. "It was like trying to have a conversation with your mates, only it's so loud that you have to shout the whole time. Meanwhile, someone's throwing buckets of cold water in your face."

So *Assassin*, 1992 Syd-Hob handicap winner, turns around and sails all the way back to Sydney. Broken bunks, broken radio, winds gusting at thirty-five knots with forecasts to an increase of fifty-five-plus—a competitive race is out of the question, might as well survive to race another day. Van Kretschmar thinks it irresponsible to go on. He says he'll never forget the line of clouds the crew can see behind them as they sail north on Sunday morning. It's the same bunch the fleet is angling toward. The clouds begin at the top of the sky and descend, in vertical columns, to just a few hundred feet above the water. They hover over the sea like a row of gray-white teeth. Kretschmar swears they're the jaws of death.

Ticehurst eventually locates *Assassin* fifty miles offshore, powering north. Because of Ticehurst, the incidents of Saturday night and Sunday morning are soon broadcast nationwide. Sydney, which went to bed with Badham's gloom-and-doom predictions, wakes to hear of five major boats quitting with structural damage and a sixth, *Challenge Again*, scooping one of their own from the drink.

And still the fleet sails toward the Bass Strait, having survived a hard night, but largely unaware that a second, more deadly storm awaits its chance to rampage—one that will make the midnight-to-dawn blow a mere footnote. The race begins to take on the earmarks of a horror film, with the audience fully aware that the hero is stumbling blindly down a dark hallway into sure death, while the hero barely suspects things are askew. It makes people want to cover their eyes.

But as with any horror film, it's impossible to turn away. Citizens of Australia begin keeping the television on constantly. Nobody wants to miss an instant of the drama. Boats that had been anonymous to nonsailors—*Sayonara, B-52, Brindabella*—are suddenly on everyone's lips. *Chutzpah*, leading on handicap, is mentioned almost constantly on the news. Bruce Taylor's seventeen years of near misses are catalogued. Roger Hickman, or "Hicko," CYCA's Yachtsman of the Year, in second-place boat *Atara*, becomes another household name. Sydney residents who have never set foot on a boat are talking knowledgeably about weather systems and sail selection and proper tactics for sailing through the Bass Strait.

Sue Psaltis is weathering phone call after phone call from concerned friends and Ed's coworkers. Glyn Charles's girlfriend, Annie, is alone in Melbourne, aware of the weather and worried in a controlled fashion, but with no one to share even the quietest anxiety. Glyn's mother, home near Portsmouth, begins getting phone calls from friends following Syd-Hob on the Internet.

The weather bomb is now obviously going to happen. It's not a matter of if, but when. Forecasters other than Badham are noting how intense the low pressure system became overnight, with the barometer dropping all the way to 978 millibars. Television weathermen are finally mumbling phrases like "weather bomb" and "East Coast low" and explaining to Australia about these hurricanes notorious for appearing from nowhere. And while the nation knows exactly what's to come, most of the fleet does not—race rules prohibit shore-to-ship communications except of an official nature. Badham broke the rule to warn his clients, and a few other boats possess WeatherFax capacity, making them aware of high winds making their way across Bass Strait. But the rest of the fleet make do with the Bureau of Meteorology's cautious forecasting.

Television weathermen are dancing around the word *hurricane*, interchanging it with *cyclone* because hurricanes typically occur at the equator. A hurricane, defined, is high-velocity winds blowing around a low-pressure center known as the eye of the storm. Hurricanes are compact, rarely measuring more than 150 miles across—almost exactly the width of the Bass Strait. They move at just five miles per hour. And they are rated, from Category 1 (winds of at least 74 mph) up to Category 5 (winds exceeding 155 mph). Technically—and this is in the name of science—weathermen reporting this storm aren't using the word *hurricane* because the BOM's still sticking with their fifty-five-knots max winds forecast. But gusts in the western edge of the Bass Strait at dawn already put the storm in Category 1.

The term *East Coast low*, however, is used. It's vague and cool. And somehow it's patriotic, as it's a weather condition specific to Australia (nowhere else on earth do East Coast lows appear). *Weather bomb* sounds even more fantastic, and that's the term newspapers are running with.

With East Coast lows characteristically descending suddenly, then sitting in one place for extended periods, the questions on everyone's lips are, When will it hit? And how long will it stay? An East Coast low hit the '93 Hobart, but it was weaker than the one forecast for 1998, with winds maxing out at fifty-five knots. But that bomb stayed over the Bass Strait for three days, making the race a war of attrition.

Television weathermen invoke that '93 Syd-Hob freely, reminding viewers that two yachts sank that year. Only 38 of 110 starters finished. No one died—all the TV anchors note this with somber faces but a "knock on wood" giggle—but many of those who finished swore they'd never do it again.

KNOCKDOWN

Now many of those same men are passing Gabo Island, sailing into the Bass Strait. Whatever security land offered was kissed good-bye at Sydney, then again at the last-chance 3:05 A.M. sked. By the time the majority of the fleet enters the Strait between nine and noon, the maxis are almost a third of the way across. The maxis are sailing into forty-knot winds, but are definitely not in a hurricane—and will never know more than the fringes of it. At the same time, Sunday-morning church services are convening across Australia. On their knees, citizens offer prayers for the brave men of the Sydney to Hobart fleet.

This as the Bass Strait toys with the fleet. Despite the incredibly deep low-pressure system, the Strait gives no indication when the bomb will drop. Some boats—*Atara, Sharp Hawk V*—even notice that the southerly has dropped. The change has been almost spooky. The wind is reduced to barely fifteen knots, but the waves are racing across the ocean at fifty miles per hour, and of a size most sailors have never seen before. What were once pleasant rollers grew to five, then ten, then twenty, and on, until the sea rises and falls forty-five feet per swell—and keeps growing larger. No one knows what to make of this—is the weather getting better or worse?

Although the wind has died down, the waves remain enormous, generating their own energy after momentum builds. However, while a reduction in wind won't reduce the size of waves, additional winds most surely increase the size of waves—and in a most peculiar fashion. Water and air are two different elements, so they operate on different playing fields. As wind increases, waves increase, too, but at an exponential rate. For every mile per hour wind increases, a wave's size increases by the power of four. So if the wind suddenly jumps from forty knots to one hundred, waves leap to astronomical heights. Such sudden increases in wind are rare unless an extremely low pressure system develops at the surface, shoving the half-the-speed-of-sound air to the surface in the Coriolis curve from thirty thousand feet up in the jet stream.

Ticehurst settles over *Brindabella* again. The clear skies of early morning are past. The camera crew captures a startling image illustrating the enormity of the waves. The skies are steel gray, with clouds reaching from sea to sky. The waves line up in neat, steep rows. White flecks the sea. *Brindabella* races up a face as long as her entire seventy-foot hull. At the wave's crest, the boat is shoved off the top. Usually a sailboat the size of *Brindabella* exerts an image of authority, but here the wave is boss. So when *Brindabella* is shoved, it truly looks like a shove—a sharp jolt from behind, with *Brindabella* unable to catch her balance. The entire front half of the boat juts out of the water, looking like some sail-propelled missile. Then it drops—and there is no better word for the way that hull splats down into that trough so far below—with all the force twenty-five tons of boat can bear. "Like hitting a three-foot-high speed bump going ninety miles an hour," one sailor describes the jarring, "for hours on end."

A shorter boat can't bash the sea with such impunity. For a small boat to shoot straight up a wave would mean the possibility of not having enough power to climb over the top. The boat would stall short of the lip, then get shoved back into the trough as the wave broke on top of it.

Sunday night's test of seamanship was wind. Sunday morning's is waves. The hours of pounding have crews constantly searching boats for signs of hull damage—leaks, ruptured hydraulic lines, bent tiller. Long discussions are held between skippers and crews about the wisdom of continuing as the storm's severity grows. Scientists that they are, the BOM is still sticking with the ridiculous fifty-five-knot forecast, even though winds of seventy-one knots are already gusting off Wilsons Promontory, that southernmost point of land in Australia jutting into the Bass Strait. Satellite photos show physical evidence of the deepening low, with clouds twisting into a tight spiral directly above the fleet—the Coriolis effect, greasing the path for jet-stream winds to get funneled down to surface level.

But the sailors know better. As their craft is a function of the atmosphere, sailors are excellent amateur meteorologists, and skippers and crews aren't fooled by light winds wafting across the decks Sunday morning. The waves are all part of the coming storm. How bad it gets depends on how far the low pressure system deepens. Assuming the worst—and all skippers are now, with the waves so monstrous—the hours between dawn and noon on December 27 are time again for hard decisions. The situation, the more honest skippers share frankly with their crews, looks hopeless.

They are in the maelstrom. Going forward means possible death. Turning around and fleeing for Eden is just as deadly. Turning a sailboat in high seas means voluntarily placing the hull broadside to a wave. There is no easier way to get rolled, especially with waves taller than some masts.

At eleven-thirty the storm gets closer. The wind returns, bringing along a rain dump. Steve Walker aboard *Business Post Naiad* says sailing through the wind and rain is like "sitting on top of your car in a downpour while racing down the highway at one hundred miles per hour."

With the exception of a few boats, skippers decide it's better to have the waves in front of them than behind them—chasing. And that means pushing on, not turning around. The question now is a matter of tactics.

Ed Psaltis is in full racing mode. Equal parts vainglorious gamble, calculated risk, and logical course of action, veering west into the storm will be the greatest test of courage and seamanship he has ever known. Subconsciously, he embraces it, despite the implications. His heart is in his throat as he sits at the tiller, bracing and hanging on as waves throw mountains of water across the decks. The wind drives spray needles into his face. He has a survival watch in place, but Ed has no plans to lower sails and adopt a survival mode. He will keep at least a storm sail flying always. Despite the weather, the 1998 Sydney to Hobart is still a competition.

Steve Kulmar on *Sword of Orion* sails no less aggressively. He stays the course twenty miles off the coast, angling only slightly westward toward the storm. *Sword*'s weather equipment includes Satcom C and WeatherFax capabilities, and *Sword* has been in contact with continental-shelf oil rigs and land weather stations in Eden. The wind is fifty knots across their beam, but moments after *Sword*'s crew reads of the seventy-one-knot blow strafing Wilsons Promontory, they receive an additional communiqué reporting that the wind has increased to ninety knots. This is a Category 3 hurricane, and the winds will reach the fleet in a matter of hours. Steve Kulmar, Glyn Charles, and Rob Kothe discuss turning around, then decide to press on regardless, sure of *Sword*'s durability. Despite the *Nokia* collision in the opening moments of the race, she is a safe vessel. This point was confirmed by a CYCA inspection on race morning, showing *Sword*'s compliance with CYCA Category One (utmost caution) safety.

Winston Churchill does not carry *Sword*'s weather capabilities, but experience and intuition has the crew following the same path, only far behind. *Winston Churchill* will push forward, avoiding survival mode if at all possible. If necessary, they will run under bare poles for a few hours, then continue racing.

Wooden boats date back to the Egyptians. Modern wood boats use a construction method first developed in the Mediterranean known as smooth-planked, or carvel-built. A framing system of equally spaced transverse frames is fastened to a continuous keel. The keel is a steering system below the boat, an inverse fin providing stability. Gunwales, or upper edges of the boat, run bow to stern. The evolution of elements to fasten the planks to the hull began with crude pegs, then nails, then copper nails, and now special lightweight metal fasteners. Wood tar or caulking material is used to seal the gaps between planks and prevent leaks.

Another form of hull construction is known as lapstrake, where the planks are rabbeted, or shaped. This way they overlap and remain smooth at the seams. But lapstrake construction has gone by the wayside as the need for extreme structural strength in fast-sailing craft increased.

Whether carvel or lapstrake, one truth remains the same: as wood rots when placed in contact with water—particularly salt water—an old wooden boat needs constant upkeep to keep her seaworthy. If just one plank fails, the entire boat sinks.

Ask a modern sailor what he thinks of wooden boats and you're not going to get some romantic dissertation on doing things the old way. Wooden boats are fine for cruising the harbor, you'll hear. But they wouldn't trust a wooden boat in big seas. Wood is less sturdy than the new space-age materials. Planks come loose. Leaks are far more common.

All those comments go double for a fifty-year-old wooden boat. *Assassin*'s Buckland joked darkly of *Winston Churchill* that a man would be suicidal to race Syd-Hob in a wooden boat that old.

Still, Richard Winning has her out in the Bass Strait with a crew of lifelong friends. She's running well, Winning notes to himself at noon. He sails under storm sail, taking the seas at a seventy-degree angle because *Winston Churchill*—quarter-million-dollar refurbishment or no—is not the sort of boat you bash straight up and down waves in. She's handling lightly, holding course well. Her deep, long keel appeared anachronistic before the race but is now an asset, providing a sense of grip as *W-C* maneuvers up and down waves.

Conditions are worsening at an alarming rate, with winds back up to fifty knots to complement the forty-five-foot seas. Each time Winning has *W-C* in a trough, he looks up at a wave as big as his boat. The consistency is good though; none of the waves are those rogues that come from nowhere to wreak havoc. As long as conditions stay consistent, things will be fine. Winning is proud of his boat and sure of his crew. They're ready for anything that can come their way.

Next to Winning in the doghouse, Steamer Stanley can't get a speech out of his head. It's Alan Payne's 1982 address to the CYCA.

It might take a hundred years, Payne warned, but a hurricane will drop right on top of the Syd-Hob. Stanley saw 1984, when gale force winds forced 105 of 150 yachts to retire, and the seventy-seven-year-old sailor washed overboard. And 1993. And he's seen enough bad weather in between to know that *W-C* is sailing into more than a normal storm. Sure, she'd survived 1945, when a gale swept the course. But in 1945, *W-C* did what all wood boats should do—hove to. Sails came down and she lolled at the mercy of the sea until the storm passed. Her deep keel provided balance to keep her from rolling.

Gentlemen's racing, 1998, doesn't allow for heaving to. Even if it did, heaving to in forty-five-foot waves is a ridiculous prospect. Far too easy to get spun sideways and rolled. The crew battens down the hatches and pushes forward, directly into the Bass Strait.

Back in Sydney, CYCA Race Headquarters issues a statement to the press saying the fleet is encountering "extreme" weather, and the worst conditions since 1993.

"Race leaders *Sayonara* and *Brindabella*," the release goes on to say, "are enduring heavy seas and winds up to 45 knots as they lead the fleet towards Flinders Island. But further back in the fleet the South Australian yacht *Doctel Rager* has reported winds of 50 to 60 knots, gusting up to 70 knots."

The last is in reference to a radio call from *Doctel Rager* to *Young Endeavour*, warning that the conditions they are experiencing are far worse than forecast. Though *Young Endeavour*'s Lew Carter passes the word back to the CYCA—and the CYCA issues the press release noting *Doctel Rager*'s transmission—Carter never relays *Doctel Rager*'s warning to the rest of the fleet, even though time is running out for boats to turn for Eden before the weather bomb drops.

This release marks the moment the fleet is truly divided in two. By the time the low deepens and the wind begins to really blow, the maxis are almost to Tasmania. They feel the conditions worsening, but not half as greatly as the smaller boats, for the maxis are sailing out the far side of the storm just as the smaller boats are sailing into it.

December 27, 2 P.M.

The real race standings (based on handicap) look like this: *Chutzpah, Atara, Terra Firma, Secret Men's Business,* and *Ragamuffin.* In sixth is *Sword of Orion.* In seventh is *AFR—Midnight Rambler. Winston Churchill* is far off the pace, but gamely continuing. *Stand Aside* is making the New Zealand end run that could vault her into Hobart, but so is *Chutzpah.* Tasmanian yacht *Business Post Naiad,* a former Admiral's Cup racer, nips at their heels. The crew of *Business Post Naiad* are a bunch of regular mates from Launceston, Tasmania, who include fifty-one-year-old skipper Bruce Guy, owner of a fittings business. It's been Guy's lifelong dream to race Syd-Hob in a boat he owns, and finally he's doing it. The nine-man crew includes sailmaker Steve Walker, public-housing inspector Rob Matthews, and Guy's neighbor over the back fence, a nonsailing locksmith named Phil Skeggs. Skeggs has never raced Syd-Hob, but the remainder of the crew have several apiece under their belts. They think conditions are in their favor. They actually laughed at the prerace weather reports, noting how the men of *Business Post Naiad* grew up sailing in the Bass Strait. They know her temper better than anyone.

• • •

At 2 P.M. on December 27, 1998, the real Sydney to Hobart race begins. At this moment the weather bomb drops. Jet-stream winds race down from thirty thousand feet in a sudden elevator-shaft deposit—forget Coriolis, these winds simply plummet—making the already boiling Bass Strait a heaving, churning death trap.

The bomb will last almost forty-eight hours. Waves eighty feet tall are recorded by oil wells on the continental shelf, just south of Gabo Island, and rescue helicopter pilots will use altimeters and other measurements of nearby mass to accurately record waves forty-five meters high—over 135 feet—in the Gabo Island black hole. Winds gust to over one hundred knots and consistently hover at eighty knots.

Once the wind plummets from jet stream to sea level, it roars east across the Strait, forming an unholy alliance with the waves and green current scraping off the bottom. Together, they hunt for the fleet. Together, they hunt for a victim.

At two-twenty, together, they find one.

NINE

LEAKY BOATS

December 27, 2:20 P.M.

The forty-one-footer *Stand Aside* from Victoria has enjoyed a banner race, and her crew is entertaining visions of winning on handicap. They make regular headway at fifteen to twenty knots, passing much bigger boats. This emboldens them. A certain reckless belief that this is their year sweeps the crew. *Stand Aside*, built in New Zealand, is designed especially to be raced in high winds. Trading on this, the crew make 240 nautical miles in the first twenty-four hours of the race, sticking them deep in the Bass Strait with conditions deteriorating. The elation of moving steadily upward in the standings bonds *Stand Aside*'s easygoing crew, makes them blind to danger.

At nine Sunday morning *Stand Aside* reduces the size of the mainsail to a triple reef, meaning a sail extending barely halfway up her mast. A small headsail flies off the bow. Still, they make more than fifteen knots, without a hint of speed wobble or vibration.

The wind and waves turn fearsome toward eleven o'clock. *Stand Aside*'s crew lower their mainsail and headsail, going with only a storm jib. This reduces maneuverability, but makes the boat more controllable atop swells. The waves are so big that, as *Stand Aside* descends to the bottom of a wave, the trough actually shelters her from wind. But as the swell carries her up again, the headsail and triple-reefed main are hoisted skyward, engaging the wind. The sudden blow pitches *Stand Aside* forward, and the crew has to be on their guard that such an occurrence doesn't bury the nose and pitchpole her down a face. Several times this almost happens, and several times the crew make a boat-saving recovery. Their elation about racing so successfully is turning to quiet fear, and to a man, the crew of *Stand Aside* would rather focus on survival than being first to Hobart.

Skipper James Hallion and navigator Rod Hunter finally make two seemingly wise decisions: first, lower all sails and run under bare poles. Second, change course from 180 degrees to 140 degrees, sailing not due south toward Hobart, but southeast, toward New Zealand. Bare-poling means *Stand Aside* is at the mercy of the sea, as she would have no sail to power her, robbing the tiller of steering. But by using the tiller to point her toward New Zealand and letting the winds push her, she is running away from the storm. Skippers call this "finding the best sea state." Indeed, Hunter is quite pleased at his boat's sudden grace and ease. The wind is pushing her along at four to five knots, and running away from the storm gives the crew peace of mind. "There's no disgrace in heaving to midrace. None whatsoever," Hallion explains to his crew as he stands at the tiller, wind searing his face like a blowtorch. With one hand, he tries unsuccessfully to cinch his hood tighter over his eyes.

The crew huddle around Hallion in the open cabin. They're just as cold and wet and could care less about the macho implications of heaving to at this point. It's Hallion who's disappointed. The only other crewman worried about competitive position anymore is twenty-eight-year-old Simon Clark, who's been grumbling all day that Hallion needs to sail more aggressively. But Clark's out on the bow now, wave watching. He can't hear Hallion's rationalizations. "All those competitive juices bubbling when we passed those bigger boats will return once the storm passes," Hallion continues. "It's a matter of waiting four or five hours."

Below, Hunter takes a break from monitoring instruments and plotting course to listen to the 2:05 P.M. sked. There's a slight weather update first, with the BOM reporting the fifty-five-knot winds it had previously forecast have arrived. High seas will follow. Hunter, like everyone else in the fleet, laughs grimly at that bit of news. No kidding. The winds arrived a long time ago. And high seas have been a fact of life since midnight. These BOM fellows need to learn a thing or two about forecasting, he thinks. In fact, their "forecast" bears no comparison to what's really happening.

Telstra Control then reports sailors should exercise caution along the coast of Tasmania, as the Tasman Island lighthouse is not working. Hunter jots this down. Then the roll call of boats begins. First is no longer *ABN Amro Challenge,* so the whole fleet finds out for the first time Iain Murray's boat is out. *Adagio* reports in. Then *Adrenalin, Aera, Alexander of Creswell* . . . one by one the boats report latitude and longitude. Hunter scribbles each down. Later he'll chart each position to see where *Stand Aside* is in the rankings.

. . . *Chutzpah* . . . Still in first place, but angling out toward New Zealand, just like *Stand Aside.* That's interesting. . . . *Dixie Chicken* . . . that's the one with the nineteen-year-old girl for a skipper. She's turning around, heading for Eden. Too bad.

The list goes on. *Innkeeper, Outlaw,* and two dozen other boats join the list of retirements. The fleet is now less than ninety strong.

Not that many hotel rooms in Eden, Hunter thinks as he waits patiently for his turn. Wonder where everyone's gonna sleep.

Because the official name of *Stand Aside* is *VC Offshore Stand Aside,* she will be one of the last boats to report in. Wait until people hear our position, Hunter thinks, smiling to himself, then wonders if anyone else will follow *Stand Aside* and *Chutzpah* eastward after the sked. People will be crazy not to see the logic. Only fools sail due south in this weather.

... Midnight Rambler ... sailing west, into the center of the low ... that takes balls, Hunter thinks.

... Midnight Special ... Miintinta ... Mirrabooka ...

Hunter yawns, glances at his watch. It's two-twenty. He double-checks his lat and long figures, not wanting to stammer or be unsure with the entire fleet listening. The sked has become disorganized, with stressed-out skippers bursting in to interrupt the transmissions of others to declare knockdowns and other minor emergencies. Radio discipline, a linchpin of blue-water racing, is nonexistent during this sked. Hunter finds this troubling—even in times of stress, professionalism is the order of the day.

Including Hallion, eight members of the crew stand watch. Four others snore just feet from Hunter. Other than for the storm, and the anxiety of bouncing at the wind's mercy in seas bigger than a jumbo jet, everything is normal. Nothing anyone can do about it. Probably better to try to sleep through it.

Someone retches. Hunter can't tell whom. Fresh barf scent trickles into Hunter's nose, makes his stomach turn and throat tighten. He's glad he can't see the physical evidence. A peek might make him heave a bit himself.

A sudden, panicked cry from up top. A scream, maybe, nipped by the wind. A monster wave is rearing up from the sea like some outlandish aquatic king cobra, though Hunter doesn't yet know. And just like men staring into the narrow black eyes of a cobra, sure that death is about to come, those crew members of *Stand Aside* on deck right now are wetting their pants as they stare at the wave, praying, mourning their demise.

Then Hunter spins upside down. He falls out of his chair and his head bounces off the ceiling. Green water pours across his navigation center, like someone opening a high-pressure valve in the nav room. Thousands of dollars of state-of-the-art computer equipment short-circuit, throw off sparks, are rendered flooded and useless. Hunter's paper maps disintegrate. All the boat's lighting is snuffed as the power generator shuts down, and Hunter is entombed in darkness.

And still, *Stand Aside* keeps rolling, rolling. A barrel in a water-fall, a toy for the ocean. The green waves are sure signs of a rogue, heaving straight up from the bottom, pulling green algae with it. The sea is always black and white, except when these freak green things pop up from nowhere like a jack-in-the-box. And they truly do come from nowhere. The Bass Strait's shallow depth causes a vertical current through upwelling, where surface water moving away from the continent is replaced by colder, deeper water pushed north from Antarctica. Upwelling is random and impossible to forecast. Hunter has heard too many stories about men unclipping their harnesses in heavy weather, sure that the coast is clear, only to have a rogue wash over the boat and sweep them into the sea. The rogues are also bigger and thicker by far than normal swells, which are predictable, even if tall.

At the same moment Hunter and *Stand Aside* are tumbling uncontrollably in the sea, *Sword of Orion* is reporting in for the sked. *Stand Aside*'s radios are destroyed, so Hunter can't hear Rob Kothe making a most unusual sked pronouncement. It's more than that, really. The maverick is breaking tradition to put out a humanitarian warning. In addition to latitude and longitude, Kothe wants to tell the fleet about the weather. Forget tactical advantage, he wants to help other men live. "We are not experiencing wind as forecast," he intones calmly, "we are experiencing fifty to sixty-five knots, and it's been up to seventy-eight."

Kothe's warning is also a competitive gesture—he's hoping boats in front of him will pass back weather information, so that *Sword* can chart the fastest tactical course around the weather. No one does. Still, Kothe's pronouncement—whatever the motivation—is extraordinary. It means the end of listening to the BOM. The fleet is in no-man's-land, and the conservative official forecast now means nothing. The only thing that matters is the here and now, and sailors alone are in the middle. Sailors alone know the facts.

There's a moment of confusion as Kothe's high-frequency-radio message is broadcast to Telstra Control on *Young Endeavour*. Nobody on board *Young Endeavour* seems to know whether it is proper sailing etiquette to respond to Kothe's insistence or to just let the maverick have his say then calmly move on to the next position report.

Radio operator Lew Carter, not normally a bold man, takes less than five seconds before unofficially taking the race in his own hands by doing what the CYCA and BOM and AusSAR and Royal Australian Navy will not do: tell the fleet it's time to go home. Quickly. He rebroadcasts Kothe's message for any ships that missed it. Then Carter goes on to note Rule 7.4 of the International Rules of Sailing, reminding skippers that it is their responsibility whether or not to continue in such situations.

Twenty-two boats listen, turning for Eden. Among them is *Midnight Special,* a high-strung crew from Queensland. But the majority of skippers figure they're too far out in the Bass Strait to turn around and that the weather will continue just a few hours more. They soldier on.

And so the bomb claims another victim. *Team Jaguar* is rolled and dismasted. A gaping hole has been opened in her decks by the mast's escape. On board is Melissa McCabe, the 17-year-old from Eden who won her spot through an essay contest. It's the second dismasting in as many years for *Team Jag.* Too late, the onboard satellite phones are found to be useless. They've been programmed for incoming calls, but not outgoing calls. So the Maydays are sent by radio. A television camera on board films the crew lying anxiously in the hold atop now-useless sails. Melissa rests between two men, staring up at the steel sky through an open hatch and not speaking. She thinks of her mom and dad and remembers how many hours she spent crafting her winning essay. She'd gone back and reread it at least fifty times, ensuring that each and every word was perfect so that the judges would know how badly she wanted to win. Her whole life, she's seen damaged boats stagger into Eden and watched on the *Today Show* as the glorious vessels unbesmirched by bad weather flew past Eden on their way to open ocean. How is it that the honor of sailing the 1998 Sydney to Hobart turned from glorious to dubious to dangerous in just a day? How in the world can something as grand as this maxi—this dream vessel—get swatted and dismembered so quickly?

Melissa isn't one of those girls who dream of breaking away from Eden. She just dreams of living life to its fullest, with adventure and travel a big part of the package. Now, drenched by the occasional rogue spilling into the hull's newly jagged maw, she longs for the safety of Twofold Bay, whose cliffs she can stare at for hours. She longs for the routine of small-town Eden, where being a budding writer means nothing—most everyone ends up on a fishing boat or in the sawmill or in the tourism industry, sooner or later. Still, it's home. So she bobs atop a lumpy, wet sailbag east of Eden, waiting for a tow home.

A fishing boat is dispatched from Eden to hunt for *Team Jag* and Melissa. On board *Young Endeavour*, Lew Carter begins devoting hours to atoning for the lack of functioning satellite phones. His conversations with the fishing vessel during the fifteen-hour search for *Team Jaguar* ties up the radio with SAR chatter at a time when other vessels are in far more need than *Team Jag*.

Back on *Stand Aside*, the rolling has not stopped. Hunter is trapped in the cramped navigation warren absorbing the chaos around him. Rushing water, shocking immersion, the moaning of the wind (Why can he hear that so clearly?), gurgled screams, the hollow thuds of bodies bending and bruising against the hull, and an awareness that the hard edges of the metal nav gear will cut his head open and concuss him for hours. He tries to swim free, but he can't, and neither can the other three belowdecks. It's like swimming inside a washing machine, with every stroke of forward motion thwarted by a gyration sending the men tumbling off bulkhead, bed, hatch, head. When the rolling finally stops, the boat is upright and flooded, with wind whooshing through the belowdecks area instead of water.

The men of *Stand Aside* are a leisurely lot, and to call them athletic would be a stretch. The four below breathe heavily from the ordeal, then wade to the stairs and fight their way up the hatch into the cockpit. Usually emerging from the hatch means entering the protective cover of the upper cabin. But that's gone now, ripped away and drifting. Pale gray light bathes Hunter. But his eight fellow crew members, the ones standing watch before the rollover, are nowhere to be seen. It's as if Hunter's on a ghost ship.

Then, above the moan of the wind, Hunter hears a cry for help. Then another, and another. The sound comes from the ocean. He stumbles to where the rail used to be and spies a most unusual sight: crewmates treading the inky water. Saved by their harnesses, the men on deck during the rollover took a lap underwater. Now, dazed, dressed in twenty soaked pounds of wet-weather gear and boots, they lack the strength to lift themselves into the boat. The broken mast lies in the water next to them, snapped rigging squiggling about the sea like spaghetti.

Hunter begins pulling the men aboard. The story of the rollover emerges with each new body on deck. The scream Hunter heard was from Simon Clark, riding the starboard bow. Feet dangling into the spray, Clark was wave watching when the rogue popped up. Clark has a theory about the rogues, that they actually appear in pairs. When the telltale sign of green appeared, he was stunned. "Bear away" was his shout. His throat hurt as he yelled, as if someone were scraping it with a file. That's how loud he screamed. But skipper Hallion couldn't hear him over the wind.

Clark yelled once more, then turned to face the wall of water rearing in his face. "This wave," Clark thought, "looks like a tennis court standing up straight."

Hallion saw the rogue by then. Unable to steer across the face, Hallion watched in horror as the tennis court suddenly sprouted a fifteen-foot wall of white water on top. The white water curled and broke. This was when *Stand Aside* rolled, getting sucked up the face, then flipped by the crest. Surfers call this "going over the falls," and that tumbling-down-a-waterfall sensation is exactly what the men of *Stand Aside* experienced.

Clark was thrown facedown into the ocean. His knee felt disconnected from his leg, and later Clark will learn he's suffered a torn anterior cruciate ligament. The same injury happens most often to professional athletes. They lie on the ground, moaning, until a stretcher comes and they're carried off the field.

No one is coming to carry Clark back to the boat. He swims back and hangs on the side until Hunter pulls him on board. To his dismay, the young wave watcher finds he can't stand.

Far from Hunter's grasp, unable to swim back, Mike Marshman, a stout father of three from Adelaide, struggles at the end of his safety tether. The fingertips on his right hand were sheared off in the rollover—something to do with the wave's force and his hand striking something sharp on his flight into the ocean. Marshman's twenty meters from the boat, reeling himself in, when his line suddenly tangles in submerged rigging. As he curses, then frantically tries to untangle himself, a wave breaks over Marshman, pushing him back under. Marshman's life flashes before his eyes, a rapid-fire montage of birthdays and loved ones and regrets and simple acceptance.

No one can help Marshman, and while he thinks it might be time, he's sure that he's not ready to die. Not here, not now, not because a jumble of rope and wire are tangling his safety harness. So Marshaman does the unthinkable and unclips his lifeline. The rigging is straining to wrap around his ankles now, straining to suck him down. Marshman disengages the clip on his chest, kicks his legs hard to shake loose from the rigging, and begins "swimming like crazy" for *Stand Aside*. His umbilical connection gone, nothing can prevent wind and waves from sweeping Marshman away. He thinks only of making the boat, not noticing the green wall of water rising behind him.

The wave lifts *Stand Aside* high in the air like Abraham lifting Isaac to heaven, then drops her back into the trough. But Marshman keeps swimming until he clings to the side and feels the firm grasp of his crewmates lifting him aboard. The sacrifice will not happen.

Hunter, a schoolteacher by trade, struggles to organize the chaos. He's dumbfounded by what the sea has done to sturdy *Stand Aside* (made in New Zealand, to be sailed in rough seas). The cockpit is sheared off. The mast is gone. The portholes are empty spaces without glass. What's left is an open boat—a forty-foot dinghy without sail, without engine, electrical power, steering, or other means of locomotion. The belowdecks area under the cockpit is flooded, with two cracks in the left side of the hull letting in more ocean.

The water in the hull makes *Stand Aside* squat low in the water, a mixed blessing actually making the pulling of the crew aboard easier, but also making her more vulnerable to rolling. Hunter sets off the EPIRB (emergency position indicating radio beacon) and passes out inflatable life jackets. He grabs a bucket to bail, then bails for what seems like hours, using the physical activity to allay fear. Somewhere in those frantic moments, Hunter finds a bag of flares. Wet, useless flares. But under the flares, a bag containing a portable VHF radio and backup antenna. With the boat's aerial deep underwater, Hunter rigs the spare and broadcasts a Mayday.

While Hunter broadcasts position coordinates, praying someone will hear, the rest of the crew deploy a life raft. This seems like a logical maneuver, but it's a task sailors employ only when all else fails. Sailors do not like life rafts. They think them flimsy and dangerous, prone to killing more men than they save. The saying "You step *up* into a life raft" implies the only time you dare enter a life raft is when your boat has sunk.

But the men of *Stand Aside* are thinking ahead. The deployment is precautionary. No one steps aboard. Instead, they secure the raft by rope to the back of the boat. Then, as the raft immediately blows to the end of the leash, the men huddle in what used to be the cockpit of their open boat, orange foul-weather gear contrasting with the yellow life preservers around their necks. They close their eyes or just open them a slit, because the wind blows so violently it hurts to look.

All order is gone. No one is scheduled for watch. No one is scheduled to cook dinner. No ropes must be secured or sails changed. *Stand Aside* bobs, emasculated, her crew waiting not to cross the finish line, but for the staccato thrum of rescue helicopters. The orange and blue Syd-Hob stickers on the bow, lovingly applied just days ago, are the only reminder that they were once racers, passing boats ten feet longer on their way to victory.

Sunday, December 27, 3 P.M.

In Canberra, Rupert Lamming and the twenty-nine other members of the AusSAR team arrive in the War Room. Lamming stoic, forty-one, stares at a map of Australia and the Bass Strait on his computer terminal. Lamming's practical bearing makes him a natural leader. His screen shows a false alarm from a Thai freighter, *Thor Sky*. The storm is breaking over her bow, and a member of the crew accidentally activated their EPIRB. As a courtesy, *Thor Sky* radioed Canberra about the mistake, with a request to ignore the transmission.

"Duly noted," Lamming thinks, fiddling with a couple items on his desk, paying no attention to the red flashing target symbol. Out of curiosity, the fifteen-year merchant marine veteran points his mouse to the signal and double clicks. He knows from *Thor Sky*'s apology that their beacon is transmitting from 406 megahertz.

Lamming double-checks this number, then stares back at his screen. The EPIRB warning flashing on Lamming's computer isn't on 406, but on 121.5 megahertz. That's the sign of an older EPIRB, a type used on sailboats. Lamming doesn't hesitate. He picks up the telephone and begins the hunt for an aircraft in the vicinity to confirm what's on his screen.

Over the Bass Strait, pilot Ralph Schwertner of Tasair, a Tasmanian charter air service, has been flying his small propeller plane since dawn, hired by Tasmanian photographer Richard Bennett. While Schwertner flies low over the ocean, Bennett shoots. Bennett's daughter, Anne, sits in back, changing film for her father so he can work nonstop.

At 9 A.M. they visited the patch of sea sixty miles east of Mallacoota. Conditions allowed Schwertner to fly just one hundred feet off the deck, and Bennett took photos of *Sayonara* and *Brindabella*. Now, six hours later, the same patch of sea is unrecognizable. Much to Bennett's professional dismay (his specialty is the captivating aerial sailing shot), conditions are too atrocious for Schwertner to fly low. Schwertner climbs to five thousand feet and prepares to return to the airfield. But as Bennett puts his cameras away, Schwertner receives a radio call from Mallacoota. Through Lamming, AusSAR has seconded the Tasair craft to the search and would like them to head in the direction of *Stand Aside*'s EPIRB to confirm their status.

Schwertner tracks the beacon and soon finds *Stand Aside*. He drops low for visual identification, Bennett shooting the whole time. Then Tasair climbs again to radio back to AusSAR: Yes, we've found *Stand Aside*. Yes, she is sinking.

Lamming immediately scrambles three civilian helicopters: *SouthCare* from Canberra, *Helimed 1* from Traralgon, and a Victoria Police Air Wing chopper, *Polair 1*. While the aircraft are all modern, none have been modified in any way to add speed or durability for flying in weather of this sort. The pilots will later tell of flying the machines to the very edge of their performance capabilities—an edge far beyond what the pilots previously knew.

The navy's Maritime Operations Headquarters in Sydney is also alerted to the severe weather and Mayday, though the navy's assistance is not requested at this time.

As he has been all day, ABC's Garry Ticehurst is the first chopper on the scene. The silver-haired Ticehurst is inexhaustible. Piloting a helicopter involves using both feet on pedals, the left hand to control attitude, with the right hand coaxing the helicopter skyward through the joystick between the pilot's legs. In addition, the pilot has a full control panel for his eyes to scan and a headphone with microphone for radio transmissions. All that sensory overload increases when the weather pushes a helicopter backward or downward or upward, the way heavy winds are wont to do. Ticehurst's long hours in the air are an incredible feat of physical and mental endurance.

Ticehurst drops the chopper down to two hundred feet off the deck of *Stand Aside*. The chopper hovers, shoves a camera out the window, records the agony for the night's evening news. Then Ticehurst ceases to be a news helicopter, electing to join the rescue effort and stay with *Stand Aside* until help arrives. By radio, he confirms that *Stand Aside*'s EPIRB is the one tracked on Lamming's computer.

"Help was on the way," Ticehurst recalled later. "But we're talking an hour away. We were lucky we'd only just refueled, so we could stay there awhile."

"*Stand Aside* being tossed about by thirty-foot waves," Ticehurst radios back in that understated monotone universally used by pilots. Their aircraft could be bullet-riddled, minus wings, with engines ablaze, but the modern pilot always behaves on the radio as if mildly bored. "The skipper is understandably distressed."

As Ticehurst hovers to keep an eye on *Stand Aside*, the thirty-eight-footer *Siena* sails past. The troughs of the waves are so deep and the roar of the wind so loud that *Siena* neither hears nor sees the helicopter. They also cannot see *Stand Aside*.

But as a wave crests, *Stand Aside* is pushed skyward. And when *Siena* skipper Iain Moray peers down and sees *Stand Aside* in distress, he elects a marvelously brave course—turning his little boat around on seas three times *Siena*'s height. Moray is an excellent sailor, in contention for handicap honors when he stops to help *Stand Aside*. He is intentionally putting an end to his competition.

"I can't believe it," Ticehurst marvels.

"I have a moral and ethical duty to help other sailors at sea,"

Moray says. "I certainly hope someone would do the same for me if I were in trouble."

Pivoting atop a forty-foot face as easily as if the sea were level and glassy, *Siena* carves back toward *Stand Aside*. But as she comes down the wave, the trough blocks the wind and *Siena* momentarily loses steering capability. The back end spins and *Siena* is broadside in the trough, the wave about to crash down on top. Ticehurst watches helplessly as Moray fights to turn *Siena*. And Moray does turn her, but just barely. The new wave throws her sideways, but doesn't knock her down. Moray's crew goes airborne belowdecks, with one crew member later diagnosed as suffering a serious head injury. But Moray keeps *Siena* upright.

An anxious Ticehurst breathes a sigh of relief. "Well done, *Siena*," he radios.

"Thanks for that," comes the casual reply.

Siena sails against the wind to *Stand Aside*. After several minutes sizing up the situation, both yachts realize the water's too big for *Siena* to effect ship-to-ship exchange. Not even throwing a rope and dragging men through the water is possible. Moray decides that only if *Stand Aside* sinks will he attempt rescue. Despite this, *Siena*'s presence is a huge morale boost to the beleaguered *Stand Aside* men. Their moods since the rollover have varied from calm to panicked, but this moment they know optimism. Moray tacks back and forth around *Stand Aside*, constantly exposing his boat to rollover, waiting for a rescue helicopter to arrive.

Ticehurst continues hovering. He receives word that *Helimed 1* is on the way. With tailwinds of eighty knots, *Helimed* makes the two-hundred-mile flight from Traralgon to Mallacoota in just fifty-nine minutes. After twelve minutes to refuel, *Helimed 1* pushes on for *Stand Aside*, arriving at 4:55 P.M.

Moray sails off, later to retire because of the crew member's head injury. *Helimed 1* takes over the rescue effort. "The whole top of the boat's ripped off," the *Helimed* pilot radios to Ticehurst, taking his first peek of *Stand Aside*. There's nothing casual or pilotlike in his delivery, merely incredulity. Behind him, paramedic rescue swimmer Peter Davidson prepares to get wet.

The standard rescue checklist rolls through the heads of pilot, winch operators, and rescue swimmer like a computer printout. First, identify the survivor and maintain visual contact. After monitoring wind direction, gusts, and the sea state, contact the yachtsmen, if possible, and instruct them to abandon the vessel if lines or rigging stand a chance of tangling the winch cable. A rescue swimmer's worst nightmare is dangling from the rescue cable and getting tangled in a boat's rigging. Not only is it dangerous to get tangled, but the protocol for pulling the swimmer clear is nothing more than pulling the swimmer clear. The helicopter flies forward, rapidly. The chance of the swimmer being sliced into several pieces is high, though such a thing has never happened.

The next step is lowering the rescue swimmer into the water with a slack line. The rescue swimmer attaches himself and cable to the survivor, then signals via two-way radio or hand signals such as a thumbs-up. The rescue swimmer rides up the cable with the survivor, an especially crucial aspect if the victim if exhausted or injured. The winch line, which runs about two hundred meters long, is rated for six hundred pounds. But while it can easily carry two people, the rotor wash from the blades puts added stress on the wire. At over one hundred knots in a hover situation, the downdraft can force the cable to spin uncontrollably as rescue swimmer and survivor ride skyward. Once they reach the chopper, a sudden gust of wind can send the cable spinning again—sometimes right into the helicopter's armored skids.

Finally, the survivor and rescue swimmer are pulled inside the chopper by the winch operator. If there are more victims, the rescue swimmer hooks up and goes back down. The victim, meanwhile, is administered first aid.

As Davidson slides his goggles over his eyes, *SouthCare* from Canberra arrives on the scene. Her two rescue swimmers make a final check of their wet suits and gear—zipping zippers, adjusting fins, tugging on gloves. Most often the *SouthCare* serves as an airborne ambulance, "life-flighting" car-crash victims to hospitals when ordinary ground transportation is too slow. They're good at what they do and have saved the lives of countless crash and other emergency victims—people who would otherwise have died. But both paramedics have a fear in their stomachs right now such as they have never known. And it's not because Kristy McAlister and Michelle Blewitt are the only female rescue swimmers hovering over the Bass Strait. It's because they're about to make their first ocean rescues. As inexperienced as they feel right now, failure is not an option. With 12 men to rescue, darkness approaching, and *Polair 1* not yet refueled, the men *of Stand Aside* need Davidson and the two rookies to make it happen.

McAlister and Blewitt watch carefully as Davidson rides *Helimed 1*'s winch to *Stand Aside*. With the *Stand Aside* rescue finally under way, Garry Ticehurst can finally disappear to Mallacoota and refuel. Schwertner's Tasair follows. Both pilots are exhausted, looking forward to a cup of hot coffee and a bite to eat, and quietly elated to have saved lives.

Any other day, this would be quitting time. But the weather bomb won't let Ticehurst or Schwertner rest on their laurels. Halfway to Mallacoota, both pilots begin picking up fresh Maydays. Ticehurst and Schwertner refuel quickly in Mallacoota then get back out over the Bass Strait. The bomb is claiming victim after victim. For the next four hours events will overlap, with multiple calamities and search-and-rescues taking place. And not everyone will make it out alive.

TEN

PARADISE

December 27, 3:30–4:50 P.M.

The weather bomb is destroying Ed Psaltis and *Midnight Rambler*. His aggressive course across the Bass Strait has taken him straight through the Gabo Island black hole. Even on a normal day, this confluence would be treacherous. Today it's sheer folly, a place for men with death wishes. The rest of the fleet stays far off the continental shelf, where the water is deeper and waves more manageable. Ed is guiding *Midnight Rambler* into the shallowest regions of the Bass Strait, where the waves will be taller, more forceful, more random.

As a welcoming gesture, the black hole sweeps the anemometer from the top of *Midnight Rambler*'s mast. Never mind the elaborate hardware bolting the wind gauge in place. The wind simply descends, tears the anemometer away, and hurls it into the face of a wave creeping stealthily toward *Midnight Rambler* and Ed's exposed, shallow cockpit.

Stunned, Ed watches the anemometer fly away. He looks straight up the mast to make sure the radio antenna is still secured. It is. Then Ed double-checks his safety harness, cinching it tighter across the shoulders and under the arms. He's wearing sunglasses in the storm because the drops of water beating against his eyes feel like bullets. The crew are all scared. They don't talk at all, but keep working as if nothing's unusual. Ed figures that at least four of them are sick, though no one's actually incapacitated yet.

With no one to talk to, and trying to avoid wallowing in thoughts of home, a line from Shakespeare—*Macbeth*, Ed thinks—runs nonstop through his brain. It's about being stuck between a rock and a hard place:

> *I am in blood*
> *stepp'd in so far,*
> *that, should I wade no more,*
> *Returning were as tedious as go o'er.*

At 3 P.M., a wave breaks over the gunwales. The hatches leading below are open just a millimeter to let in fresh air, and the water forces itself in, drowning everything electronic except the radio. Bob Thomas's navigation role is suddenly superfluous, as he has no gear to navigate by. Boat speed, wind direction, wind speed, GPS position, bearing and distance to Tasman Island, apparent wind angle, electronic digital compass, water temperature, direction and speed of current, and cross-track error indicator—all gone. The only item remaining is a tiny, old-fashioned compass mounted on deck. It's like something—and Ed thinks this thought clearly—Ed's ancestors used when Australia was first discovered.

The compass is so small Ed can't even see it from where he stands five feet away. He decides that the wave watcher will have to perform double duty, keeping one eye on the ocean, then creeping across the deck to the compass now and then to make sure Ed is still bearing due south. Usually, in the event of an electronics failure, Ed would have traditional navigation aids. But neither sun nor stars nor land on the horizon are available as reference. It's like horizontal vertigo, with waves coming from all directions and the horizon one steel-gray mass.

Ed's making seven to eight knots under just a storm sail. He stays at the helm for extended periods, but rotates wave watchers frequently. The cry "Wave" is constant, and he's developing a simple method of attack. When a wave is called, Ed bears into it, sailing up the face at seventy to eighty degrees. Then he shoves the tiller so *Midnight Rambler* can pirouette atop the crest and slide down the backside.

Ed's not getting cocky, but after several hours of nonstop waves, he figures he has it wired. So when the rogue hits, Ed is a hair less poised than he should be. The green wall surprises him. One minute *Midnight Rambler* is moving along smoothly, the next she's knocked flat. Below, Chris Rockell is slipping into wet-weather gear, preparing to go on watch. The knockdown throws him across the boat like a rag doll. His scalp finds the only exposed bolt on the ship. Head wounds are known for being extremely bloody, and when the taut flesh atop Chris's head is ripped open wide, blood flows rapidly into his eyes and follows the sharp contours of his nose. Except Chris neither feels nor suffers from the blow. He's unconscious. The blood now mats his hair, permanently stains his bear suit.

At least Chris is still in the boat. Ed isn't. Ed's in the Bass Strait, praying his safety harness doesn't snap. It's stretched the full length, the tight harness straps limiting Ed's ability to swim back to the boat. All he can do is dog-paddle and kick and pull on the harness. No one knows he's out there, and he feels stupid wearing sunglasses and seaboots and ten tons of clothing while trying to swim. The water sucks him down. When he opens his mouth even an inch to scream, salt water invades him.

And then he sees a second green wall rising next to *Midnight Rambler*. The rogue's twin has come to finish the job. Ed Psaltis feels foolish—stupid—for having dared the black hole. And now his boat is going to sink. And now Ed is about to die.

• • •

Sunday, December 27, 3:20–3:50 P.M.

Since the sked, *Sword of Orion* has become the picture of self-lessness. Boats sending Maydays are using *Sword* as a radio relay vessel. Boats knocked down have lost their high-frequency-radio antennas atop the mast. Using VHF, distressed boats send their Mayday, *Sword* picks it up and broadcasts the message to Telstra Control, then Lew Carter passes Mayday information along to AusSAR.

The mavericks are still racing. Despite the storm, *Sword* is still making record time—but their efforts are equally focused on help-ing others. Amazingly, a moment comes when the wind drops, the sun comes out, and seagulls land on the bow. The sea is bright, happy blue. The crew is ecstatic, and all clamber on deck to soak in the calm. The moment is serene, surreal. It happens suddenly.

"Bigger sails, boss?" Darren Senogles yells to Kothe.

The ingenue skipper doesn't even look at Kulmar or Charles. His years as a glider pilot have taught him the fickle nature of weather systems.

"Wait."

"But we're out of the storm," Senogles yells back.

"Wait."

Sword of Orion bobs lazily, glad to finally be free of the bomb. Glyn Charles comments to Steve Kulmar that he can't wait to get some extra sail up there. Time to be racing again.

The wind picks up a notch, then the sun slowly squeezes off, as if a giant hand were rotating down a dimmer switch. The waves roil and spit. After twenty minutes of calm, in a place they now realize is the hurricane's eye, *Sword of Orion* sails back into the storm. The rain pisses down. The waves again grow like mountains, rising seventy-five feet into the air.

Moments like the eye are rough on adventurers. The illusion of serenity weakens their resolve, as they feel they've given their all to conquer the opponent, whether it be mountain, rapid, or ocean. To have the challenge reappear is not just disheartening, it's almost fatal. The depression a man feels is total.

And so Rob Kothe, the competitive skipper bent on nothing less than victory, stands on the heaving deck of his expensive boat, crushed at the realization that the worst is yet to come. Something inside him dies a little. It was easy to keep resolve and race to Hobart when the storm raged nonstop. But that time in the eye let him relax. *Sword* had endured—beaten—the storm and seen sunshine. Kothe was all set to hoist the main and race hard. Hopes were so high. The mood of relief was total. The crew was cheering.

Now to be back in the storm again . . .

Kothe doesn't feel up to fighting the beast. He's had enough. He wants to go home. He will turn on the TV and sit in his favorite chair and remain very still for a long time. He will revel in the sensation of being dry and warm. Nothing around him will be moving, and seasickness and its attendant smells will be far away. Rob Kothe wants very much to be someplace quiet. Right now. He wants to be someplace calm.

Kothe assembles his paper-wondrous crew. "It's time," he gives the order, "to turn around." Then Kothe disappears to the radio station to begin relaying Maydays again, leaving Steve Kulmar to oversee the slow turn for Eden.

There will be a survival watch, Kulmar decides. If we're not racing, there's no sense in risking everyone's life on deck. Kulmar selects Darren Senogles to ride the bow and watch for waves. Glyn Charles will take the helm. Charles settles behind the wheel tiller, adjusting his safety harness so that the straps are tight about his torso, and the clips are attached securely to himself and the boat.

Glyn plants his feet squarely for leverage and begins scouring the horizon for rogues. Under these conditions, going home isn't such a bad notion.

Down below, Rob Kothe feels *Sword* turn around. When the deed is done, he radios the *Young Endeavour* that *Sword of Orion* is retiring from the 1998 Sydney to Hobart Yacht Race. The mavericks are heading for Eden. They will race no more.

ELEVEN

KINGURRA

The more you head into the maelstrom, the more vulnerable you are, of course. But it's what you owe to whatever gift you have.

—Author unknown

Sunday, December 27, 4–7:30 P.M.

The AusSAR War Room is filled with men wearing the unofficial AusSAR summer uniform: short-sleeved white shirts, dress slacks and shoes, neckties. The mood is controlled chaos. Phones ring, with media and loved ones and the just plain curious pleading for specifics about race conditions. The bomb has exploded, and things are happening quickly. With every satellite pass overhead comes more notification from the fleet that ships are in trouble.

Civilian rescue personnel are recalled from holiday. Seven helicopters and twenty fixed-wing aircraft are assigned to the Syd-Hob storm. A search grid covering four thousand square miles of Australian coastline is laid out should things get worse. The order is given for sonar buoys to be dropped in the Bass Strait to test for current drift.

By 5 P.M. the imprints of activated EPIRBs—those targets on a computer screen—have gone from one to a dozen. The only rescue helicopters in the air are focused on *Stand Aside,* so Garry Tice-hurst and Ralph Schwertner are the eyes and ears of AusSAR at sea, relaying radio messages from the fleet, passing along eyewitness weather reports. Each report from this communications cross fire—be it firsthand or fourth—ends with the War Room recipient crossing the room with a dry-erase pen in hand. As per standard AusSAR practice, the names of ships in trouble are written on the huge white board. Each is assigned a high, medium, or low priority. By dusk the number of ships on the board will climb from a dozen to fifteen—a record.

Several of those boats radioing Maydays are high priority, desperately in need of assistance. The medium-priority Maydays are those ships setting off their EPIRB because they're unlucky, such as *Ninety-Seven,* which lost its steering and was almost run over by a freighter. Lowest priority is given ship setting off EPIRB because they're scared—scared to death aboard a boat that's getting slapped silly. All alone in seas taller than two houses, thinking about the wife and kids, and wondering what kind of legacy would be left. When these folks call in, it's just to let the world know where they are. We're turning around for Eden and the seas are pretty fucking big and we're down to two men on deck and a storm jib. The coordinates are these, and if you'd like to send a helicopter immediately and fly us off to a safe place, we'd be happy indeed. The reputation of the hard-core Australian sailor takes a beating from these men.

One high-priority boat is *Solo Globe Challenger.* Tony Mowbray is the skipper and owner. He's a laborer from Newcastle, a coal-mining town north of Sydney, who has always longed to sail the world. And not just a leisurely cruise, but a nonstop, unassisted, single-handed global circumnavigation—one man, alone. His voyage seeks to raise money for a Newcastle charity, the John Hunter Children's Hospital Kids Club. As a personality, he is alternately gregarious and inward, like all who seek solitude on the sea.

His boat, then, is more than just a pleasure craft, it is Mowbray's haven. After finally finding a craft worthy of bearing such a distinction, Mowbray sold the lesser *Polaris*, mortgaged his home, and purchased this yare forty-three-footer. He has thirteen Syd-Hobs to his credit and spends every minute of every day planning for October 1999, when he will sail from Newcastle, then return six months to the day later. Syd-Hob 1998 is both a test run for the newly christened *Solo Globe Challenger* and effort to raise the John Hunter charity's profile.

Mowbray has dipped into his savings to purchase $50,000 worth of mast, navigation aids, and other accoutrement. Because Syd-Hob is not a solo race (at least six crew members are required; three must have Syd-Hob experience), he invites seven buddies from the mines. Two, David Marshall and David Cook, have never raced Syd-Hob. Marshall, a father of five, carries a good-luck charm: his four-year-old's plastic dolphin. He comes to rely on the token when things get rough, staring at it as if it were magical.

Things started out well enough for the men of *Solo Globe Challenger*, but Sunday afternoon is the worst weather Mowbray has seen in thirty-two years of sailing. He sails under bare poles, eyeing the cliffs—and that's how he thinks of the waves—coming to get him. Wave after wave breaks over his precious new boat, and each time Mowbray angles *Solo* just so, avoiding destruction.

But Mowbray can't man the helm forever. And things go wrong suddenly when Mowbray ducks below for a moment, leaving four crew on deck. Two waves hit his boat, the first a fifty-footer on the nose that spins her sideways. The second comes from behind. All sixty-five-feet of wave collapse atop *Solo*, knocking her down. A seven-foot skylight in the cabin shatters, and cold, black water pours into the void. Meanwhile, *Solo* lies flat on the surface, her new aluminum mast bent like a cheap coat hanger.

As *Solo* rights herself, Mowbray stumbles onto the deck. Keir Enderby is pinned beneath the mast and boom, legs crushed. "Get it off me!" he screams at anyone who will listen.

Tony Purkiss's blood is turning a puddle of seawater crimson.

His head has been smashed open by the collapsing boom. Glen Picasso dangles over the side, unable to climb on board because several ribs are broken or cracked.

Mowbray lifts the injured men in his arms and carries them below. After strapping them into bunks and covering them with blankets, Mowbray activates the EPIRB and tries to turn on the motor. It doesn't work. Nor does the radio. David Cook looks hard at Mowbray. "How the hell are we going to get out with no sail, no power, and no electronic communication? There are blood and bodies everywhere. We could sink. If we don't fix this boat up, we could lose everyone, especially with the injuries."

"Keep calm, mate. We're not losing anything," Mowbray replies.

Mowbray stays calm. It's the only way of ignoring this incredible loss—all this work, all the money, all the dreams. He rigs a sail and turns his craft toward Eden, then directs the crew to stop the flow of water by stuffing sleeping bags into the skylight.

"Once you've finished that, bail," he barks. "And don't stop. Bail until this boat is dry."

And they do. Marshall, meanwhile, wishing desperately to be home, settles into a corner and begins to pray. All the while he clutches the plastic dolphin, somehow sure it will deliver good luck. He's not petrified so much as questioning his motivations for sailing. Why does a man who has it all leave home to chase adventure? Cook stares to the skies, searching for that rescue aircraft that will make everything all right. The hard questions can wait until later—if that moment comes.

Mowbray stays at the helm, staring and listening incredulously to the sound of waves. "I'll never look at waves the same again," he says. "Those waves are out to kill us. You can see death working in the water."

As the crew of *Solo Globe Challenger* scans the sky for rescue, Ticehurst and Schwertner are back in the air, peering down into the water in search of *Solo Globe Challenger*. The process is daunting, as the sea is vast, whitecapped, and ever changing, and from the sky a forty-three-foot boat doesn't look like much more than a matchstick.

EPIRBs might make the task easier, but the current is pushing boats along so quickly that no one's where he's supposed to be. *Solo* is no different. Normally, EPIRBs act as a homing device. But there are so many EPIRBs currently activated that helicopter and aircraft radar is confused. It can't zero in on boats. The only method of finding boats is flying to their last known location and searching visually. Canberra can do no better—the AusSAR War Room is chaos, what with all the Maydays and EPIRBs and aircraft being launched and the constant ringing of phones.

The one constant is Ticehurst. AusSAR has come to depend on his radio relay and search efforts more than they'd like to admit. Television helicopters are nowhere to be found in AusSAR's national search-and-rescue plan.

At 5:18, Ticehurst is still scouring the sea, eyes bloodshot and body bone-tired. He's been in the air over twelve hours. A glance at the fuel gauge shows ABC needs fuel again, so Ticehurst breaks off the *Solo* search. The sixty-mile flight back to Mallacoota is a battle into the wind. Ticehurst feels as if he's barely moving. Then he picks up the radio message that will shake all Australia: "Mayday, Mayday, Mayday—here is *Winston Churchill, Winston Churchill.*"

Ticehurst stays calm, but his eyes go wide. *"Winston Churchill, Winston Churchill.* ABC chopper. Go ahead with your position, over."

"Twenty miles southeast of Twofold Bay, over."

"Nature of your Mayday? Over."

"Affirmative. We are getting life rafts on deck. ABC chopper, we are holed. We are taking water rapidly. We can't get the motor started to start the pumps."

"Roger. How many on board?"

"Niner. Niner."

Ticehurst immediately relays the message to Canberra. Because of his fuel situation, he's unable to fly directly to *Winston Churchill*. Ticehurst radios back to Winning to apprise him of this, but receives no answer. AusSAR immediately dispatches the Victoria Police Air Wing helicopter, *Polair 1*, originally bound for *Stand Aside;* and even sends the brigantine HMS *Young Endeavour* and Telstra Control.

But it's not that simple. AusSAR's sudden confrontation with a multiple-target scenario is overloading its resources and it doesn't have enough helicopters to rescue everyone. *Stand Aside*'s men are being slowly hoisted off, with Peter Davidson personally responsible for the first eight to be rescued. But Davidson's *Helimed 1* is now almost out of gas and heading back for Mallacoota, meaning one less chopper in the air for the next three hours. Events are happening far too fast. Three hours is too long to wait for a new chopper.

AusSAR knows every minute of every rescue in place, often speaking with the chopper pilot while the swimmer is in the water. A typical conversation goes like this actual dialogue overheard from one helicopter trying to hover low over the seas while effecting rescue: "Look out for that fucking wave! Look out for that fucking wave!" and then, calmer, apologetic. "Sorry, mate. Bit of a problem there. Trying to stay between the waves and the clouds, you know."

AusSAR knows Rod Hunter was the last man lifted by Davidson before *Helimed 1* was forced to leave the scene. Even after seven—seven!—rescues, Davidson saved Hunter in textbook fashion—the horse collar draped under Hunter's arms, the lightning-speed upward jerk out of the raft, the slow spin ("Take a bit of a look down, just to bid the view adieu," victims are advised), a bit of a swing under the helicopter to avoid the skids, then up into the cabin.

AusSAR is concerned about the two women, Michelle Blewitt and Kristy McAlister, hoisting the four remaining sailors from *Stand Aside*. The men are tired and in poor physical shape, and both women are strong but slight. Tired men in heavy seas drown. To make things worse, the wind is tumbling the life raft roped to *Stand Aside*'s stern. But there's nothing anyone can do about that. Blewitt and McAlister will have to make the rescues. AusSAR would like to focus on helping them, encouraging them, but Aus-SAR has other rescues to worry about. A new report from Telstra Control states that *Business Post Naiad* may have been rolled and dismasted. No comfirmation yet, but early word shows no crew hurt. Now *Winston Churchill*—national treasure, symbol of Sydney to Hobart—is taking water. Who knows if she's really sinking or not, but a good sailor such as Richard Winning doesn't hop into life rafts at the first sign of trouble. Something must be up, but how bad is it really?

John Constable isn't panicking, but the coordinator of aerial rescue scours the War Room board for any—every—conceivable craft capable of effecting search. He needs to find *Solo Globe Challenger*, *Business Post Naiad*, and *Winston Churchill* immediately. In addition to those unrescued sailors on *Stand Aside*, these three boats are the high-priority Maydays. Action must be taken now. But how? No rescue boats or even fishing trawlers are in the vicinity of the fleet yet. Fixed-wing aircraft can't effect rescue, though sailors on several boats harbor a belief that PC-3 Orions are capable of dropping a tow cable and pulling boats to safety. This bit of wishful thinking would destroy any boat being towed, as the Orion's stall airspeed of 150 knots would decimate the unlucky craft dragged through the monstrous seas. The only method of rescue, then, is helicopter. And the only available chopper is the Victoria Police Air Wing *Polair 1*—and she's on the way to *Winston Churchill*. If just one other boat reports a Mayday, Constable will have to start selecting who gets rescued and who doesn't. Playing God. Choosing who lives and who dies.

The *Polair* was called on duty at 3:50 P.M., after the *Stand Aside* roll. A normal three-hour flight from Essendon to Mallacoota is accomplished in just two hours, courtesy of an 80 mph tailwind. The

Polair, with a maximum speed of 120 knots, averages 205 all the way to Mallacoota. The crew hears *Winston Churchill*'s Mayday as they fly.

After a quick fuel stop, they leave Mallacoota at six-thirty. Their assignment is to assist the final rescues on *Stand Aside*. Garry Ticehurst in the ABC chopper is getting refueled at the same time, taking off two minutes later. The blue-and-white *Polair* is making 220 knots with the tailwind, but Ticehurst soon comes alongside. The pair fly in formation toward *Winston Churchill*'s Mayday location like air cavalry riding to the rescue.

John Constable tracks the helicopters back at AusSAR. The situation is holding together well, albeit with dumb luck, the logistical equivalent of chewing gum and baling wire.

Then comes the distress call Constable fears: a crewman washed overboard. It's from *Kingurra*, a twenty-five-year-old pleasure boat. Skipper Peter Joubert radios that the man has been swept away. The crew have a visual line of sight on him, but he's unconscious, not wearing a life jacket, adorned in long underwear, drifting four hundred meters from the boat . . .

Probably a dead man, Constable thinks. It'll be dark by the time a chopper can get there. If exposure doesn't get him, he'll drown. Even if he does manage to live, finding him without a satellite location beacon will be impossible. Needle in a haystack.

But Constable can't just ignore the guy. Does he divert *Polair 1* from *Winston Churchill* or does he let the unlucky man overboard drown? The decision is important enough that Constable asks Lamming, the man in charge of all maritime search and rescue, to make the call.

Lamming studies the situation. Ideally, the *Polair* should proceed directly to *Winston Churchill*. But *Winston Churchill* is nowhere to be found. In fact, they could all be drowned. Or maybe they're fine, floating in life rafts someplace out of radio contact. Or maybe *Winston Churchill* is A-okay—the crew saved the boat and are motoring placidly into Eden. The thing about the *Kingurra* crewman is that people think they know where he is. That makes it a no-guesswork rescue. Fly over, drop a swimmer, hoist the sailor, go home.

Lamming agrees with Constable about the *Kingurra* rescue. Dark by the time a chopper arrives, needle in a haystack. This poor guy—a kid really, some twentysomething American—can't possibly be saved. To save him would mean sending a chopper there. Now. And attempting the impossible by finding a half-dressed crewman bobbing in the water without an EPIRB. Impossible. But, Lamming thinks, isn't that the nature of the rescue business—doing the impossible? Lamming knows he won't be able to live with himself if *Winston Churchill*'s found all right and the kid is ignored.

Lamming makes his decision: divert *Polair 1* to *Kingurra*. Constable makes the radio call. The *Polair* immediately changes course and goes after one John Campbell of Seattle, Washington, unconscious and unaware of how or why he's in the water. With *Kingurra* just east of *Winston Churchill*'s last reported position, Lamming asks the crew to search for *W-C* as they divert. The *Polair* reports back that they see no sign of *W-C*. They've most likely sunk. With no sign of life rafts, loss of life is probable under these conditions.

That Campbell is in the water and the rest of *Kingurra*'s crew isn't can be attributed to one of nature's fickle quirks that makes blue-water racing as deadly as mountain climbing. And that makes sailing Sydney to Hobart as deadly as climbing Mount Everest.

Campbell is on deck. The cockpit. Minding his own business, trying to make conversation with a couple of the guys. They're all amazed at how the *Kingurra*'s anemometer, like the more low-tech wind-speed indicators throughout the fleet, is maxed out at sixty-eight knots. Spume blows across the sea in wispy entrails. Campbell perches alongside three other crew members, clipped in by safety harnesses, shrouded in wet-weather gear. Every fifteen minutes or so a colossus rumbles across the deck, soaking everyone in the cockpit. These waves are tiresome, but predictable, and when one breaks, the routine is simply to brace on some fixture aboard the boat and lean into the wave. Campbell finds that sharing the suffering with three others makes the misery bearable. In the ocean all around them, men are fighting for their lives. But these four on deck aren't in a position to hear the radio, so they know nothing of *Stand Aside* or *Team Jag* or anyone else. They just know they're cold, wet, tired, hungry, and miserable. Blissfully unaware, bracing for waves.

Suddenly: "Watch out!" It's helmsman Anthony Schniders, who sees the Big One. It comes from nowhere, all of a sudden. Campbell braces on the cockpit, ducks. The other three do the same.

But ducking and bracing are not enough this time. The wave spins *Kingurra*, shoves her sideways down the forty-five-foot face. She tumbles, white water arcing over the top. She's caught in the tube. If *Kingurra* were a surfer instead of a yacht, this would be a magical moment. The cylinder surrounding them would display light on both ends, dark water, and a roar so deafening it feels like silence in the middle. The tube's force would shove the surfer from one end of the cylinder to the other. He might drag a fingertip across the tube as he shoots to daylight.

But *Kingurra* is a yacht, broached. The cylinder does not shoot her to daylight. The tube closes atop her, getting smaller and smaller until water meets water and whirls and whirls down into the trough. It's a horizontal centrifuge, and *Kingurra* is caught in the middle.

All goes dark for the crew. Campbell's chin and face slam into something hard. Peter Meikle, who was standing next to Campbell, notices it's dark and wet *and* he's breathing. Strange. Then Meikle figures the boat is upside down, and he's in an air pocket.

Below, skipper Peter Joubert, a cantankerous, seventy-four-year-old engineering professor at the University of Melbourne, feels his chest cave in. A crewman has been thrown on top of Joubert, crushing his chest cavity. As if the pain weren't misery enough, seawater pours into the hold from a hole someplace. Men are screaming, praying out loud, swearing a blue streak.

Then *Kingurra*'s rolling again. One, two, three, four seconds pass. Daylight replaces the dark water and she is upright. Meikle sees no one, thinks he's the only one not washed away. He gulps air like a thirsty man who's found a babbling brook. Spume blasts across the deck, the salt spray burning Meikle's face. Wind noise and spume. Sensory overload that feels more like sensory deprivation. God's little reminder that Meikle's alive. He feels relief, worry, fear.

Damian Horrigan was hurled forward. Now he struggles back to the cockpit. Both Schniders and Campbell were pitched over the back of the boat. The open transom is topped by a thin braid of safety wire. Schniders and Campbell hang over the safety wire by their safety harness, legs dangling in the water.

Both men are limp. Then Anthony Schniders mumbles something, hoists himself back on deck.

But Campbell still isn't moving. Deck pitching and slick, Meikle half-walks, half-crawls to the back of the boat. Campbell's safety harness has ridden up around his neck, cutting off his oxygen supply. Blacked out, he dangles in the water. Limp. Dead weight. His chin is bleeding badly and his eyes are already black and swollen.

Meikle shouts below for help. No one answers. They're all too banged up. Too stunned. The same crew that dined on beef roast the first night out, and for whom the race was supposed to be more of a pleasure cruise, are suffering from bruised ribs and battered arms. Their heads—craniums, brain buckets—are ajar from bouncing off hard corners and sturdy surfaces. Vomit. Overflowed toilet. Salt water. Clothes and dry bags. Disarray. Joubert's ribs are broken, a lung is punctured, and his spleen is ruptured. Still, he's crawled to the navigation station and sent the Mayday ("We need a helicopter!"), then helped his twenty-two-year-old grandson turn on the bilge pumps.

After a moment, navigator Tony Vautin answers Meikle's call for help on deck. Vautin knows that Meikle's the one who invited Campbell and thus feels responsible. Even as Schniders grabs the tiller and steers away from a sixty-footer, Meikle and Vautin are at the back of the boat pulling on Campbell, trying to hoist his limp form up over the three-foot wire and back into *Kingurra*. Vautin is having a hard time getting a grip, so Meikle begins doing the majority of the hoisting.

Meikle is not a strong man. He's barely in his twenties. Still a boy, really. Slight, middle-sized, athletically average. Campbell is thin, but long. Probably outweighs Meikle by twenty pounds. Meikle's problem is that Campbell rides so far over the safety wire that the only part of his body Meikle can grab is the harness around the upper torso, under the arms. And that's a stretch, forcing Meikle to lean far over the wire and pull upward, with leverage working against him. Campbell's legs are underwater, dragging behind the boat so far that Campbell's almost prone. The legs are attached to boots, and the boots are filled with water, increasing the drag as Meikle fights to pull his friend over that silly wire.

Seeking a bit of comfort before beginning his watch, Campbell unwittingly made Meikle's chore tougher. The wet-weather gear is layered. The intent is to trap body heat between layers and increase warmth. Adventurers from mountain climbers to deep-sea divers follow the same principle.

First Campbell slipped a liner over his clothing. That's the initial layer of warmth. But instead of putting the bulky outer shell on next—the slicker—Campbell put on his safety harness. Then he put on the slicker. Previous experience tells him that putting the safety harness on over his slicker is too binding. He can barely breathe. Better to wear it underneath, looser. More freedom of movement, especially with all this weird weather.

Campbell discounts the fact that linings are slippery by design. The idea is to repel water totally. Only a slippery, impermeable membrane serves the function. Now, with Meikle pulling Campbell on board by the harness, that soaked, slippery lining provides no friction. Campbell's right arm slips out first. Meikle grabs on to his friend's hand. Campbell's body drags behind the boat, slipping the rest of the harness over his head. Meikle is now Campbell's only connection to the boat. The safety harness and slicker dangle useless and empty atop the safety wire.

Horrigan and Schniders are too busy evading waves to heed Meikle's calls for help. They can't hear him, anyway. The wind has not let up. Some weird acoustic of clouds and sea and jet-stream pressure shoots a loud moan through the sky.

Meikle has Campbell firmly by the hand. Then not so firmly. Then just the fingertips. If only Campbell could wake up and return the grip. Fight, John.

The sea wants Campbell. He's yanked from Meikle by a sudden bite of current. Meikle, calm, realizes his friend is definitely gone. Nothing anyone can do about that now. But if things aren't done properly, Campbell's chances of rescue will disappear altogether.

While Horrigan steers, Schniders keeps an eye on Campbell—there's no chance he'll live if they lose sight of him. Meikle quickly pops below and confirms Joubert has made the man overboard (MOB) call. Then it's back up top to discuss strategy with Schniders. All the activity has Schniders feeling a funny sort of pain, though he can't figure why. Later he will discover that his knee was shattered in the rollover.

Meikle and Schniders decide to bring the boat around, but this course of action is all but impossible. First, the storm jib was shredded in the rollover, meaning *Kingurra* is without sails. The motor is dead from all the water below, eliminating turning under power. Schniders will rely on the tiller and force of the waves to push him around. He's sure it can be done.

Instead of throwing their EPIRB toward Campbell so rescuers can locate him, Meikle and Schniders decide to save the beacon in case something else happens to the boat itself. "As long as we can see him," Schniders tells Meikle, "we can direct rescuers by radio."

Meikle looks off the back, sees his friend facedown ten meters off. Not a perfect situation, but there's still hope.

Then Campbell lifts his head. His boots, pants, and liner bob away from his body. Yes, Meikle thinks, yes! He's doing it. He's shedding the heavy gear and swimming for the boat.

But Campbell is still in a fog. Not conscious, not unconscious, he treads water in his long underwear and slips farther and farther from *Kingurra*. Peter Meikle begins wondering how long they can keep watching him. Soon, Campbell is visible just a few seconds out of every thirty.

When Campbell finally comes to, he's six hundred meters and a wave trough away from *Kingurra*. He decides he's dreaming. No way he's bobbing in the Bass Strait in sixty-to-ninety-foot seas. You *must* be dreaming, John, he tells himself. I'm wearing my long underwear for crying out loud. That's right. I'm in my bunk, lashed to the windward side of *Kingurra*, dreaming a horrible nightmare about being swept out to sea. There must be some Jungian meaning behind this most disturbing dream. Definitely have to write this down in the morning so I can check it out later.

The veil lifts slowly, a nightmare in reverse. Instead of waking himself to find the nightmare over, he slowly wakes to find the nightmare reality. He is drifting. He is in the Bass Strait. The wind is so loud he can't hear himself think. Death by drowning will come the minute he gets too tired to tread water. Campbell figures that gives him an hour. Surely, *Kingurra* can steer back and throw him a line. He sees her. The bare poles pop atop a crest once in a while. At least he's not alone. Somehow, that faraway boat is reassuring.

The hypothermia thought comes next. Nothing saps body heat like cold water. As Campbell's core temperature plummets, he will shiver—this is the body's way of generating heat—but when that doesn't work, a feeling of elation and calm will overwhelm Campbell. Being from Seattle, near the base of Mount Rainier, he's heard the stories of climbers in the later stages of hypothermia. That sense of well-being causes many to strip off their clothes and wander naked in blizzards. Many die flat on their backs, hands folded under their heads as if reclining in a hammock.

It doesn't work that way for sailors. As the body cools, Campbell's heart will stop pumping blood to his extremities. It's a preventive measure, designed to preserve the vital organs. Feet will go numb, then hands. Then legs and arms. He won't get the chance to lie back in that pretend hammock because his arms and legs will cease to tread water. And John Campbell will sink to the bottom of the Bass Strait, where his body will rocket along on a current until it decomposes or he becomes fish food or he flies back up to the surface on the face of a green wave.

Campbell has less than an hour before hypothermia will kill him entirely. One factor in his favor is the Bass Strait's relative warmth, about seventy degrees. Thank goodness for summertime.

A swell lifts him. It's like an elevator pushing him skyward. He strains for a glimpse of *Kingurra*. There she is. Hope. Then the elevator goes down and Campbell is in a trough, walls of water before and behind. But he has hope and tries not to despair. He's been in the water twenty minutes.

TWELVE

RIDING THE WIRE

Sunday, December 27, 5:30–7 P.M.

At the same moment, paramedic Michelle Blewitt is tangled in ropes dangling from *Stand Aside*'s life raft. The final four members of *Stand Aside*'s crew are dispersed between the raft and the boat. A rope connects them. Various other ropes dangle from the raft as attachment points for drogues—or sea anchors. But the crew hasn't attached the drogues in their haste to inflate the raft and float it clear of the yacht. Now the ropes curl unseen in the black water like snakes waiting to entangle all stumbling into their grasp.

And that would be Blewitt. The life raft flips, tosses the men in the sea. She struggles to right the raft, then gets tangled in the ropes. Panic, but just briefly. Then a quick flick of her rescue knife and she's clear.

She winches one crewman up. Rescue procedure holds that she rides up with the victim, her legs wrapped around his torso to prevent spinning. He's swallowed a stomachful of seawater and immediately vomits it back up onto Blewitt. Too engrossed in the rise and fall of the seas to notice, she sees that he's secured inside the chopper, then unclips him. She rests a moment, sitting in the door

158

of the helicopter looking out. The view is horrifying. One minute the ocean's a hundred feet below the hovering helicopter, then a swell rears up, missing the chopper by just ten feet. She trembles with the awareness that she's about to willingly enter that dervish again. Adrenaline jacks her heart rate, stopping the trembling, providing an odd sense of calm. The only familiar sensation is the way the air outside smells: salt spray and JP4 jet-fuel exhaust, just like on training missions.

Timing the rising swell so her descent is ten feet instead of one hundred, Blewitt impulsively unclips herself from the line and decides against riding the winch back down. She checks her mask, snorkel. Then, pushing off with both hands, she jumps. After what seems like a mere second of free fall, she is in the water, sinking way under, feeling the pull of the swell dragging her left and down. Then she frantically kicks to what she thinks is the surface. But the turbulent conditions are inducing a sort of underwater vertigo, and Blewitt isn't sure if she's kicking upward or down into the Bass Strait's depths. Even when her heads pops out of the water, spatial perception is fleeting. The sea is black and white. The sky is black and gray. The wind shoves her from above and the current shoves her from below. Only the life raft in front of her provides perspective. Blewitt swims hard to it, grabs the inflated rings, and pulls herself up and over until she lands atop the hard rubber floor. Then Michelle Blewitt rests, allows herself to feel alive and safe—but only for a second—then gets back to work.

The men littered about the raft's interior are traumatized, subdued. They just want out. Some are terrified of the ride up, afraid they'll slip from the harness and fall back into the sea. But Blewitt, now with help from Kristy McAlister, pulls the last two guys from the raft. Both women ride the winch up with the victims, then sit in the doorway again, timing swells for the leap back down. A final crewman remains below, standing on the deck of *Stand Aside*. Blewitt drops into the water again. Salt water forces itself into her mouth as she sinks under. She swallows two mouthfuls, the bitter, lukewarm fluid expanding her stomach involuntarily. Waves keep her under, and the combination of breathlessness and salt water in her stomach and fatigue and spatial disorientation feels like a harbinger of death.

But when Blewitt fights back to the surface, she tries her best to look calm. She's more experienced than McAlister, who's been on helicopters just two months. Staying calm and setting a good example are a sign of professionalism. At the very least, it keeps Blewitt's mind off her own fears.

Blewitt makes her way to *Stand Aside*. It sways, rising and falling with the swells. The final crewman leaps in the water. Blewitt slips the collar on and the pair rockets skyward with Blewitt's legs around his chest. Soon she and Kristy McAlister are safe inside their helicopter, heading to Mallacoota. Then Blewitt and McAlister spend the better part of fifteen minutes vomiting salt water.

In between retching, they high-five each other—the rookies came through.

The call goes back to AusSAR: all twelve crew of *Stand Aside* safely on board. A whoop echoes through the War Room. Twelve men! The standard has been set. The goal of AusSAR for the duration of this storm is to pull men from the sea with the same efficiency and professionalism displayed during the *Stand Aside* rescue. There will be no loss of life. Weather reports show the storm strengthening, but thirty-five boats are now en route to Eden. Out of harm's way. That includes the dismasted *Business Post Naiad*. It's just been confirmed she's motoring in. Her Mayday has been reduced to medium priority.

John Constable applauds along with the others after the *Stand Aside* rescue, but his job has not gotten easier. With night falling, he can't use *SouthCare* or *Helimed 1*. Both lack night-vision equipment. The only groups with that capability are the navy Sea King and Sea Hawk squadrons, the 816th and 817th, respectively. As the search for *Winston Churchill* takes shape—and Constable can see a small group planning it against one War Room white board—he'll need the navy. The search so far has been devoid of military involvement, but it's time. Constable needs those two squadrons, and word filtering into Canberra from Maritime Headquarters in Syndey is that HMAS *Newcastle* and the naval air station in Nowra are recalling personnel from leave. They're definitely on the way. Maybe by midnight.

Not soon enough, but at least *SouthCare's* and *Helimed 1*'s pilots and crews can rest. That's one problem taken care of. That kid is still missing from *Kingurra*, with the Victoria Police Air Wing *Polair* and ABC chopper due on-scene any minute. Constable worries they've made the wrong choice sending *Polair* to *Kingurra* instead of *Winston Churchill*. Still no word from *W-C*. That's not a good sign. One high-profile loss like that will stay in the public's memory, wiping out the fantastic success already achieved on *Amro Challenge* and *Stand Aside*. If only the public could realize the difficulty of multiple rescues in seas this size . . .

Nothing Constable can do about that now. Best thing to do is wait for word from *Polair*. Sure hope they find that American kid.

The American kid is cognizant of two things: he's in deep trouble, and *Kingurra's* circling in search of him. He must not let them lose sight. Every time a swell lifts him he waves his arms wildly. As best he can, he swims toward them. With the current, it's like swimming in place, but it's better than doing nothing.

A flare arcs over the water. Odd. Maybe they think he can't see them. Campbell swims harder to *Kingurra*. He looks a mess—his jaw is broken, his right eye socket is broken, and his right cheek is crushed inward. Adrenaline coursing through his veins shuts out the pain, and he's unaware of any injury. Swimming to *Kingurra* is Campbell's only focus, though he's beginning to accept that it's as impossible as swimming to New Zealand. A long way from Seattle, he thinks. Campbell shoves images of his folks, Wally and Sally, from his head. Swim. Swim. Swim. Why'd they fire that flare? Swim. Swim. Swim. Water's not too cold, but I'm really, really tired. Having trouble feeling my toes. Swim, swim, swim.

Campbell's heightened sense of awareness means he hears the *Polair* helicopter as it arrives on-scene, even above that obscene moaning of the wind. He waves his arms, swims hard, shouts giddily—as if that's going to help—and generally behaves like a man about to die who's been given a second chance. All the effort exhausts Campbell, makes it harder to tread water. He doesn't care. Got to be seen. Swim, swim, swim.

But the *Polair* doesn't see Campbell. In fact, they don't even see *Kingurra*. The boat is white. The seas are almost entirely white foam. Black rain tendrils join sky and sea. The sun, wherever it's hidden, is setting.

There are three men aboard *Polair*. The pilot is Darryl Jones, a senior constable. The two rescue swimmers are Senior Constable Barry Barclay, a reed-thin man with a mustache so big it seems to cover his entire face; and Senior Constable David Key, a burly veteran officer and family man. As per procedure, Barclay and Key take turns performing rescues. The one who doesn't go in the water operates the winch. Today it's Key's turn to go in the water. Barclay doesn't argue.

Jones, Key, and Barclay have considerable ocean rescue experience. They are friends, both on and off work. When Barclay or Key speak with Jones during a rescue, asking him to move left or right, up or down, all three speak in shorthand. No need for formalities. The three have total faith in the others' abilities and carry a quiet professional pride. They've seen it all and done it all, and when the call goes out for a crack rescue team, they believe *Polair* is as good as they come. The navy and guys like Shane Pashley get all the glory, but *Polair 1*'s professionalism will stand up with that of any navy crew.

But as confident as they can be, the men of *Polair 1* are shocked and afraid as they approach *Kingurra*'s position. This weather and these seas, all three swear, are the biggest and baddest they've ever seen.

Jones flies to *Kingurra*'s approximate location. He doesn't see them, nor do the pairs of eyes in back. Using GPS coordinates, Jones begins flying in circles, slowly spiraling outward. That's when *Kingurra* fires the flare.

"Got him," Barclay cries, making visual contact with the boat. Raising *Kingurra* on VHF radio, Barclay works with Tony Vautin to direct *Polair* to Campbell's approximate location. They should find him, Vautin says, six hundred meters away.

"In which direction?"

"I'm not quite sure."

What Vautin neglects to tell Barclay is how Campbell's head performed an amazing act of demolition during the rollover. Flying through the air, Campbell's face knocked a life ring from it's metal support brackets. The brackets broke all those cranial bones, but Campbell's head exacted its revenge, dislodging the brackets and sending the life ring into the sea. Perhaps Vautin is unaware of this, seeing as how something more important to a navigator—namely, the primary compass—was also destroyed by Campbell's right eye and cheek in the rollover.

Either way, Barclay and Key aren't given the information about the life ring. So Key is understandably euphoric upon spotting the life ring, believing it to be Campbell. Key's sitting in the open door, dressed in wet suit and fins.

"Got him," Key says breezily.

But there's no man inside the life ring. Key's heart sinks. A plume of white water shoots through the ring's opening every few seconds. At dusk, from the air, that plume originally looked like a man. At dusk, from the air, almost any shape inside a life ring can look like a man. Key wonders if the men of *Winston Churchill* have died because of *Polair*'s diversion.

"Wrong on that," Key tells Jones somberly. "Just a life ring."

Jones exhales a dejected breath, then eases off the throttle and prepares to take the search in a new direction. It's getting dark. A look at the fuel gauge shows that fighting this wind is causing the chopper to suck gas at twice the normal rate. If they don't find this kid soon—

"Wait." It's Barclay. He sees something out of the corner of his eye. With special night-vision goggles, he scopes in on the object. What Barclay sees are a pair of arms waving like crazy. Not a man. Just arms. Waving. Deliriously. Like you and I would wave if our only hope for rescue—a beautiful blue-and-white, state-of-the-art helicopter with a big white spotlight beaming down—is about to turn around and fly away forever.

"I got him."

"You're sure?"

"Right. Definitely him. Unless some other bloke's bobbing around out here."

Campbell has been in the water thirty-five minutes. He's exhausted and injured. Hypothermia is shutting off blood to his extremities, and his arms and legs barely move. When he tries treading water, his mouth is just an inch out of the sea. Spume and oxygen enter this opening in equal portions. In the few short minutes it takes Barclay to spot him, Jones to fly overhead, and Key to clip onto the winch and ride down, Campbell disappears under the surface twice.

Jones settles into a hover. The wire spins as Key descends. He wears a yellow, plastic face protector with his goggles, the kind skiers wear to protect their skin from freezing. Still, fork-tine stabs of wind burrow into chin, neck, ears—places the mask doesn't cover. So he moves one hand from the wire and places it over his nose and mouth, because if he doesn't, Key fears the pain will distract him from doing his job properly.

The staccato of the helicopter blades deafens Key. And while the deafening never decreases, the closer Key rides to the surface, the more that dreadful moaning of the wind replaces the churn of the helo blades.

Then baptism as a ninety-footer (Jones records the height with a special altimeter noting the proximity of mass to *Polair*) grabs Key by the ankles and yanks him underwater. Let's play, the wave seems to sneer maliciously. A sudden washing-machine agitation corkscrews Key under, rolls him around to disorient him, spits him back toward the surface. Key is unsure if Barclay has unclipped the cable from above. Probably has. That's the prudent thing to do. No sense the whole chopper getting sucked down by a big wave.

Should things go terribly wrong, such as the helicopter crashing, rescue swimmers are trained to survive in the water. Standard gear is wet suit, fins, flight helmet, mask, and snorkel. In case of emergency, they also wear an inflatable life jacket and carry an EPIRB, two-way radio, flares, and strobe light. Rescue swimmers left in the water within thirty miles of land are always prepared to swim to shore.

But, as salt water forces its way into Key's mouth and nose, the last thing on his mind is swimming to shore. He just wants to reach the surface. His wet suit provides buoyancy, but the wave still holds him under. He doesn't know up from down. Claustrophobia washes over Key, a sensation intensified by the plastic shield across his face. Key knows a feral panic, and he fights a monstrous desire to rip off the mask, spit out his snorkel, and breathe. He's been underwater for almost a minute. What he'd give for a lungful of that spume-laden ocean air . . .

As if the wave wants Key to take a breath so it can toy with him longer, the wave rumbles mischievously at the exact instant Key feels he can take no more. Key is rocketed to the surface, his head is forced above water so he can gulp air. Amazingly, the cable is still hooked to him, and it didn't tangle around him when he rolled. A small miracle.

The swell rises to the sky, carrying Key along for the ride. Okay, Key tells himself, time to refocus. As the swell peaks, Key pirouettes, searching for Campbell. There he is, still waving those arms and trying to keep that gaping mouth of his above water. Campbell looks pale. Key aches to swim to him, to rescue him.

Only Campbell is one trough over, with eighty feet of wave separating him from Key. In fact, *Polair* is hovering over the same trough. It's Key that's in the wrong place.

Darryl Jones remedies the situation in a hurry, guiding *Polair 1* through a quick zig that drags Key into the proper trough. Instead of up and over, Key is pulled straight through the separating wave. He closes his eyes. The feeling is like hitting, then being swallowed by, a brick wall. Key once again feels his insides bulge from saltwater infusions. He'll have a word with Darryl about this stunt later. Dragging him across the water is one thing, but directly through a wave . . .

Key opens his eyes. John Campbell is the first thing he sees. Pale, almost lifeless, Campbell flails his arms, trying to swim. Keys goes to him. They hold each other, resting. Key is exhausted after just five minutes. How Campbell survived as long as he has is unfathomable. Key settles the horse collar over Campbell. It takes a while—a pair of mighty waves heave them up, then send tumbling down the face—but they cling to each other like life itself. Finally it's done.

A quick thumbs-up from Key, and Barclay slingshots them skyward. Jones holds his hover exactly as long as it takes for Key and Campbell to tumble inside the door, then, because *Kingurra* reports their situation stablizing, he's headed for home. As the soggy pair heave salt water, Campbell covers Key and Barclay with hugs and kisses. He's ecstatic.

Jones pushes *Polair* back to Mallacoota. He hasn't told anyone yet, but *Polair*'s running out of fuel. The same tailwind that propelled them to *Kingurra* at 220 knots is now in their face. He honestly doesn't know if they'll make land.

In back, Key and Barclay strip Campbell. They rub his body down vigorously, trying to draw blood back to his limbs. Campbell lies on the floor, a senior constable on either side, flagellating his limbs in a desperate attempt to get the body functioning properly again. When he tries to sit up, they force him back down. Experience has shown that sudden movement of hypothermic victims can kill.

The duel dramas continue all the way to Mallacoota, Jones glancing at his computer screen (forty-five minutes to get to Mallacoota, with eighty minutes' worth of fuel) as Campbell rejoins the living, slowly being warmed and wrapped in blankets. Then it's thirty minutes to Mallacoota with fifty minutes of fuel. Then Jones is calmly speaking with his mates in that casual pilot way about the checklist for ditching at sea. Just suppose, he says. Not that we're going to, but if we were about to ditch, how would we prepare?

No land in sight. A squall pushes them backward. Twenty minutes to go with twenty-five minutes of fuel. Then ten and ten. Then Jones doesn't even bother shooting for the airfield. He radios the ambulances to meet *Polair* at a bare patch of earth short of the runway.

They land safely. An ambulance arrives to trundle John Campbell off to a hospital.

"That fella gonna be okay?" an exhausted Key asks an ambulance doctor just before Campbell is whisked off.

"Yeah."

"Good. He's a tough one."

The next morning, Darryl Jones and Barry Barclay and David Key will see their exploit splashed on television and in newspapers worldwide. Somehow the reports will get it wrong, so that Key will be the winch operator and Barclay the heroic swimmer, and Jones won't be mentioned at all. But they're a team, so none of them will mind. Nor will it really matter that their names—instead of Shane Pashley's—will be synonymous with daring rescue, if only for a fortnight. All that's nice, but it's not why they do the job. If asked, they'd probably say they fly search and rescue for the same reasons Syd-Hob sailors race the Bass Strait—something to do with pushing to their mental, physical, and emotional limits. In a really weird way, a way they only admit to each other when the day is done, SAR is fun. Not when you're in it. But when it's done. A sensation of calm passes over the body. Incredible well-being. And the body begins to miss the rush, even minimize the danger. That's the way of adventure.

Then Darryl Jones and Barry Barclay and David Key will admit to each other—but only to each other—that rescuing a man from those seas was the hardest thing they've ever done. If they can pull off one of those, they have nothing to fear. Ever.

But tomorrow's another day. And that nagging in the back of their skulls is the realization that tomorrow always brings a rescue just a tick harder. And just as Darryl and Barry and David have no idea their exploit will be splashed in papers and on televisions around the world in the morning, they cannot possibly know that another rescue is waiting that makes the John Campbell hoist look simple.

THIRTEEN

MIDNIGHT RAMBLER

Sunday, December 27, 4–7 P.M.

Ed Psaltis is alive. He found the strength to swim back aboard *Midnight Rambler* after the knockdown. She righted herself as Ed hauled himself into the cockpit. Then Ed grabbed the tiller and steered *Midnight Rambler* out of danger a split second before a second rogue washed over her decks. Now Ed's strapped in a bunk below, damaged, sleeping. Bob has the helm, taking over after Ed barely survived a second knockdown at five-thirty. Bruises cover Ed's body. Wave after wave has pushed him around the cockpit, bouncing his body off the tiller and stanchions. Getting swept overboard, even attached to a safety harness, is a new sensation to Ed. He doesn't admit it to the crew—even Bob and Arthur—but that glimpse of mortality shook him. The knockdown happened so fast. Just like that he was over the side. Ed sleeps, enduring nightmares of being thrown overboard without a harness, and swimming through waves as green and thick as pea soup while *Midnight Rambler* sails into the distance. He shouts for help, the whole crew stands on deck and sees him, but instead of turning the boat around, the crew just waves and sails away. The despair Ed knows is incredible.

The nightmare wakes him. The pain on his left side is too great, so Ed rolls over and leans his cheek against the hull. The laminate feels cool against his skin. The smoothness is somehow reassuring, as if connecting with the known in the midst of the unknown implies safety.

Arthur lies in the bunk below, his head just nine inches from Ed's. Chris is across the way, concussed, lashed into a bunk. Ed and Bob seriously considered turning around when they saw the depth of Chris's gash, but Chris wouldn't hear of it. "This boat will not turn around on my account," he stated defiantly. Then Chris tried to charge up on deck and pull watch, open head wound and all. A compromise was reached, with Ed and Bob deciding not to turn back for Eden so long as Chris promised to stay in a bunk for at least six hours. Arthur even volunteered the lone dry blanket on board if Chris would comply. And so it was done.

Ed fingers a puffy welt running up and down the left side of his ribs. Six or seven inches long, ripening quickly into a bruise. Probably from when he smashed into the stanchion. Ed's mouth feels dry and his lips are cracked. He chuckles grimly at the irony—he's dehydrated. All that water out there and Ed's drying up inside. He shouldn't be surprised—fighting the tiller in weather like this is tougher than any rowing or running workout back home, and he's sweating buckets under three layers of clothing. But that would explain the incredible fatigue. Even with adrenaline providing extra oomph, Ed just feels so tired. He remembers that dehydration saps a body of energy quicker than going without food or sleep, then vows to drink more water before going on watch again.

But then they come again: thoughts of Sue. He can't help it. Sue and Benjamin and Matthew. And his dad. The whole crew's thinking about their families, so at least Ed doesn't feel alone in his worries. No one talks about the weather, other than the occasional joke about the wind being so nice and mild, but everyone lets slip with a family reference once in a while: Wonder how the wife's holding up? Wonder if we're making the news? Hope the CYCA's letting them know we're all right. The crew are all either married and have kids or are related to another crew member. Worry is normal. Even that subconscious fear of sinking is normal.

Ed wonders if Bill Psaltis ever lay with his cheek pressed to the hull like this, ruminating about family and thinking quiet thoughts of death. The notion is so preposterous that Ed almost laughs out loud. Bill cared most for his boat. No way on earth Bill would think of family during a race. Why, even now, Ed imagines Bill back in Sydney, calmly telling Sue to calm down and wondering what all the fuss is about. Bill would be more concerned with whether *Midnight Rambler* is still racing competitively than about the safety of Ed and Arthur.

As if one cue, Ed hears Arthur whispering something. "Listen to that."

Ed can't hear anything. His mind races. Does Arthur hear something he can't? Maybe some piece of broken equipment or machinery that, in this storm, could mean fatality for one or more of the crew.

"I don't hear anything. Tell me what you hear."

"Listen . . ." And now, strangely, Arthur is weeping. "Can't you hear it?"

Ed hears . . . nothing. Nothing! And *Midnight Rambler* is barely moving. Ed rolls out of bed and slips on his wet-weather gear. He climbs up the hatch into bright sunshine. Birds. Blue seas sparkling with the sun's reflection. Only ten knots of wind.

Bob smiles and takes one hand off the tiller and spreads it out toward the seas as if he's responsible for the weather.

"What do you think, mate?"

"Beauty."

Arthur charges on deck. One by one, the crew comes up top, even Chris. They strip their shirts off and feel the warmth of the sun on their chests, realizing for the first time how cold and miserable they've been these past twenty-four hours. A couple of the guys talk about going below and slipping into shorts.

"Not quite yet, mates," Ed says.

Ed drinks in the peace and quiet. Yes, this is the eye. He knows that for sure. And there will be more calamity. But for now, the sense of calm is wondrous. He looks to heaven and smiles, beaming a thought back: I'm okay, Sue and Benjamin and Matthew. Know this: Ed Psaltis and *Midnight Rambler* are okay. We are beating this storm. The worst is not over, but *Midnight Rambler* is pressing on.

• • •

Glyn Charles was once a "sailing bum," willing to sail for anyone, anytime, but has now transcended the category. In fact, Glyn is busy developing a category all his own: sailing Renaissance man. He is a man of many talents and interests, thinking with the right and left sides of his brain. He has the mind of a mathematician, constantly appraising angles, calculating odds, strategizing. Charles can sail any kind of boat, short of a clipper. He is also a popular writer. Articles and advice columns of Charles's appear monthly in British sailing magazines. His 1997 book, *Keelboat and Sportsboat Racing*, shows others how to follow his path from dinghy sailor to Olympic yachtsman and is considered by many the premier text on boat handling.

In addition to sailing, Charles is an accomplished all-around athlete. His swimming prowess is well-known, and he thinks nothing of dropping in the ocean or pool for two consecutive miles of stroke. His body is lean and strong. He always avoids the dissipation of too much food and drink, the downfall of many a sailor, but especially now that the Olympics are just twenty months off.

Softened by Annie Goodman, Charles enjoys living in artsy Emsworth. He is on the verge of settling down, or at least as close to settling down as an international sailor is capable. Royal Yachting officials quietly say Charles has ten years left in his Olympic career, by which time his knowledge of sailing's intricacies and politics, on and off the water, will make him an ideal candidate to become an elder statesman. This will happen by default if Charles wins his Olympic gold, but is likely nonetheless. Charles is too well known and liked, has too much to say, to go gently into the good night. He is all passion and fury, living for the purity of the perfect tack and the simple wonder of true love found.

Like all sailors, Glyn knows his astronomy and has a passive reverence for the stars' mysteries. If need be, Glyn can navigate by sun and stars, just like old-time mariners. Glyn knows that Orion and his sword are the very image of the manly hunter. In ancient Egypt, the appearance of Auser, as it was called, marked flooding of the Nile. The "belt" was used as an orientation marker for the three great pyramids at Giza. The Maya referred to them as "hearthstones." The Hebrew Book of Job mentions Orion by name, in connection with God's power when angered: "He . . . who shakes the earth out of its place and its pillars tremble; the One speaking to the sun and it does not rise, and He sets a seal around the stars; . . . who made Orion and the chambers of the south."

Glyn knows there is rich history in the name of this boat he pilots on this dreary Sunday afternoon. The eye is but a distant memory, and the storm is worse than ever. But this is his link with history—it's a sailor's job to persevere through bad weather. Glyn knows that with his skills and knowledge he might have been a Cook or Magellan in another era, and that instead of piloting this slender sailboat he would be at the helm of a stocky bark such as *Endeavour*, exploring new lands. Captain James Cook and Glyn Charles are remarkably alike. Like Charles, Cook was born of modest means, the son of a Scottish farm laborer. He fought his way up through the sailing ranks, becoming the first enlisted man given command of a British sailing ship. Like Glyn Charles, Cook was a Renaissance man, both a sea captain and a physician, and on his ships there were as many botanists and scientists as sailors. Cook would die a grisly death, hacked to death by angry warriors in the surf zone of Hawaii's Kealakekua Bay.

Glyn isn't thinking of heritage nor history nor grisly death as he steers *Sword of Orion* back to Eden. He's just glad to be driving the boat with the wind in his face and the fate of the crew in his hands. He likes that Kothe and Kulmar have given him the helm in this time of immense pressure. Much preferable to champagne sailing; fighting the elements is what sailing is all about. Charles likes the thrill of sailing with following waves. Coming from behind and right, they're likely to appear suddenly and without warning. That's good, though. This is the kind of situation that will make Glyn a better sailor. Sailors with experience in seas this tall—and they rise up behind *Sword* anywhere from forty-five to ninety-five feet—are rare. Even the Royal Ocean Racing Club on St. James Place in London, that bastion of all things British and sailing, has few men able to claim such experience. And those guys have been sailing all their lives. They even named the meeting room adjacent the second-floor bar the Fastnet Room. Glyn allows himself a smile as he imagines walking into the RORC bar, settling into one of those comfortable wingbacks, and calmly regaling blue-blazered members with tales of sailing a forty-three-footer through seas twice the boat's size, during winds twice those of the '79 Fastnet. Glyn Charles has been hearing '79 Fastnet stories for as long as he can remember. Time for Glyn Charles to tell a few of his own. Experience like this will help next time he solicits sponsorship or patronage. Experience like this will definitely help in getting a Whitbread slot after the Olympics are over.

The thoughts of the future and success are warming, even as rain soaks him to the skin. Glyn's toes are getting cold, as drips and drabs of water trickle into the seams of his wet-weather gear then run down his legs into his seaboots. Bowman Darren Senogles— "Dags"—has clipped his harness to the safety jackstay, allowing him to move freely around the boat. Glyn is clipped to a strong point behind the wheel. The storm jib is up, but nothing else. Kulmar has advised a northerly angle of sail, so that the waves come predominantly from the west, with the rogues coming from all directions. He has, however, given Glyn the option of choosing a better course if he so desires. Kulmar sits toward the center of the boat now, belowdecks in the nav station. Kothe sits nearby, manning his state-of-the-art radio system as he relays Maydays to *Young Endeavour.* Glyn thinks of how everyone aboard thought life would get easier once *Sword* turned for Eden. But it hasn't. They've actually doubled back into the worst of the storm—all in a quest to reach someplace called Eden. Glyn would laugh at the irony if the wind weren't hurting his face so much.

"The storm," Kothe remarked to no one in particular just before turning around, "doesn't give a rat's ass whether we're still racing or heading to port." And Glyn knows this to be true.

Glyn searches for his rhythm, steering *Sword* across the face of wave after wave. He appraises the angle carefully, looking for patterns in waves. There doesn't seem to be any, but past experience tells him that, with patience, a pattern will soon emerge.

Instead of making a beeline back to land, *Sword* is S-turning through the waves like a skier navigating a mogul field. Fighting the seven-foot wheel, Glyn decides to make a course change. He motions for Dags to scurry back to the cockpit.

"Go below," Glyn yells to Dags. "Find out if there's any new weather information. I'm thinking of charting a new course and I want to know what the weather's doing."

"Right," Dags yells back. Dags slides on his butt to the forward hatch, using the left hand for stability on the deck, the right to pull his safety harness along the guide wire. The wind keeps trying to push Dags overboard, and the rain makes the textured deck feel as slippery as waxed linoleum. He concentrates with all his might as he scoots forward. Finally even with the hatchway, Dags reaches to open it.

The wind is pushing the hatch shut, and Dags looks down to focus on the task. It's a struggle, but he finally pries the hatch open. Dags prepares to drop below, then remembers to make one last check for waves. He lifts his eyes. A green wall of water stares back at him. It's huge, at least eighty feet, and seemingly inches away. The wave came from nowhere, rising up in the ten short seconds it took Dags to move forward and open the hatch.

Glyn doesn't see the rogue yet.

Dags open his mouth to scream a warning, but *Sword of Orion* is scooped up before the first syllable escapes. The wave is vertical, more like a waterfall than a curling, breaking patch of ocean. For a split second, *Sword* is affixed to the wave like a rock climber roped to a cliff. Just sticking there sixty-five feet up, defying gravity.

When the wave breaks, Dags is thrown off into the white water. His tether stretches. Below, Kothe and Kulmar and the rest of the crew are hurled into radio and navigational equipment. The force of the wave wraps the mast neatly around the hull, into the exact curvature of the boat. The boom, attached to the base of the mast, swings horizontally across the deck like a giant baseball bat as the mast is crushed. The boom thuds hard into Glyn's ribs at the same time the wave's crest breaks over the cockpit. Glyn is fungoed overboard. *Sword* goes airborne, falling for two full seconds down the face of the wave, twisting as she goes. All her tonnage splats into the trough. The wave's tonnage follows a split second after, shoving *Sword* under.

When the wave finally passes, Kothe lies facedown below, wrapped in electrical wiring and writhing from a knee bent sideways at a ninety-degree angle. Dags is up top screaming about a man overboard. Really screaming, as if maybe Glyn isn't anywhere near the boat but getting swept away.

The entire crew of *Sword* scrambles up top, even Kothe, who has torn knee ligaments and who makes the journey in a half-crawl. The crew finds Dags screaming still, pointing to the horizon. The remainder of the deck is destroyed, with the wheel entirely gone and the mast twisted over the side. Glyn's harness dangles over, too, one end still attached to the deck's strong point. The harness's stitching was sheared clean off by the wave, and now Glyn's in the ocean, thirty meters from the boat. Dags is yelling for Glyn to swim. And as the whole crew watches, Glyn is trying, or at least tries, for about six strokes. But he can only move one side of his body. The boom has broken the other side. Glyn treads water, not speaking or yelling, and looking dazed and in deep pain. Dags ties a rope around his waist and affixes the other end to *Sword*'s broken mast.

"I'll swim to him," he yells. "I can make it. Just be ready to pull us back in."

But a second wave blindsides *Sword* before Dags can leap. No one was looking for it. All are knocked from their feet. *Sword* doesn't roll, but she squirrels away across the surface like a surfboard without a rider. By the time everyone stands again, Glyn is two waves and 150 meters away. Dags can no longer swim to him. Glyn will be impossible to find in all the spray and trough.

Because boats can't just slam on the brakes, the man-overboard procedure for all racing sailboats dictates a figure-eight return to the man. This is accomplished through tacking and jibing. The man-overboard procedure can be effected more quickly by turning on the engine, though turning on the engine in a sailboat isn't as fast as starting a car's ignition. Batteries need to be switched to the starter, and the fuel cock must be opened. But none of this matters to *Sword*. They can't tack and jibe because they have no mast or steering wheel. The crew can't motor to Glyn because the mast wrapped around the bottom of the boat means ropes and sails everywhere, fouling the prop. Besides, the area belowdecks is underwater, likely shorting the engine's wiring. Helpless, the crew watches Glyn get swept away. He wears wet-weather gear and seaboots, no life jacket. He just treads water, looking at the crew hopelessly, waiting for them to do something. With just one good arm, it doesn't take long for Glyn to get weak. He starts going under. Each time he resurfaces, it's for shorter and shorter periods. Dags, overcome with emotion, has to be restrained from leaping in after Glyn.

"He's too far away," Kulmar reminds Dags. "You'll just kill yourself."

"I can do it, though. I can get to him."

Glyn watches the commotion. He rages inside, impotent and confused. This can't be happening. His body has failed hm. He can't move his left arm, and most every rib on that side of the body is broken. The crew is doing everything they can to save him, but there has to be something more they can do. It's all very simple. Someone needs to have the balls to swim over and rescue him. Forget the odds. He knows he's a stranger to most of them, but Glyn would risk his life for a fellow sailor in a heartbeat. Now he's swallowing seawater and can't keep his head above water, and the guys on deck watch him go under as if he's some sort of absurd entertainment. This is happening. Glyn is drowning. He can barely breathe or cry out. His clothes weigh a ton. He's got just one good arm to swim with and won't be able to hold on much longer.

But *Sword* is in trouble herself, and the crew cannot help him. In between watching Glyn slip farther and farther away, they bail. Seventy-knot winds still rake the decks, and the waves aren't getting any smaller. The starboard afterdeck separated from the hull during the rollovers, most of the internal bulkhead supports within the boat were broken, and water pours in at the points of damage—the hull/deck join and wheel well. The mast and rigging need to be cut away.

Sword of Orion is sinking.

Rob Kothe activates the EPIRB. He actually takes it up top and ties it to the deck with a piece of twine. He argues with the crew, who are distraught about Glyn and who scream at the novice sailor that the fucking EPIRB doesn't belong up top. But he tells them it's his fucking boat and he'll do what he wants with his fucking EPIRB.

Hostility and confusion and despair and a crew that wants off—now. And all the while, Glyn Charles is still visible, bobbing farther and farther into the distance.

Kothe goes below. The man who's played humanitarian all afternoon, alerting the fleet to danger and acting as radio relay for so many vessels in distress, begins sending Maydays of his own. His mast wiped out the high-frequency radio, so he can only send VHF.

"Mayday, Mayday. This is *Sword of Orion*. Mayday, Mayday."

But the radio is jammed with useless chatter between the fishing boat searching for *Team Jag* (who will later say they were never in real distress) and Lew Carter aboard *Young Endeavour*. Kothe, who swears he will Mayday until losing his voice, gets no response to his frantic cries that a member of his crew is dying. Right now. Would someone send a fucking helicopter right now? What's wrong with you people?

In the meantime, Glyn Charles disappears. One minute the crew sees him, the next he's swept away on a wave, still waiting for someone to swim to his rescue.

When Captain Cook was in great danger off Hawaii, he could have saved his life by swimming back to the ship. But, like Glyn Charles now, Cook was injured and unable to swim that fateful day. His crew watched helplessly from his ship's deck as their leader died a slow death at the hands of local warriors, who passed around a single knife to plunge into Cook's body rather than kill him all at once. What terror Cook must have known as he slowly deteriorated, his body finally settling beneath the waves for the sharks to find.

And so it is that *Sword of Orion*'s crew helplessly watches Glyn Charles die. Even with just one good arm, Glyn's too angry—too much of a fighter—to cross his arms, stop the eggbeater kick, take one last deep breath, and offer his body to the sea. Instead, hypothermia claims him slowly. It begins with his body shivering uncontrollably. His legs shut down next, then his arms. Glyn's angry in the early stages, seething at the injustice and the stupidity and senselessness. And then remorse washes over him like a bad drug as time passes and his body temp lowers. Then mourning. Finally, the salve of well-being fills Glyn Charles as his core temperature slips below ninety degrees and his body stops that awful shivering. Glyn's mind still functions, and he is able to appreciate the sky and waves and wind with the love of a lifelong sailor up until the very end. Finally, his limbs no longer moving, his mind knowing contentment after a life of rage and battle, Glyn Charles slips beneath the waves one last time.

FOURTEEN

THE PERFECT LIFE RAFT

Sure I am this day that we are masters of our fate; that the
task which has been set before us is not above our strength;
that its pangs and toils are not beyond our endurance.
—Winston Churchill

Sunday, December 27, 5:15 P.M.–Midnight

The perfect life raft for a sailboat would be lightweight so it can be
stored below. Anything over one hundred pounds must be lashed
to the deck. The perfect life raft would have an EPIRB of its own,
separate from the mother ship's, so rescuers could find the raft
once the ship sinks. There would be metal ringlets anchored inside
the raft, allowing sailors to clip in with lifelines. A Gore-Tex
canopy would provide shelter from rain and sun. A drogue would
deploy beneath as a sea anchor to prevent the raft from getting
rolled by heavy winds. A survival kit would be built in, with fresh
water and freeze-dried food and a flare gun and anything else the
crew deems essential for survival and rescue.

The perfect life raft would also be inexpensive, so crews would be more likely to buy it, rather than opting for something flimsy and lightweight that barely meets sailing regulations—figure about $3,000. On top of the price of a yacht, that's a small price to pay for peace of mind. But many sailors go to sea their whole life without boarding a raft. It becomes a bragging point, something to share with the mates over a beer. Sooner or later the logic of the perfect life raft gets watered down as a tonic for lesser sailors. Real sailors don't need the perfect life raft because real sailors never sink.

John Stanley, Richard Winning, John Dean, Jim Lawler, Bruce Gould, John Gibson, and Mike Bannister are all real sailors. Real good sailors, with a corner of their minds occupied since boyhood by sailing knowledge learned firsthand. They have sailed everything from dinghies to Laser to eighteen-foot skiffs to blue-water boats. Michael Rynan and Paul Lumtin lack that experience, but both have spent enough time sailing Sydney Harbor to know their way around a boat.

But now the *Winston Churchill* is in dire straits, and the nine men bob aboard two life rafts in the horrendous seas. Their longest night is about to begin.

Two Hours Earlier

At dusk on December 27—27, just like her sail number—*Winston Churchill* is bearing south, to Hobart. Steamer Stanley sits in the doghouse, right in front of the helm. Steamer is a benevolent man, round in the face with a salt-and-pepper mustache clipped short. He's the man who rebuilt *Winston Churchill*, lovingly refurbishing the Huon pine hull, making it stronger by adding an additional thirty-five hundred fasteners. Given his time at sea and knowledge of *W-C*'s limitations and abilities, Stanley has the honorary title of sailing master. Theoretically, all matters tactical should be referred his way. It doesn't always work that way—Winning is comfortable with leadership and knows his boat well enough to make decisions himself—but often it does. So Stanley perches in the doghouse as *W-C* rolls up and down monstrous seas, taking waves at the prescribed sixty-to-seventy-degree angle up the face. *W-C*'s extralong keel digs in, providing far better control on the wave face than the smaller keels of modern racing boats.

Stanley finds comfort in *W-C*'s sturdy character, but she's fifty-six years old. She can't bash up and down waves forever. Maybe it's time to change strategies. With night coming on, the odds of getting surprised by a wave will increase. Stanley decides the options are to keep running south, turning around and running away under bare poles toward Eden, or heaving to. *W-C* heaved to quite nicely during the 1945 gale. No reason she can't do the same now.

Rogue waves have increased. From one of every fifty being a rogue, now it's one in fifteen. Winning is a few feet back, steering. John Dean, a rugby fanatic and father of two teenage boys, is wave watcher. Looking out a doghouse porthole—the portholes are small pieces of glass, each just eight inches across—Stanley lazily watches *W-C* climb a wave. More accurately, he feels *W-C* climb a wave. It's an eighty-footer, and gravity pushes Stanley against the right wall of the doghouse as *W-C* climbs and climbs. The only thing he can see through the porthole is the black-and-white water of the wave's face.

W-C climbs up, up, up . . . and just before Stanley should feel the lip pass under *W-C*, and the hull top the crest to take the long ride down the backside into the trough . . . *Winston Churchill* stalls. Just stops. She's not over the top, but fifteen feet below. She's run out of speed. Stanley doesn't see the glossy black and white of the wave face through the porthole now. He sees the churning foam of a breaking wave. The wall of foam arcs over *Winston Churchill*, about to break directly on top of her. Stanley can feel *Winston Churchill* slide backward down the wave as the wave continues to curl above. She is halfway between crest and trough when the wave throws the twenty-five-ton boat through the air on its side.

Water shatters the doghouse portholes. Stanley is thrown across the doghouse and pinned against the left wall, ocean pressing him flat and caving in his chest. He can't breathe as salt water is forced into his mouth and nose and ears. The force of his ankle slamming against the wall bruises it to the bone, and the pressure of driving water—imagine lying flat on the ground and having a tanker-truckful of water fall on top of you—rips muscles in his groin and surgically repaired hips, splaying his legs in a sadistic plié.

Instead of rolling, *Winston Churchill* has been flung into the backside of another wave. As if the waves were playing catch, using a sailboat instead of a baseball.

The waves collapse into each other, then pass over *W-C*. She rights. Stanley hears his name being called. A look out the dog-house shows Winning and Gould dangling from the rigging by safety harnesses, their feet swinging above the deck like men in a gallows. Stanley limps to them. He untangles both, then assumes control of the ship. Winning is told to start the motor. Stanley will head below to flip on the bilge-pump valves. The helm goes to Bruce Gould, whose thirty-two Syd-Hobs are the most on board.

Below, Stanley sees for the first time that *Winston Churchill* may be lost. The mast has drilled straight down through the bottom. Six feet of bulwarks are missing from the left side. Water is pouring in. Planks have come loose, and over a foot of water covers the floor. It's imperative to get the motor running immediately, both to power the bilge pumps and dry the hold, then power back to Eden.

But when Winning turns on the engine, it shuts down after twenty seconds. He tries again, with the same result. And one more time. Water rushing in has swamped the engine. Everything else below is destroyed as well—paper charts, navigation aids, on-board computers.

Lumtin, sleeping below, wakes up thinking a bomb has gone off. He almost hadn't sailed this year, having been laid low with the flu Christmas Day. But not wanting to let Richard down, he ignored the sickness.

Now he's in the hold of a flooded ship. Blood is everywhere. The world is in black and white. He staggers from the bunk in his underwear; the water reaches above his waist as he fumbles in search of his wet-weather gear. When Lumtin finally bumps into Winning, the owner doesn't look him in the eye to give him the bad news. "We're sinking, mate. Best to get your things together and make your way up onto the deck."

The news makes Lumtin's chest tight and stomach hurt, as if he's been kicked hard in the balls. You wanted a challenge, Paul, Lumtin thinks. And now you've got it.

By now, all the crew's getting the life rafts on deck. It doesn't take a rocket scientist to see that *Winston Churchill* is sinking. *Winston Churchill* has a big ugly hole in her side. She flies no sails. Islands of food and gear and shit and vomit float about, latching onto Winning's calves and thighs as he wades to the radio. This yacht that represents a living history to all Australia—sailing, World War II, ties to England, Sydney-Hobart—is about to become history. It's with sadness that he picks up the microphone. The HF is stuck on the weather-fax frequency and Winning can't change it. Digsusted, he picks up the VHF instead.

"Mayday, Mayday, Mayday . . ."

Stanley moves up onto the deck. "Gather round, boys," he says as calmly as possible, feeling very much like the activities director on the *Titanic* as he passes out life jackets and pretends that quality time in life rafts is going to be good for the crew. These lifelong sailors don't trust life rafts. No control. Too flimsy. Definitely an item of last resort. Sometimes, they've heard stories, the wind picks up an entire raft and sends it skipping across the ocean surface like a smooth pebble on a pond.

Gould steers *W-C* under bare poles, though the hull's halfway underwater. Winning is still radioing the emergency. ". . . here is *Winston Churchill, Winston Churchill* . . . we are holed. We are taking water rapidly. We can't get the motor started to start the pumps . . . niner. Niner."

The life rafts are inflated, tied to the stern by rope. Winning comes back up on deck. He's wet to the waist from the rising water.

"Any luck, Richard?" Steamer asks his good friend.

"I spoke with the ABC chopper. I gave them our position, but I have no idea when they're coming to get us."

"All right then, boys, into the rafts," Steamer orders.

The life rafts bob, waiting. They are not perfect life rafts. Nor are they even in accordance with SOLAS (Safety of Life at Sea) specifications, such as those used by sailors in around-the-world sailboat races. But *W-C*'s rafts are in accordance with the Australian Yachting Federation's Category One safety requirements, which makes them good but not perfect. They're lightweight, more subject to the whims of heavy weather.

Stepping from the deck of a sailing ship—their home, in effect, since leaving Sydney—into the water to swim, then step up onto their flimsy life rafts, the gentlemen of *Winston Churchill* are scared to death. If only there were some way to save *Winston Churchill* . . .

But that's never going to happen. The wind and swells pitch *Winston Churchill* about mightily, sucking her down. Gould stays at the helm, even as the decks are awash. All that pokes above the water are the doghouse and cockpit roofs. As sailing master, Stanley oversees the boarding of the life rafts. Winning, Gould, Michael Rynan, and Paul Lumtin swim to the first raft.

Winning is the last to go. He shakes Steamer's hand, saying good-bye without saying what's on both their minds. "See you soon, mate."

"Good on you. Be careful out there."

Winning pauses, about to step off his beloved boat for the last time. "She really was a beauty, Steamer. I'll miss her."

"We'll all miss her, Richard." Then, nodding to the raft and the rising water, Steamer shakes Winning's hand again. "Off you go."

As Winning immerses himself in the Bass Strait, Paul Lumtin swims the last strokes to the round raft with the millimeter-thick floor and paper-thin roof that is to be his refuge. All Lumtin can think of is his family, and how badly he wants to see them again. He curses his predisposition toward adventure, realizing too late that he's been trying to prove something to himself through all his crazy antics. Before going to work for Richard Winning—and being introduced to sailing four years prior—Lumtin worked at a Sydney theme park named Wonderland as a stuntman. His job required him to leap backward off the eighty-foot mainmast of a pirate ship three times daily. If that wasn't enough, he spent his spare hours looking for excitement—scuba diving off the Great Barrier Reef with the great white sharks, flying acrobatic planes, extreme skiing. He knew the Sydney to Hobart wasn't going to be a "teddy bear's picnic," but this is absurd. Nine men are swimming to life rafts, fighting for their lives. Some of them, Lumtin is sure as he pulls himself aboard, won't make it. He feels lucky to be young and strong, but knows even that won't prevent the weather from drowning him and this lovely orange-and-black raft. Lumtin curses his adventurous bent—it feels so stupid, so selfish, all of a sudden—and tells himself he has nothing more to prove in life. Not a thing. And then Paul Lumtin swears that if he makes it back to shore alive, he'll never leave Nancy and the girls again.

Richard Winning, flopping in beside Lumtin, activates the EPIRB.

A line connects the first raft and the second. Jim Lawler, Mike Bannister, John Dean, John Gibson, and then Steamer Stanley swim to the second raft. Waves immediately push the rafts from the sinking *Winston Churchill*. Thirty seconds later, she goes under.

After seventeen Syd-Hobs, fifty-six years, one collision with a whale, countless dockside parties and weekend cruises, with perhaps a child or two conceived on board and the benediction of her historical namesake, the *Winston Churchill* is no more. Steamer Stanley and Richard Winning watch her slip beneath the surface. Their fifty-two-foot, Huon-pine, copper-nailed, split-backstayed, doghoused . . . relic.

The stranded sailors peer for a sign of her—a section of mast, the doghouse roof, maybe a shiny white section of gunwale—thinking maybe a wave will lift her momentarily for a last look. But there's nothing. Just the sea, angry as ever, closed up over her, ignoring her regal bearing. It's a desecration. She deserves better.

All that's left are nine men floating on two rafts. It's as if *Winston Churchill* never was, and these fine gentlemen have been mysteriously dropped into the Bass Strait amidst a hundred-year storm.

Winning and Stanley are left to address the situation at hand: living. These gentlemen aren't sailing bums, but men upon whom others depend. They absolutely must pull through. All the men have families, with the exception of Michael Rynan, the son of two caring parents. Lawler is a grandfather. John Dean coaches an under-seventeen rugby club. Winning owns an entire company. Survival is not an option, it's mandatory. It's up to Winning and Stanley to make that happen.

The first raft is round. The second is larger, rectangular. Independent air chambers mean that a hole in one section won't sink the entire raft. There's a canopy on top, orange-colored for rescue planes to spot, jutting above in a cone shape. Each raft has two paddles, a first-aid kit, emergency rations for each person, survival mirror, seasickness tablets, flashlight, parachute flares, chemical lights, orange-smoke flares, sponges, a whistle, repair kit, sea marker dye, thermal protection aids, and a hand pump.

Within a few minutes of setting out, one wave sends the round raft to the left, while the rectangular raft drifts right. The rope connecting them stretches, tenses, breaks. The drogues beneath both rafts, intended to slow drift and provide a solid underpinning to prevent the rafts from flipping, break, too. Then, suddenly, the rafts are airborne. Like beach balls, the wind bounces the drogueless rafts across the seas. Waves lift them up and down their faces, rolling and dunking the rafts. By dark, the crews can barely spot each other. Even if they could, they're too busy keeping their rafts afloat to check more than once every half hour. Water pours in through the roof flap, and the men bail nonstop.

On board Winning's boat, Paul Lumtin is overcome with guilt. He promised his daughters Jacinda, four, and Brianna, eleven months, he'd be home for New Year's. Whatever it takes, he'd told them, I'll do it.

But the most recent flip has emptied the raft of her survival contents and stolen some of his resolve. Water, food, first-aid kit, flares—gone. The nitrogen canister used to inflate the raft had even punctured the floor, allowing water to gush in from above and below.

The men of the second boat—Stanley's—are having more trouble than those in Winning's. Steamer Stanley can barely move from the ligament damage to both hips during the initial rollover. John Gibson—Gibbo—had his fingers filleted to the bone by a length of rope while launching the rafts. The five men all wear life jackets with strobe lights attached. They sit around the perimeter of the raft, facing each other with legs interlocked. They intitially sat cross-legged, but an early roll of the raft sent them all flying. Steamer even thinks his ankle is broken.

So now their legs are stretched. When a wave rolls them, they quickly reassume their positions, even with the raft upside down. It's actually more comfortable with the raft upside down. The hard rubber bottom prevents water from rushing in. The only problem is a diminishing air supply, as the small area only contains about ten minutes of fresh air.

Their square raft is a German model named ProSaver, bought by Winning for $3,000 in July. In Stanley's opinion, it leaves a lot to be desired regarding safety. Now, upside down, Mike Bannister, John Dean, Jim Lawler, John Gibson, and Steamer Stanley debate the logical course of action. Do they swim outside the raft and flip her back over? They'd seen Winning do the same thing to his raft earlier, and it seemed a right idea.

Or is it better to keep the ProSaver upside down and cut a small hole in the roof to let air in? The notion of cutting a hole in the floor of a boat is heretical, but seems like sound logic, given that Stanley can barely move and none of the men are in position to swim outside and flip a hundred-pound raft in these seas.

"Look," Jim Lawler says. He's fit and tanned and confident, easily the most athletic of the bunch. "I'll dive under, then swim out through the opening in the canopy. I'll climb on top and use the drogue rope to flip us over."

"That's no good. That opening is bloody small. You'd have to take your life jacket off to squeeze through. Should a rogue come along, you'll be swept away just like that."

Argument ensues. Not heated, but intense. "I won't be swept away."

"There must be a better idea."

"What if we cut a small hole in the roof? Just a gash, you know? We'll let in a touch of fresh air without letting in the waves. How's that sound to you?"

"Who's got a knife?"

"I do." Lawler removes his pocketknife.

"We're going to cut a hole in the bottom of a raft? What kind of nonsense is that?"

"It's not the bottom now, it's the top. And if we don't do something, we'll run out of air in about three more minutes."

"I say we flip it over."

"And I say that flipping it over means a man taking off his life jacket to swim out the hole. That's as daft in these seas as slicing a hole in the raft."

Finally, light-headed from diminishing oxygen, unwilling to sacrifice Jim Lawler to the sea, the five agree that Lawler should use his pocketknife to open a small slit in the roof. He carefully unfolds the blade, careful not to drop it in the water. The tip is poked through the hard rubber bottom—now roof—and the blade dragged ever so carefully for four inches. All five watch the operation as if Lawler were performing open-heart surgery. His movements are precise, cautious.

Then it's done. A cold puff of fresh air slips through the crack and the men breathe easily. They feel cocooned, protected. The upside-down raft feels safe.

They bob this way for two hours, making small talk and listening for the rescue craft that's sure to come their way momentarily. But then a wave rolls them upright. The weight of five men falling and tumbling stresses the floor. The four-inch air hole begins increasing in size. The men settle into their interlocked sitting position carefully, but it's too late—the floor's slow disintegration has begun. In a moment it ceases to exist. The men, cursing their logic and this blasted twist of fate, cling to the square perimeter. Their legs dangle in the water. The orange roof shelters their heads.

The sun is down. There's no sound of rescue helicopters. The carry no EPIRB nor other method of relaying a distress signal. The storm shows no sign of abating. Mike Bannister, John Dean, Jim Lawler, John Gibson, and Steamer Stanley hold on to what's left of their raft with all their strength. Rescue in the dark is unheard of. It's going to be a very long night.

• • •

All four of Australia's national networks—ABC, Channel 10, Channel 9, and Channel 7—make the disappearance of *Winston Churchill* their lead news item Sunday night. Film of the *Stand Aside* rescue is played, but there's no footage of *Winston Churchill* because she hasn't been located. The devastation of the fleet is total, with rumors swirling that *B-52* and *Solo Globe Challenger* have disappeared, *Sword of Orion* has rolled, a Sydney man is lost at sea, and forty-five boats are running for Eden.

Channel 10 sports reporter Bill Woods, reporting from Constitution Dock in Hobart, passes along the grim word. His drawn expression is genuine, as the horrified Woods has covered Syd-Hob for years. Usually there's a carnival atmosphere at Constitution Dock, but he's overwhelmed by "a sad and sound mood" along the waterfront. Many sailors' wives and families are already in Hobart, waiting for the finish. Now, they inundate race headquarters—already moved from Sydney to Hobart—with queries about status.

All the networks are dispatching crews to report live from Mallacoota, site of the helicopter refueling and rescue return. Camera crews are also dispatched to find *Winston Churchill*'s families.

Bruce Gould's family takes an optimistic approach, saying, "He's been through so much at sea, we have faith he'll pull out of this okay, too." But John and Robyn Rynan, nineteen-year-old Michael's parents, are the picture of parental worry. It was Michael's first Sydney to Hobart, Robyn tells reporters. Before this he was a top sailor on Flying 11 yachts in Sydney Harbor. Racing to Hobart was a big leap, but we're sure he was ready. No, we didn't expect such a thing to happen. Yes, we have high hopes he'll come back safely.

In Melbourne, Annie Goodman searches for news of *Sword of Orion*. She hears that they've been rolled and dismasted, but have been spotted by fixed-wing search-and-rescue aircraft. A Sydney man has been washed overboard, reports say, which isn't good. But at least, she thinks, Glyn's all right.

Sue Psaltis fears the worst. There's been no word, and with all the rollovers she's afraid Ed's lost his mast and HF radio. She packs the boys in the car and drives to her in-laws, so she won't have to spend the night alone. The next sked isn't until 2 A.M. She prays that Ed reports in all right. When she arrives, she sees a look on Bill Psaltis's face she's never seen before—fear. Though he pretends nothing's bothering him, Bill paces.

"They'll be all right, Sue," Bill says over and over. "My boys are excellent sailors. They know how to handle a blow like this. They'll be all right."

"I'm sure they will, Bill."

"Of course they will. My boys are excellent sailors. They know how to handle a blow like this."

Bill Woods in Hobart, even as he reports on-camera, feels strange. There's a lack of awareness of the disaster's scope. Whenever people feel it's as bad as it can get, or the storm has passed entirely, something new and more awful happens. First it was *Amro Challenge*, then *Team Jag*, then *Stand Aside*. Now it's not just *Winston Churchill*, but several boats. There's even a dark rumor that the man overboard from *Sword of Orion* is drowned. And what of all the boats no one has heard from? People Bill

Woods knows are dying, and no one knows how many. When the camera switches back to the Channel 10 studios in downtown Sydney from Woods's remote location, it's a stark juxtaposition: from grim-faced Woods to cheery studio anchors.

"It was one of those nights," sports nut Peter Gearin said later, "when all the regular cricket scores and horse-racing results just seemed plain frivolous."

Finger-pointing has begun between the CYCA and BOM. The CYCA is taking a curious stance, saying that skippers should decide when to sail, but also saying the race would have been postponed if they knew how severe the weather would be. The BOM fires back that their prerace gale warnings should have been sufficient. It would have been irresponsible to forecast hurricane winds and hundred-foot seas.

At the AusSAR War Room in Canberra, the men just want to take a deep breath. Between 3 P.M. and 7 P.M. they saw every worst-case rescue scenario played out—boats sinking, boats disappearing, multiple rescues in high seas, a lost man found, not enough helicopters, and even a shortage of helicopter fuel that had a tanker specially diverted from Sydney to Mallacoota to resupply air crews. The AusSAR team are overwhelmed, as if they're drinking from a fire hose. No matter how grand and spectacular the rescue—and by anyone's measure, *Stand Aside* and John Campbell were kick-ass rescues, sure to make front-page news on any other day—it doesn't matter.

Because for every man hoisted aboard or boat sighted, there's another Mayday. The silver lining on the cloud has turned out to be the fleet's proximity to land—rescue centers in Mallacoota, Merimbula, and Eden are less than an hour's flight by helicopter to the damaged boats. But for that proximity—say, were the fleet one hundred miles farther out to sea—the rescue helicopters would be low on gas almost as soon as they reached a rescue site. They wouldn't be able to stay on site as long as they had. *Stand Aside* would have seen just half their crew rescued. John Campbell would have been lost, or the rescue never attempted at all. There would be fatalities where there are none. This disaster that is the 1998 Sydney to Hobart would truly be a massacre if the fleet weren't so close to shore, and AusSAR takes solace in that.

The disappearance of *Winston Churchill* and the man overboard on *Sword of Orion* are the most ominous occurrences in an escalating series of catastrophes. As *B-52* didn't send so much as a Mayday, her location is a true mystery. AusSAR decides to split their resources, with one-half beginning a search for the MOB encompassing *Sword's* position at the time of rollover; the other half will focus on finding *Winston Churchill* and *Solo Globe Challenger*. AusSAR makes a formal request for naval assistance—immediately acted upon—and then seconds fishing boats from Eden to the search. The *Polair* crew are resting and refueling in Mallacoota. They'll be in the air soon, using infrared television cameras to search. Other rescue helicopters are arriving from civilian organizations across southeastern Australia—*Helimed*s, *Careflight* choppers, *Westpac Lifesaver*.

Royal Australian Naval Maritime Headquarters in Sydney reports to AusSAR that two Sea Hawks and one Sea King are on the way. HMAS *Newcastle* will sail from Sydney with just half the crew—anything to help. Seventeen fixed-wing aircraft will launch at dawn, among them the most sophisticated weapons in the search-and-rescue arsenal, two PC-3 Orions from the Tenth Squadron and two C-130 Hercules from the Thirty-seventh Squadron. Both will launch from Edinburgh. One aircraft, an air ambulance, has been set aside for patient transport.

In Berry, Shane Pashley's phone rings at nine o'clock, while he watches TV. Get a good night's sleep, comes the command, and report to the base at 7 A.M. Pashley's usual crew from the HMAS *Newcastle* is still on leave, so he'll join a Sea Hawk crew from the HMAS *Melbourne*. His pilot will be Nic Trimmer; Rick Neville will fly copilot. Aaron Abbott will fly left seat in the back, as winch operator. Pashley, the order comes, will ride the wire. He's to be the rescue swimmer.

■ ■ ■

I resented the phone ringing at what must have been 6 A.M. It kept ringing and ringing. And when no one in the house answered, I begrudgingly arose.

"Hello, it's Nigel Russell," a voice said. "You told me that if our mast ever broke, you'd come over and pick us up. Well, here I am."

"Where's here?"

"In Pambula Hospital. My gear's soaked. I've only got fifty dollars. Can you loan me some clothes?"

My trip to the hospital revealed dozens of tired and battered men sitting silently in blue-striped flannelette pajamas. Unable to sleep, they perched on vinyl couches, eyes focused on the humming TV, where the *Today Show* relayed the enormity of the unfolding disaster.

—Stacey George, whose family farm is
forty miles north of Eden

FIFTEEN

EAST OF EDEN

Sunday, December 27, 11:30 P.M. to Monday, December 28, 8 A.M.

Eden was once Eden—idyllic and unspoiled. Now it's a half-holiday, half-industrial coastal "frontier" town perched between the northern shores of dramatic Twofold Bay and the Australian Alps. Large, deep, and protected, Twofold Bay is an amazing natural harbor. Whaling was once the predominant local industry, then tuna fishing, and now, with tuna overfished for decades, it's logging of nearby old-growth forests for export to Japan.

Locals enjoy Eden's redneck qualities and how it's always followed its own path. Huge trucks loaded with half a dozen or so giant tree trunks ply the local highways on their way to the nearby logging mill. The large marina boasts a lineup of hardy fishing boats. The waterfront also offers an array of cheap tourist hotels, a few arts-and-crafts shops, milk bars, assorted stores, and a couple of pubs where the emphasis is on service instead of decor.

Eden gets cold and desolate in winter, when the whale watching from Twofold Bay's rugged, sheer cliffs is best. The climate is ideal in summer, and worth the nine-hour drive from Sydney. Still, the tourist and retirement industries have pretty well passed it by.

When they do come, the tourists are from government-cinder-block Canberra or staid Victoria, soaking up local history for a day, then spending the night farther north along the surf beaches.

Until December 27 the biggest news in Eden lately has been the ongoing clashes between loggers and environmentalists. But at midnight, there are no contentious voices in Eden. It has become a refuge. Boats in all condition motor into her sheltered harbor. The official tally is thirty-seven, but nobody really knows. All that matters is dry land. Sailboats dock, the boat is tied off, and men with years of blue-water experience climb ashore and kiss the ground. They laugh, making as if the ceremony is half in jest. But it's all real, and though they don't show it to their mates, more than one sailor has a good cry on the telephone when he rings the family to let them know he's okay.

Eden's 17-year-old Melissa McCabe, stepping ashore from *Team Jag*'s dismasted vessel, has become a mother hen to the fleet. She arranges accommodations, drives sailors to the hospital or airport, and at a time when many sailors are having trouble thinking clearly, sees that sanctuary must be accorded the battered men of the fleet.

Around town, dual missions are taking place, with sailors drifting in from the storm, as fishermen—believing the waves too big for fishing—steel to set out before first light and rescue less fortunates. The fishermen and the yachting crowd don't usually mix well, but in the bars, after several beers, they are all mariners. Nothing more, nothing less. The fishermen listen as yachties recount horror stories, not quite feeling a brotherhood, but acknowledging that the mood is one of relief instead of tension. Leaning against the bar, blue-water sailor after sailor swears he'll never attempt another Sydney to Hobart. And, they add with gravity, this is the year they mean it.

Many of the boats in port had sent Maydays and activated EPIRB. They're usually the ones without masts. With total body fatigue and brains still not trusting the reassurance that safety has arrived, the crews of dismasted, rolled, and knockdown boats have that faraway stare of combat veterans. When they lean against the bar and swear they'll never again race Syd-Hob, people believe them. Most of them get pretty drunk the night of December 27.

Eden is not officially a part of the Syd-Hob itinerary, so there's no official place to check in. Eventually the CYCA will send a representative and begin coordination with Sydney and AusSAR, but now there's no one. And without established protocol for alerting organizers, most sailors feel their job is done once they kiss the dock. So the CYCA and AusSAR have no idea who's safe in Eden and who's not. When many of the boats still actively being hunted by SAR choppers are found safely in Eden, one AusSAR official even makes light. "Must've run out of beer," jokes night-shift supervisor Steve Francis.

That Francis can joke is a sign that the situation seems to be improving. Seems to be. AusSAR is effectively shut off from the world. Their perception stems solely from hard data pouring in, the most significant being EPIRB markers on computer screens— the number has dropped from fifteen to six. Another sliver of good news is the discovery of *B-52*. She was pitchpoled (shoved nose down into a trough) at six-thirty, with several crew washed overboard, then recovered. The dismasting knocked out her radio, so even after a second wave rolled her back over, *B-52* couldn't make contact with AusSAR. The shaken crew thinks they've seen the worst of it. And though a Sea King could begin hoisting off crew by midnight, they've elected to stay on board and motor back to Eden.

Every AusSAR employee in the War Room is also cognizant that no serious Maydays have been signaled since seven o'clock. Either the sailors are adapting to conditions or they're through the worst of it. Actually, AusSAR notes, this could be a symptom of a trend: the boats getting hammered were almost all turned and headed for Eden. They've quit the race. The waves are behind them, not before them. Instead of being in a race mode, they're in a mental retirement mode. Their guard is down. Most Fastnet fatalities occurred similarly.

For two reasons AusSAR hopes more than ever that the rollovers and knockdowns are over. First, the fleet is past the halfway point in the Bass Strait now. Those seeking shelter in Eden have already turned. The remainder are shooting for Tasmania.

Second, with the fleet so far out in the Strait, immediate rescue will be impossible. The crew of a sinking ship would have to man life rafts and wait for a rescue ship. The weather makes prolonged time in a life raft downright perilous, chance of survival slim.

One glance at recent BOM satellite photos shows the weather certainly hasn't gotten better. The weather bomb roosts over the fleet, showing no signs of dissipation. *Winston Churchill* and *Solo Globe Challenger* are still lost somewhere in the whirl of clouds.

Search helicopters have established contact with *Sword of Orion* and discovered that intense bailing has stabilized her situation. The man overboard, an Englishman named Glyn Charles, is definitely missing. That's a negative, and the search for him will continue past daylight. All traffic—military, commercial, and otherwise—in the Bass Strait have been notified to be on the lookout. Until that search has been called off, Syd-Hob—and AusSAR—haven't officially lost anyone to the storm.

While the Glyn Charles search continues, injured crew will be lifted from *Sword* by a RAN Sea King, commencing at 2 A.M.

A bit of bad news is that the navy doesn't have the anticipated night-vision capability. They have something called night autohover, which allows them to make a rescue if a boat is located. *Polair 1*, then, is the only functioning search helicopter with night-vision capability. Only they're not flying. They have to rest sometime, and AusSAR needs them up at first light. Out of necessity, Darryl Jones, David Key, and Barry Barclay are currently snatching six hours of sleep, even as *Winston Churchill*'s EPIRB has disappeared off computer screens.

Finally, an activated EPIRB confirms that *Business Post Naiad* is motoring safely to Eden while awaiting rescue helicopters. Half the mast is still standing, but is nonfunctional because the boom is bent. The crew that thought the Bass's tantrum would work in their favor is pulling out.

BP's problems began just after the 2:05 P.M. sked. They were following the high line through the black hole, same as Ed Psaltis. *Sword*'s sked observation of high winds brought knowing nods in the *Business Post* nav room, and the strategy of skipper Bruce Guy was to bare-pole for a few hours, then race hard for Hobart. These native Tasmanians were racers, not tourists. Summer regatta wins on the Bass Strait confirmed their sense of athleticism. In their minds, aboard this special championship boat, they represented the hopes and dreams of all Tasmania.

But a miscalculation by Rob Matthews early Sunday evening cost them. He was at the helm, angling her up a wave. *Business Post* leaned too far into the fifty-footer, which didn't allow her keel purchase on the near-vertical face. She slid sideways, then rolled upside down as the wave broke on top. Though the wave passed and the boat righted itself, the five men on deck were thrown overboard. Luckily, their safety harnesses held.

More angry than scared, the men pulled themselves back on board. As Tasmanians, they have a proprietary feeling about the Bass Strait. They know her quirks and fits. She is their secret pride, and their ability to sail her is their mark as sailors. How dare she buck them? How dare she end their race? And their race was definitely over, that much they could tell. The top half of the mast had broken off. The boom was bent so badly it looked more like a boomerang. Water covered the deck and had flooded below. The stove was off its mounts. Cutlery littered the water. And the refrigerator had blown open, spilling the contents. They bobbed now, the watertight jars and watertight plastic bags, giving belowdecks the appearance of a grocery store after a flood.

The men of *Business Post Naiad* hid their disappointment (this could've been our year!) and set to making things right. Bruce Guy turned on the motor, which, miraculously, had not flooded out, and began steering north. Matthews, Phil Skeggs, helmsman Steve Walker, and Tony Guy lashed the mast top to the left side of the boat—it was the polite thing to do; tearing it off and letting it float about the seas would be hazardous for other boats—and lashed the boom's tip to a port stanchion. Bruce Guy decided to take his chances on salvage. And after a new antenna was jury-rigged, a Mayday request for helicopter rescue was radioed. The EPIRB was activated.

Business Post Naiad's VHF signal was too weak to reach Lew Carter aboard *Young Endeavour*. The yacht *Yendy*, a four-hour sail from *Business Post Naiad*, relayed the Mayday.

The sun went down while *Business Post Naiad* waited for help. It was a time of overlapping Maydays—*Sword* was getting visual helicopter verification of status, the *Stand Aside*'s last man was being winched off by Michelle Blewitt, the John Campbell rescue was being effected by *Polair 1*, and *Winston Churchill* was nowhere to be found. As badly damaged as *Business Post Naiad* was, they were low man on the totem pole for rescue because of their seaworthiness. Namely, they weren't sinking. If they were lesser sailors, or aboard a lesser boat, help would have come right away.

Young Endeavour checks back an hour later to see if *Business Post Naiad*'s condition has stabilized. If so, would they like to downgrade their Mayday? The *Business Post Naiad* response was that they would like another boat to come alongside them in the darkness, as they were floundering.

Telstra Control, busy coordinating the fishing trawler's search for *Team Jag*, never hears *Business Post Naiad*'s request. For the better part of Sunday evening, Telstra Control and the fishing-trawler skipper monopolize the radio. With *Yendy* now too far away to act as relay, *Business Post Naiad* has no method of repeating the request for a companion vessel. The frustrating thing for *Business Post Naiad*'s crew is that, although Telstra Control can neither hear them nor seems interested in paying attention to them, they can hear Telstra Control and their chatter with the fishing boat loud and clear. The more cynical members of the crew note that *Team Jag*'s skipper is on the CYCA board and hint at proprietary treatment.

In the darkness, the men grow scared. Listening to the freight-train sound of waves in daytime is one thing. But at night, when the waves are unseen, but rumble no less ominously, the sensation is petrifying. The moon pokes through for an instant, a sign that the storm might be letting up. But it's just a ruse. The moon—puppeteer of wind and waves and tide and current—is just stepping from behind the backstage curtain to count the house. Then it slips behind a cloud bank so totally that the night is once again opaque. The friends and neighbors on board *Business Post Naiad* are alone with their thoughts and the freight-train rumble and the waves coming to get them.

At eleven-thirty it's locksmith Phil Skeggs, a goateed, athletic young man, on deck with the more experienced Rob Matthews. Skeggs is new not just to sailing, but travel, as well. On Christmas Day he was so homesick he phoned his family twelve times just to hear the voices of his wife and children. Even as the storm rages around them, Skeggs thinks only of getting home so he can celebrate his fourteenth wedding anniversary.

Matthews is at the helm, with Skeggs a few feet away, reading the compass and shouting out bearings. Normally, the skipper does this himself. But with the waves nearly invisible in the darkness, Matthews must focus entirely on squinting into the storm to discern where horizon ends and waves begin. The best indicator, in fact, is noise instead of sight.

Then they roll again. Just like that, an unseen force rears up and throws them upside down. Neither Matthews or Skeggs hears the wave. It just is. The boat free-falls upside down for a second. The trough finds her still inverted, and it's lucky for Matthews and Skeggs that they've been thrown clear or they'd be crushed. Steve Walker, trapped upside down in the cabin, tries to force his way on deck, but the closed hatchways seal his path. Two of the guys wear headlamps, so the darkness isn't total, only more eerie and strobe-like. Bruce Guy kicks out the hatch. Water pours in until pressure equalizes. The six men inside the boat are up to their waist in water now, with Guy moving toward the life-raft storage. He jerks the rack down, then waits for the boat to roll back over so he can carry the raft on deck and prepare for abandoning ship.

Directly in front of Guy and Walker, beyond two layers of opaque laminate, and one layer of foam core, Matthews and Skeggs are underwater, tangled in the ropes and broken mast and rescue harness. Each tries to unclip his harness. Skeggs has deck ropes around his chest and arms, preventing him from reaching the chest clip on his harness. Matthews, feeling his air supply run out, is still tangled, but bobs to the surface. He's in an air pocket underneath the cockpit. He gasps, sucks air, gets his strength back.

"Phil," he cries out, thinking Skeggs has surfaced in the dark air pocket. He doesn't know that Phil is just a few feet away, wriggling out of his harness and disengaging himself from the rigging's tentacles. "Phil."

There's no answer, and then the boat gets hit by another wave. It shoves the boat farther into the water, still upside down, and pounds down on Matthews's head like a hammer hitting the tip of a nail. The air pocket is gone, and now Matthews is back under.

Matthews is almost right next to Skeggs now. Both men continue their lone battles, unseen by the other. The need to breathe is incredible, bringing on panic. The ropes drag both men under, and just when one arm becomes untangled, some other section of rope lassos them. The battle is never ending, and Matthews and Skeggs are calling on every athletic reserve in their body to fight their way free.

Another invisible force rights the boat. In the cabin, Walker rolls from ceiling to floor, holding his breath as more water pours in. Like *Winston Churchill, Business Post Naiad* is sinking, which becomes obvious once *Business Post* is right side up. Walker prepares to sprint up the hatchway, but Bruce Guy beats him to it.

Guy takes one step, then another, then collapses. It looks as if he's stumbled, but in fact he's having a major heart attack.

"Bruce? What's up, mate? You all right?" It's Steve Walker, bent over his fallen friend. Guy's limp form sinks back into the water. Other crew members, panicked and thinking Guy has slipped, step over their leader as they fight their way from the claustrophobia of the water-filled hold onto the deck. Only Steve Walker, right next to Guy, sees that his friend is in trouble. Guy's face slips below the water. Walker immediately grabs Guy by the shoulders, cradling him in his arms. Their faces are just inches away.

"Bruce? Can you hear me, Bruce? Are you all right?"

But everything is not all right. And before Steve Walker can scream at his mate to fight, Bruce Guy is dead. Walker floats Guy to a bunk and attempts mouth-to-mouth resuscitation, but there's no response.

Walker, devastated, leaves Guy. He trudges up top to tell the mates, only to find them busy saving a life themselves. Rob Matthews is all right. Phil Skeggs, still trussed in rigging and rescue harness, has drowned. Unable to open his chest harness, he was ensnared by rigging and held underwater until he simply ran out of air. The affable young man with an overwhelming case of homesickness leaves behind a wife, Stephanie, and children, Kirsty, nine, and Joshua, six. His body is taken below and lashed into the bunk above Bruce Guy.

The rescue helicopter arrives two hours later, the *NRMA Care-Flight*. Spotlight shining on the stricken vessel in the midnight blackness, Pilot Dan Tyler makes the snap judgment that *Business Post Naiad* will go under if she takes another broadside. He directs winch operator Graham Fromberg to expedite a quick rescue. Fromberg does, dropping the horse collar and hoisting men aboard with clinical efficiency, or what passes for clinical efficiency at midnight during a hurricane. When the men of *Business Post Naiad* come aboard, Tyler and Fromberg are struck at how somber they are. No smiles, and certainly no kisses. Just tired bodies covered with oil and fuel, murmured thank-yous and sighs of relief, and the palpable presence of loss. Their one request is that Tyler hurry back to land so they can find pay phones and reassure their families before the media releases news about the tragedy.

The bodies of Bruce Guy and Phil Skeggs, still lashed below, are left behind. They bob in the boat, even as the storm rages.

Two days later, the Sydney police launch *Nemesis* finds *Business Post Naiad* drifting one hundred miles northeast of Eden. The yacht is towed through the night to a privately owned wharf in Eden, far from the boats seeking shelter. Coroner's officials bring Phil Skeggs and Bruce Guy ashore for the last time, lifting their bodies into stretchers, then up onto the dock.

"Dad loved sailing," Guy's son, Mark, tells reporters when the news reaches their home in Launceston. Mark Guy usually sailed with his father, but other commitments prevented the twenty-six-year-old from racing Syd-Hob in 1998. Now he eulogizes his father in a manner all men, adventurer or no, would be glad to hear. "He loved the competition. He loved a beer and a talk after a race. He simply loved life. Dad has always been there for Mum, my sister Karen, and myself. He has given me unbelievable support in everything I have done."

• • •

Arthur Psaltis clambers on deck at 2 A.M. "Go below, Ed," he shouts in his brother's ear. They've been out of the eye for six hours now. The moaning and violence have returned. A new sound has been added: buckshot. That's the thousands of pellets of spray blasting against the hull. The pellets don't impact, they ricochet. Ed knows, because the pellets are doing the same to his face. The sunglasses have come off with darkness, and now water drives into Ed's eyes. He looks down at the tiller most of the time, only peering into the wind intermittently. Even when he looks away, the residue salt stings, makes him blink hard and tear involuntarily.

To Ed, he's just pulling his load. That's why he refuses to leave the helm. But exhaustion overwhelms him and the entire *Midnight Rambler* crew. Ed can barely sit up straight in the cockpit, his legs are so wobbly from fighting the seas. His eyes hurt from trying to discern wave and horizon. Arthur's crew management skills have become as important to *Midnight Rambler*'s battle against the storm as Ed's helm skills and Bob's navigation. But how long can that last? The tendency of *Midnight Rambler*'s crew toward over-work is leading them to tragedy, Arthur contends. Fatigue causes mistakes, and even a single screwup could kill them. All it takes is one second's distraction for a rogue to flip the boat.

"I'm all right, Arthur."

"Shut up. You are not. Get some sleep."

Ed's quiet a minute. He places his face near Arthur's and speaks as softly as he can, so there's no possibility of anyone else hearing. "How does our position feel to you?"

"What do you mean?"

Ed licks his lips. "I don't know where we are."

"What does Bob say?"

"He doesn't know either. All the nav gear's broken and it's too dark to shoot the stars."

A wave washes over them, a small, black nuisance intent on drenching. Ed and Arthur are soaked. Chris, wave-watching for-ward, looks back and yells an apology they can't hear. That's okay, Ed thinks. No one saw that wave.

"So where do you think we are, Ed?"

"Well, the waves are still to starboard, so we're headed south. But the current is shoving us east. We could be well off course."

"Seriously?"

"Seriously."

"How far?"

"I don't want to think about it."

Despair in the form of crushed dreams hangs unspoken. No one aboard *Midnight Rambler* has said as much, but the motivation for fighting the storm has always been winning. If not, they would have turned for Eden the instant Chris cut his head. The second knockdown would have been another indicator.

But now the race is lost. Being thrown off course means almost a day fighting the wind toward Tasmania. Going high and west into the winds was a major miscalculation on Ed's part, it now seems. Not only did they face the storm earlier and with more severity than other boats, but the current pushed them sideways across the Bass Strait, negating their risk. They might as well have run for New Zealand like *Chutzpah*. It seems as if *Midnight Rambler* is halfway to Auckland, anyway. No more Peter Pan, sailing by the second star on the left and straight on until morning. *Midnight Rambler*'s crew are just a bunch of fools who risked it all and will have no reward beyond their lives to show for it. There has to be some greater motivator than mere glory for attempting a Sydney to Hobart, and now, chances of winning gone, Ed finds himself searching his soul for that motivation.

Finally, Ed agrees to get some sleep.

• • •

By 4 A.M., Richard Winning is exhausted. He's a responsible man, used to looking after others. He directed Rynan and Lumtin to ride his raft because he feels personally responsible for their fate. How he would face their families if something happened to them, he hasn't a clue. Same goes for Bruce Gould. The man is a treasure.

So whenever a wave flips their raft, Winning swims out the small roof opening and rights the raft. Then he pulls himself up over the side and flops in with his mates. No one talks much, other than commenting on the sounds of coming waves. Nothing anyone can do when waves hit, of course, except hang on and wait until the rolling stops, but they listen hard because it's nice to have warning before taking flight. Conditions have been like this for eight hours now, and not once has a rescue helicopter choppered into their vicinity. Enough with the waves—a helicopter's the one sound they all want to hear.

Lumtin has had enough of thrill-seeking, especially when a particularly large wave rolls the rafts and sends all four men tumbling in a chaos of elbows, knees, water, and tangled bodies. When the situation settles, the raft is filled with water and Lumtin is at the bottom of the pile of bodies. His face is pushed into the floor. For a few moments his world is quiet. His single thought is that he's drowning. In a panic, Lumtin squirms and wiggles and punches and kicks—anything to find air. Bodies fall off him slowly, and it feels as if he's been underwater for hours. Like doing a push-up with an anvil around his neck, Lumtin forces his head skyward through the weight of bodies into a small air pocket. This happens in slow motion, but Lumtin—once sure his head is really out of the water—throws his mouth and eyes open wide. He sucks in air until the panic stops, then curses the night and the waves and the Sydney to Hobart race and sailing, in general.

Winning, once the scrum is untangled, has the men bail, using seaboots as buckets. But instead of ridding the raft of all its water, Winning has them leave a few inches on the floor as ballast. "I guess no one has ever died from hypothermia of the ass," Lumtin cracks, settling against the side in six inches of ocean.

But terror still fills Lumtin. He dreams of giving up. All the men do. Exhaustion weakens their resolve. When more water forces itself through the small roof opening, the crew bail and bail, not sure how much more of this they can take. All are thirsty, their tongues and mouths dry like cotton. If they had to pinpoint the source of strength that keeps them bailing hour after hour, some of the men might cite God, but Lumtin, candidly, believes he is motivated by fear. More exactly, fear of the big waves bowling for life rafts outside the thin orange flap. "It's like nothing I've ever heard in my life," Lumtin says of the deep, thundering sound that keeps building and building. "Too awful for words."

Hard as it is to believe, the five men of Steamer's raft are even more exhausted. They've been clinging to the sides for hours, and it's all they can do to hang on. Hypothermia's setting in, though having their heads protected by the roof is slowing this. Legs are numb from dangling in the water, hunger prevails, and there's no fresh water, so dehydration is robbing their strength, too.

Like everyone else on the ocean tonight, the ears of Steamer's boys are tuned to the roar of coming waves. They've all become quite good at figuring which waves are close and which are far. Some are small and some are very large, and how much you hold on depends upon the wave's size. Sometimes it's possible to barely clinch the inflated tubes and just let the swell wash over the boat. Sometimes the wave breaks like Niagara Falls during a spring thaw, white water unleashing itself with a power seen nowhere outside nature. "Boys," Stanley says when they hear the big ones coming, bold and furious, "we just have to hang on like grim death."

It's impossible to hear the rogues, of course. They just scoop up off the Bass Plains and rear to the surface, all vertical current and green algae and the remnants of some aborigine campfire from thirty-five thousand years ago. And so the five men in the square German life raft never hear the rogue that forever changes their lives. They're just sitting still, legs dangling in the water, listening, when the raft begins descending. It's as if they're on an elevator and the bottom's dropped out and they're plummeting down a shaft. The ProSaver falls, falls, falls, into a trough. The ProSaver lands with a thud, with a million gallons of water landing on top of them moments later. The raft is forced under, then pushed hard to the east. Mike Bannister and Jim Lawler are ripped from the raft. John Dean is thrown off, too. Stanley and Gibson are forced under, still clutching the ProSaver as hard as they can. Gibson's open wound stopped stinging from the sea salt hours ago, but he still can't make the kind of grip he'd like. He has to use both arms to hug the inner tube, protecting the bad hand.

The wave sweeps Steamer and Gibson along, shooting them across the ocean surface as if they've been shoved down a water slide. Stanley feels as if he's been holding his breath forever when the "almighty" wave plays out.

"Is everybody here?" Stanley sputters.

"Me—Gibbo. I'm here."

Stanley looks around the life ring—and that's all it is now, because the roof has been ripped away. There's no sign of Jim Lawler, the grandfather and a good friend of Bill Psaltis's. Nor truck driver and husband Mike Bannister, nor John Dean, the lawyer and rugby coach whose two teenage sons adore him and model their behavior after his.

The white water from the wave stretches four hundred meters. Back where they started the wild ride, Stanley sees two life vests. Wind and current are pushing Stanley and Gibson farther and farther from the life vests, as if they were sailboats scudding across the ocean surface. Whoever they are back there, they're on their own now. There's no way for Steamer Stanley and Gibbo Gibson to hook up with them again. Swimming against the current is unthinkable. Trying to kick the life raft, considering Stanley's broken ankle—the pain is starting to feel specific—back to those two men is unthinkable.

"We can't do anything," Stanley laments, thinking out loud. "The wind is going to blow us so fast they're not going to be able to catch up with us. It's impossible."

"I know."

Stanley looks square at Gibbo. They're all each other has in the world. They have to keep each other going. "There's two of us. Three boys didn't hang on, and unfortunately, we can't do anything about it. It takes a lot, but if we want to survive, we have to hang on to this raft."

The night is black, and as they talk, the two look right and left for waves. It's become second nature. Gibbo takes a deep breath and speaks with conviction: "Then let's hang on. For ourselves."

How awful. They look at each other. This is it. They are two middle-aged men, not far removed from being senior citizens, experiencing advanced hypothermia, clinging to inflated rubber as if it were life itself. The wind blows almost one hundred miles an hour. They ride up and down hundred-foot waves. It's several hours before dawn. If they fall asleep and let go of the ring, they will drift away and die a lonely death, bobbing in the Bass until hypothermia claims them. They have no EPIRB to summon help. No flares, parachute, or otherwise. To eat, they had one biscuit in Stanley's pocket when *Winston Churchill* sank, but that's long since been divvied. They have no water, other than the salty sea all around trying to kill them.

Only three other people in the world are more destitute than Steamer Stanley and Gibbo Gibson right now: Mike Bannister, John Dean, and Jimmy Lawler. There haven't been people in such a hopeless situation for years. Even Isabelle Autissier and Tony Bullimore had the comfort of a floating vessel. But Bannister, Dean, and Lawler have slipped away from the raft and from each other. Each is alone. Bannister and Lawler bob in their life jackets. Dean lost his—an empty life jacket is still clipped to the ProSaver, and in all likelihood it's Dean's—so he treads water in the dark. All three men feel small and long for the security of the life raft. Compared with the isolation of fighting these seas alone, that flimsy bit of rubber was positively homey. Somehow, being alone makes the hypothermia creep in that much quicker. How could this be happening?

Neither Steamer nor Gibbo are big talkers, so all five men bobbing in the Bass Strait are effectively alone. Silently—though they want to rage and scream and ask God why he's selected them for such agony—all gird for the mental fight ahead, convincing themselves that if they can live to see one more dawn, help will find them. And so the night drags on.

• • •

Midnight Special is the other half of the "Midnight" equation. Unlike Ed Psaltis's *Midnight Rambler*, *Midnight Special*'s prerace plan resembled nothing remotely competitive. The forty-footer is officially based at the Mooloolaba Yacht Club, crewed by nine

Martin Dugard

middle-aged friends with a combined seven Syd-Hobs. Two men have never raced across the Bass at all, but veteran blue-water racer Neil Dickson (at forty-nine, the youngest crew member) and Mooloolaba Yacht Club commodore Roger Barnett have a reassuring depth of experience. The official race guide proclaims *Midnight Special* "a boatful of regular blokes out to have some fun and avoid having midlife crisis in the middle of the Bass Strait."

Something like a midlife crisis happens anyway. Dickson's and Barnett's expertise see *Midnight Special* into the Bass Strait in eighteenth place overall Sunday morning. The crew can't believe their luck (maybe this is our year!), and even when seasickness immobilizes four men and sends them to bunks for good, turning around is never discussed.

Midnight Special is jointly owned by five of the crew, and just before the 2:05 P.M. sked Saturday, Dickson gathers them below to argue for turning around. And argue they do. The *Midnight Special* is a crew of rookies buckling under pressure. Some stand, while others lie in their bunks. The cohesion of the fun-loving blokes is no more, and words are heatedly exchanged. The more competitive crew members see no need for turning around, while the incapacitated would gladly sacrifice vital regions of their anatomy to get back to port and stand once again on solid ground. And so they are divided.

But just when the stalemate gets most vicious, the storm makes the decision for *Midnight Special*. She is knocked sideways by a sudden wave. Ian Griffiths, a lawyer in favor of pushing on, is heaved into the ship's cupboard, breaking his leg and destroying the hutch. At almost the exact same time, the voice of Rob Kothe broadcasting his wind warning comes over the radio. Needing no more encouragement, Dickson abruptly ends the argument. He turns *Midnight Special* toward Eden and switches on the motor, officially ending their race. The call of abandonment is placed to *Young Endeavour* by HF radio. *Midnight Special*'s position, Dickson reports, is forty miles off Gabo Island, pretty much in the center of the black hole.

212

KNOCKDOWN

The journey through this infamous patch of sea wrecks her. Waves knock her down twice. The men of *Midnight Special*, older and not agile, get mugged awfully. Peter Carter suffers cracked vertebrae. Two men break their noses. Broken ribs, torso and facial bruises, and open wounds all around. Blood stains the walls where heads have opened. Blood drips onto the floor, mixing with seasickness vomit, giving the bile a wretched crimson chunkiness no one can stand to look at.

The midnight rollover shatters any remaining morale, turning inexperienced and veteran alike openly fearful. Anger, confusion, hopelessness, fear, and sickness swirl into a claustrophobic tension, then morph into outright panic. Then a hundred-foot rogue spins *Midnight Special*, breaks the mast, shatters portholes, floods below, threads lengths of rigging into the propeller. The hull delaminates in long, jagged sections, letting water sneak in even after the wave passes. Dickson is knocked unconscious and concussed, but when he comes to, he immediately begins shoving sleeping bags and lengths of spinnaker in the cracks. The sleeping bags work for a while, soaking up water until saturated, then rendered useless. But the sails staunch the flow for good. The men in the lower bunks struggle to their feet, as the seawater's level is higher than all but the top rack.

Dickson directs a bailing brigade. Everyone has either broken a bone or endures seasickness, but those ills are superfluous now, as a sinking boat means sure death for all. They work the lower companionway in shifts that will last through the night. Trevor McDonagh, a sixty-year-old bricklayer, activates the EPIRB. A Mayday is impossible because everything electronic has been flooded. Dead in the water, *Midnight Special* waits for rescue and hopes another wave doesn't come get them.

Dawn brings hope and an honest appraisal of the boat. The bailing has reduced the flooding, but *Midnight Special* is incapable of making land. The only hope is for someone to dive overboard and untangle the propeller. Maybe they can start the engine again and jury-rig a steering system. But no one wants to dive overboard, because the waves and current are just as powerful at 6 A.M. as they were sixteen hours ago when the weather bomb dropped. Jumping into hundred-foot seas is like signing a death warrant.

Then a new sound.

Not the moaning of the wind, nor the slow rumble of the waves, but something thrumming and monotoned. An airplane. A PC-3 Orion, flying low and slow, wagging its wings from side to side in the international symbol of recognition. Cheers and sudden love for their fellow men breaks out all over *Midnight Special*. The crew knows further elation when a *SouthCare* medevac chopper hovers over their deck moments later. Paramedic David Dutton jumps into the water and quickly motions for the crew to leap from the boat and swim to the horseshoe collar. There isn't much time, he tries shouting over all the noise. We're low on fuel and have to do this quickly. The crew sends dermatologist David Leslie first. As a physician, he can report their condition.

Leslie takes a deep breath, calculates the distance to Dutton, then jumps feet first into the water. It settles over him, and he has to fight his way back to the surface. Leslie spins, only his head above water, looking for Dutton. There he is, directly beneath the chopper.

Behind Leslie, on board *Midnight Special*, bricklayer McDonagh and nursery owner Bill Butler wait their turn to leap. The rest of the crew, unable to squeeze on deck, wait below for their turn to ride the winch. All those hours of tension are finally gone, replaced by the relief of imminent rescue. With their smiles and backslapping, they look and act like a boatful of regular blokes again. The midlife crisis has passed.

Leslie slips the strop over his arms and shoulders. Dutton gives the thumbs-up and the winch ride begins. They spin slowly as the cable lifts. Leslie is turned away from the chopper, toward the boat, so that he can see his mates below, all happily watching the lift. Leslie is all smiles himself. He spins slowly, glances up at the open door, feels the brace of Dutton's knees on his ribs, and is awash in a security and happiness like none he has ever known. More than anything, Leslie feels alive. What a wondrous sensation.

The cable continues to spin. Leslie looks at his mates again, just in time to see another rogue roll *Midnight Special*. The entire crew has been watching Leslie and Dutton. No one saw the wave. Now the boat is upside down, with absolutely no one in the water. There is nothing Leslie can do. And while he's thrilled to find himself safely in the chopper, his spirits sink even lower when the helicopter begins speeding away. Almost out of fuel, the pilot is running for shore. Both Leslie and Dutton peer out the door as *Midnight Special* disappears into the distance, still upside down.

• • •

Roughly forty miles away from *Midnight Special*, Steamer and Gibbo watch the sunrise—a misnomer, as the horizon simply fades from black to dark gray—back to back. They've worked out a system through a night of rolls. They sit back to back, pressing their legs against the outer rim of the raft. This keeps them both inside the ring, surrounded from smaller flecks of water by the raft. Each keeps his own thoughts, constantly searching the skies for aircraft. And while the presence of the other is reassuring—what must the others be going through all alone?—they hear and see nothing. The greatest emotion is abandonment, as if the world somehow misplaced them and hasn't seen fit to find them yet.

"How you doing, Gibbo?"

"I'm alive, Steamer." Gibson's tongue is thick from swallowing salt water. The words come out like syrup.

"Good on you, mate."

• • •

Polar 1's crew overnights in Mallacoota. They're back at the airfield for preflight and briefing at four-thirty. They take to the skies at six, once again headed for *Winston Churchill*. And once again, they're diverted, this time to *Midnight Special*. Neither David Key, Barry Barclay, or Darryl Jones knows what to expect. The last reported sighting from *SouthCare* showed *Midnight Special* inverted after getting hammered by a brute wave. If need be, Key—again the swimmer, with Barclay on winch—can climb on top of the boat and pound on the hull to see if men are trapped inside.

But there's no need. *Polair 1* finds *Midnight Special* righted. Except time is short. Everyone is on deck and she's sinking quickly. Well versed in the art of weather-bomb rescue after his *Kingurra* experience, Key is almost nonchalant about the challenge, remarking seriously to pilot Jones that the waves are "only" fifty feet and the wind "only" seventy miles per hour. But as the rescue begins, Key begins fearing for his life. The waves knock him against the hull of *Midnight Special* again and again. He swallows so much salt water that nausea overwhelms him, and he feels without the strength to finish the rescue. But he forces himself to work faster rather than slow down—the job has to be done, there's no time for Barry Barclay to slip on his wet suit and take over, and *Midnight Special* is sinking. Key hauls up exhausted crew, one by one.

When Key finally rides the wire down for the last rescue, he sees a monster wave bearing down on the boat. It's a half mile away and moving quickly. Key drops in the water, swimming quickly to the sailor. The man is exhausted, and too hypothermic to say his own name, so Key never finds out who it is. The sailor's core temperature is so low that he doesn't even realize he's in trouble. When Key tries to coax the man into the water to slip the rescue strop on, the sailor refuses. He tells Key he'd rather go down with the ship.

Midnight Special is barely above the water now. In the end, the sailor doesn't leap into the water so much as wade over to Key. Collar on. Thumbs-up to Barclay, and then the winch jerks skyward. *Midnight Special* is still afloat. But less than thirty seconds later, and well before Key climbs into into *Polair 1*, *Midnight Special* slips beneath the Bass Strait forever.

Darryl Jones points *Polair 1*'s nose into the wind. It's time for everyone to go home. At least this time he's got just enough fuel to get there.

● ● ●

By 11 A.M., not a single plane or helicopter has flown in the vicinity of Gibbo and Stanley. The hypothermia is getting worse, with both men shivering violently. They have never known such exhaustion and hunger. A scan of the horizon shows no sign of their shipmates' bobbing vests. And while neither says anything to the other, each is shocked at how pale his companion looks. Yet their spirits have lifted, if only slightly.

The waves are small, the wind is calm, the rain is intermittent. The longest night is truly over for Gibbo and Stanley. Somewhere, alone, Mike Bannister, Jimmy Lawler, and John Dean notice a change in the sea, too.

The weather bomb is no more.

■ ■ ■

Rough Seas Barrage Race; 2 Dead

Sydney, Australia—Two sailors died, 15 were missing, and an American was among the 56 who were rescued after gale-force winds and two-story-high waves battered yachts Monday in the 725-mile Sydney-to-Hobart race.

The two dead were Australians, found on the 40-foot vessel *Business Post Naiad*, 60 miles off the New South Wales state town of Merimbula.

Bruce Guy, the owner and skipper of *Business Post Naiad*, and first-time race participant Phil Skeggs, were killed, Australian Maritime Safety Authority spokesman David Gray said. Guy had a heart attack during one of the two occassions the boat rolled, Gray said, while Skeggs drowned when he was unable to free himself from a safety harness. Their bodies were left on board the boat, but attempts were being made to recover them as soon as possible.

The 70-knot gales snapped masts, tore holes in decks and hulls, and devastated crews as at least 37 yachts were forced out of the race, which was narrowly led by American maxi *Sayonara.*

Nine crew were aboard the missing cutter *Winston Churchill*, and contact was lost with the five crew aboard *Solo Globe.*

British sailor Glyn Charles was swept off the *Sword of Orion* on Sunday night when the boat rolled in wild seas and remained missing.

Race officials said Charles had sailed in four Admiral's Cups and represented Britain in the Star class at the 1996 Atlanta Olympics, finishing eleventh.

One of the missing yachts, *B-52*, was found heading toward Eden on the New South Wales coast. The nine crew on board were thought to be safe and the vessel was sailing unassisted.

American John Campbell was rescued by a police helicopter after being swept overboard when *Kingurra* rolled 22 miles south of Gabo Island.

—*Los Angeles Times,* December 28, 1998

SIXTEEN

THE MAELSTROM

Monday, December 28

The *Sydney Morning Herald*'s headline screams "Man Lost As Fleet Takes a Battering," but the debacle of the 1998 Sydney to Hobart becomes more than just a local piece on Monday morning. The world soon knows about the weather bomb. Accurate details are hard to come by, and many incidents happened late Sunday night, so the stories appearing in newspapers from Los Angeles to Paris to Tokyo have conflicting accounts of how many men and boats are missing. No one knows, actually, not even AusSAR or the CYCA. When *B-52* motors into Eden, Don Buckley phones his wife, Fiona, by cell phone. She's been waiting anxiously for word of him, calling the CYCA at all hours for status. They know nothing and can tell her nothing. When Don relays the word that he's fine, she passes along the news to the CYCA.

"Don's in Eden?" comes the incredulous reply.

"Just spoke with him."

"Would you mind calling him back? If possible, we'd like him to get the names of all boats in port there."

Because his boat was without radio, not even CYCA commodore

van Kretschmar knew of the storm's severity until late Sunday night. While sailing *Assassin* back into port, he finally raised the CYCA by cell phone when the crew passed Wollongong. "I knew something was wrong when I called the club at ten P.M. and a director answered," he recounted the next day. "When they told me what was happening, I was devastated. The whole crew was. People were dying—people that I know were dying."

Van Kretschmar, a tall man with a casual air, announced that an inquiry would be conducted by the CYCA. Skippers would be solicited for comments on everything from conditions to boat construction. Privately, van Kretschmar suggested that few remedies were available. The problem lay with weather forecasting and skippers making improper decisions. "We need seminars to instruct people when it's proper to go out. But we also need more real-time data from the weather people. The East Coast low doesn't fit into meteorology's deliberate delivery—they happen too fast. Kenn Batt and Roger Badham both intuitively started to get concerned about East Coast lows, but couldn't send out an official warning because it was deemed too subjective. It would be hugely beneficial for Sydney to Hobart to have guys like this allowed to speculate."

In the future, van Kretschmar would take greater control of the race by installing a rounding buoy off Eden or Gabo so the fleet wouldn't stray so far from shore. "If there's trouble, they can seek shelter immediately."

At no time during the storm did van Kretschmar or any CYCA official consider canceling the race, whether out of respect for the dead or as a safety precaution. Spokesman Peter Campbell noted that "had the Cruising Yacht Club of Australia acted to stop the race at that stage after the bomb hit, many more yachts and their crews would have been lost as they turned back into what became the worst part of the storm." Campbell went on to point out that all skippers, via official CYCA documentation, were reminded of Rule 4 during the prerace briefing December 24.

A public furor rose in Australia when Prime Minister John Howard defended the race's right to continue. "I'm not a yachtsman. I have to respect the views of people who are and understand the sea. It sounds pretty sensible to me that the only principle you can work by is that each skipper is in command of his ship and he alone has to decide what the boat is going to do. I'm persuaded of that."

It would become a point of contention in the weeks to come, with the country divided. On one hand would be those empathetic about those lost at sea (and Howard's apparent heartlessness), placing special focus on the loss of national treasure *Winston Churchill*. These people would say Sydney to Hobart should have been canceled the moment the storm hit. They will say Howard has no right to defend yachtsmen. They will make the case that as long as public monies are being spent on the rescue (and AusSAR will later announce a tab of $650,000 for civil resources. The cost of assistance by defense aircraft and the HMAS *Newcastle* is not included), the nation has both the right and duty to enforce codes of behavior on adventurers.

On the other hand were those who believed that Australia was a nation founded on self-determination. This attribute is displayed best by her athletes and adventurers. The sailor was a special breed, not given to backing down in the face of incredible odds. Like the eighteen-foot-skiff racers duking it out in the waters of Sydney Harbor long before, Sydney to Hobart skippers were only taking competition to its logical conclusion.

The government, seeking to quell the outrage, will launch a Coronial inquiry into the tragedy. The Bureau of Meteorolgy will launch an inquiry of their own and in May 1999 declare themselves exempt from all blame. The sailors alone were responsible, the BOM report would say, due to their inability to fully comprehend "the severity of conditions when a storm warning is issued."

The report would go on to promise that the BOM would intensify its efforts to insure that the sailing community had access to high-quality weather information and "a high level of understanding for them of that meteorological information." The bureau's staff in Sydney, the report will conclude, performed to a high standard throughout the event.

The CYCA will fire back with their own report a week later, blaming the BOM for vague and unreliable forecasting. The CYCA's report concludes by noting that at future Syd-Hobs, BOM forecasts will be supplemented with expert weather information broadcast regularly to the fleet from the radio-relay vessel *Young Endeavour*. The individual hired to do those broadcasts will be Roger "Clouds" Badham.

Throughout Monday, December 28, the scale of worldwide media coverage expands, even though the storm is passing. The disaster touches a nerve. This was more than just a bunch of sailors blundering into a storm. What struck so many, and what made this disaster different from the Everest tragedies of 1996, which also rocked the world, was how completely average Sydney to Hobart sailors were. Just regular guys with regular jobs pushing themselves to their mental, physical, and emotional limits. Many had everything—career, family, money—yet the allure of risk drove them past a limit where normal men would stop. And so tragedy struck some, as it inevitably would. Was this an object lesson or a call for people everywhere to examine their lives and ask why they weren't asking more from themselves?

Journalists of all stripes—photographers, writers, TV types—camped on the CYCA doorstep or in Eden and Merimbula and Mallacoota. Every major news organization in the world covered the story. The AusSAR issued information through an official spokesman, letting a select few journalists into AusSAR's War Room to watch the SAR team in action. The BOM put a gag order on all meteorologists, instructing journalists to seek a department spokesman. The BOM Web site, once the scene of up-to-date weather photos and forecasts, suddenly became impossible to access. The Telstra Sydney to Hobart Web site was deluged. Every group knew a little about the status of their piece of the puzzle, whether it be weather, boats, or rescue. But each shared little with the other, and even less with the press. Hence, the original death toll was predicted to be as high as sixty, and the number of boats equally grand. It was all grand and surreal, the disinformation. Nine crew members of the *Winston Churchill* were bobbing like corks in the Bass Strait, location unknown, and battered sailors filled hospital beds from Merimbula to Mallacoota to Perimbula District's thirty-bed hopistal, where the lone doctor worked non-stop for a day tending over forty wounded (broken bones, cuts, and deep-tissue bruises the predominant complaint), but people were already trying to cover their tracks to escape blame.

The conflicting information could be insidious. Sue Psaltis was inundated when news of *Midnight Special*'s problems were aired, as many thought newscasters were speaking about *Midnight Rambler.*

In Melbourne, Annie Goodman learned of Glyn's disappearance Monday morning. *Sword* had not lost a Sydney man, but a British Olympian, eleventh in Atlanta and projected to medal in Sydney. Annie cringed as Glyn's life and death—was he really dead? They hadn't given up already, had they?—were vividly recounted. Official word of the search was front-page news, second only to *Winston Churchill*'s disappearance. Britain went into mourning over Glyn's death. London newspapers made Charles front page news, as well, right alongside a piece about four climbers killed by an avalanche in the Scottish Highlands the same afternoon. Editorials about the adventures and men and women pushing themselves too far and public monies being spent to rescue private individuals crept into papers everywhere, but especially in Sydney. When Glyn's death was confirmed, Annie flew back to London and went into hiding with friends. She refused to speak with anyone about Glyn's death.

Margaret Charles, a sweet woman suffering the loss of her only son, watched in horror as camera crews and journalists tracked her movements. "He was a good boy and he died doing something he loved," she said publicly, while politely asking the journalists to remove themselves from her flower beds. "He was a wonderful son and a loyal and supportive brother to his sister, Merrion, as well as being devoted to his girlfriend, Annie."

Glyn's loss wouldn't sink in for almost six weeks, and Margaret Charles finally dropped the stiff upper lip to blurt out how horribly she missed him. "What I have the most trouble with," she confided, "is that he's not coming back. Not ever. That thought sinks in so slowly, and I'm only now coming to grips with it."

• • •

Sword of Orion's crew never saw her go under, but she is assumed sunk. "*Sword of Orion* has not been recovered. The crew is of the opinion she would founder in any significant seaway," Kothe said in a statement. Despite his injured knee, Kothe was not lifted off in the night with the first group of *Sword*-sailor rescues by Sea King. He went with a second group hoisted off three hours later.

Steve Kulmar, taken aback by the tragedy, rethinks his lifelong commitment to blue-water racing. "My brand-new seaboots and wet-weather gear are still aboard *Sword of Orion*," Kulmar, the last man lifted from *Sword*, said. "She has sunk. There is no better place for them. I will never do another Hobart race."

The rescue of *Sword*'s crew was not without incident. The crew leapt into the water to await the rescue strop. When it was dropped to Kulmar, his life jacket interfered with his ability to slip the sling over his shoulders. Three times he thought he was ready to go, and three times the winch began lifting, and three times he dropped back into the sea. Kulmar, disgusted and scared, fought the last fall hardest and separated his shoulder. The current had forced Kulmar away from *Sword*, and he was floating alone two hundred yards from the boat when the navy Sea King finally decided to lower a swimmer to help.

Dazed, broken, Kulmar felt the rescue swimmer attach the

strop. Lifting to the heavens, he saw brilliant flash of white light above him. It was the Sea King's spotlight, but Kulmar was convinced it came from heaven. He was unable to decide whether he was living or dead. "That was the defining moment," he said later. "I knew that if I were alive, I would never do another Hobart. My wife, my children, family, and friends meant too much to me—nothing else."

In Newcastle, the families of *Solo Globe Challenger* are heartened to hear that Tony Mowbray's crew is being lifted off by helicopter. Mowbray tries to sail her back to Eden, but finally gives up and accepts rescue by the HMAS *Newcastle*. His dream boat is salvaged by an Eden fishing trawler and towed back to port.

Two other boats send Maydays Monday. Roger "Hicko" Hickman's *Atara* is in trouble off Gabo Island at 9:55 A.M. And the yacht *Miintinta*, whose owner Brian Emerson's prerace plans for the run to Hobart included "plenty of time for baked dinners and lots of chilled wine to make the going that little bit easier," is floundering farther east of Gabo's black hole. Waves are swamping her and she's taking on water. The *Atara* later rescinds her Mayday and continues to Eden on her own power. But *Miintinta* continues taking on water and sinks. A fishing boat rescues the crew before she goes down. Emerson, miffed, immediately declares he's going to sue the CYCA and the boat's manufacturer to recover costs.

Little by little, loved ones across Australia breathe a sigh of relief as the whereabouts of all sailors and vessels become known. The last boat on her way to Eden is *New Horizons*. She should be in port by dawn Tuesday. During one of her four rollovers, *New Horizons* lost her radio to an infusion of salt water, so she calls in Maydays by cell phone. Her boom is lost and her engine doesn't run, skipper Mike Keliher tells AusSAR. A police launch is sent into the Bass to tow *New Horizons* home.

The only nine men not accounted for are the crew of *Winston Churchill*. Their search is updated hourly by radio and television newscasters. Crew relatives go into hibernation, waiting for word of raft spottings. Shirley Bannister, Mike's wife, has a bottle of champagne ready to uncork when the rescues are made. The couple met at a CYCA function twenty years prior, and Shirley likes to joke she married Mike "for better or sailing." She repeats it even now, though with a self-conscious grimace. Bruce Gould's family repeats their belief that he's been through a lot before, and he'll pull through just fine this time. His daughter Nancy believes that the sea is Gould's life. He's attuned to it, prepared for it. That, she thinks, will give him an edge.

• • •

None of the men lost at sea feel as optimistic. On Winning's raft, despair reigns. They haven't seen any sign of rescue. Everyone is severely dehydrated, hypothermic, and exhausted. Their biggest fear is falling asleep and not waking up again. Lumtin knows he's going to die if they have to spend another night in the water and fights the depressing thought of never seeing his wife and girls again. Every time he closes his eyes, he sees his daughters' faces staring back at him. He's sure the other men are thinking the same things.

The men are hallucinating, too, constantly imagining ships and planes. Lumtin feels himself separate from his body and imagines he sees his dead body floating facedown in the raft. So this, he marvels, is what I look like dead.

By the time 3 P.M. rolls around, men on both life rafts foresee another night in the ocean. Winning's raft is almost deflated, and the men make mental preparations for bobbing in just life jackets. Steamer and Gibbo—who has secured himself to the ring by cinching his rescue harness around the perimeter—swear a plane passes overhead at 3 P.M. But the plane doesn't see them, and they continue drifting. While the men of Winning's raft are younger and not injured, Steamer and Gibbo are almost dead. The combination of injuries and hypothermia has weakened them severely, and neither is capable of fighting the sea one more night. Even though the storm has passed, the waves are still roiling at ten to twenty feet and the wind whips at thirty knots. If a plane doesn't get to them before nightfall, neither man will last.

High above the Bass, Shane Pashley is focused on finding the men of *Winston Churchill*. Oblivious to the whirling intrigue, the world waking up to headlines about death on the Bass Strait, and the dire condition of *Winston Churchill*'s men, Shane Pasley fights to concentrate as his Sea Hawk flits above the waves. Forty aircraft are over the Bass Strait, most searching for *Winston Churchill*. Shane flies in the back with Aaron Abbott, scanning the sea for hour after hour. They've been in the air since early morning. The drill has been the same: sit in the open right-side door, cast eyes to the horizon, then reel them in slowly, scrutinizing every wave peak and dark spot on the way. Pilot Nic Trimmer flies a search grid that takes him back and forth over the seas. The only breaks in the monotony come from the occasional PC-3 passing overhead, or the runs back to HMAS *Newcastle* to refuel. When things get really boring, Aaron and Shane switch sides to get a fresh perspective. Shane finds it's easier to look out the left side. The door isn't open there, so he peers out a window. But while that wind isn't tearing into his face, it's almost easy to nod off. Not that he would. The helicopter's rotor roars and vibrates more than a bad roller coaster, a phenomenon enhanced by the wind.

Sometimes they chase EPIRB, sure that it's *Winston Churchill*. But time after time it's an abandoned boat, the occupants already lifted to safety. One of the boats is *Business Post Naiad*, the bodies of Guy and Skeggs still riding inside like a pair of Vikings on a modern pyre. They spot *Solo Globe Challenger*, empty, awaiting tow.

A few more hours and we knock off for the night, Pashley thinks, eyes moving to the horizon and slowly journeying back. Maybe one more refuel on *Newcastle* and we head back.

A search plane passes over Winning's raft at 4 P.M. Hastily, Winning steadies the flare gun and arcs a flare. The plane gives no indication it's seen them, however, and again the four wallow in the deflating raft, awash in misery. The sky shows no signs of clearing and the waves are still rolling high and hard. The men wonder if that plane was their last chance.

Twenty minutes later another plane. Winning fires another flare. This time, the aircraft flicks its landing lights on and off—hello. The four men cheer. Tears are in their eyes, and they allow themselves to dream of family and warm beds and food and dry land. Hope, a sensation they haven't touched in a day, courses through their veins. They've been floating in purgatory, not among the living and halfway to death. Suddenly, death feels so very far away.

The same plane flies directly over Steamer and Gibbo. Steamer waves the spare yellow life jacket madly. He's also wearing a white jacket, so he's sure the plane spots them. "He's seen us, Gibbo. We're right."

That's when they hear the rescue helicopter. Their spirits soar. The drama is finally over, and the two old friends finally relax. They've done it.

But the helicopter passes right over. It's *Helimed 1* and flies, oblivious, directly over Steamer and Gibbo on its way to pick up Winning's group. Both rafts have been blown one hundred miles in the twenty-three hours since *Winston Churchill* sank. The search has taken so long because no one thought to look so far away.

Incredulous, their morale lower than ever, Steamer and Gibbo keep their eyes on *Helimed 1*. Surely she's turning around. But she choppers over the horizon in a beeline, sealing the two men's destiny. They're to die in the Bass Strait atop the shreds of a German raft. This is it.

The mood is contrasted sharply over on Winning's raft. Tears of happiness and cheers all around as the rescue sling drops down. No sight or sensation in their lives—first kiss, wedding day, child's birth—compares. It's not until safely in the chopper that the men think of their crewmates and find that they're still out there somewhere. The men from Winning's raft are taken to Mallacoota, where all of Australia begins celebrating their rescue. Michael Rynan's tearful mother and father get in the car immediately to make the drive south. Robyn Rynan collapses in tears when her son's rescue is relayed. Champagne and beer flow freely in the homes of Richard Winning, Paul Lumtin, and Bruce Gould. Their joy is tempered by the notion that another raft is still missing. But to have the men safe . . . the four families' joy is sublime and wondrous. Hearing the news of *Winston Churchill*'s raft being found, Michael Bannister's family pops champagne of their own. Surely their dad is among the rescued.

It's dusk now. A pair of PC-3 Orions zoom over the ocean, trying to find Steamer and Gibbo before sundown. There was an earlier sighting, but that proved inaccurate. When the plane returned to the site, the men were gone. No raft. Scanning the seas with a special heat-seeking device, the RAAF Orion gets no readings. It looks like another night at sea for Steamer and Gibbo.

But at 8 P.M., just before the sun goes down, an Orion crewman spots the raft. Still no readings from the heat sensors, and the crewman thinks the men are dead. The real reason is that the body temperatures of Gibbo and Steamer have sunk so low. The call goes out for a rescue helicopter.

Shane Pashley's Sea Hawk is about to call it a night when the PC-3 call comes. Nic Trimmer has just refueled on the HMAS *Newcastle* and has plenty of fuel to effect rescue, but the important thing is to make it happen quickly—darkness is falling. In fact, by the time the Sea Hawk hovers over Steamer and Gibbo, it's definitely nighttime. Trimmer radios a visual identification, saying he's spotted two survivors. Shane Pashley is already suited up and rides the wire down to the raft. Trimmer, looking down from the pilot's right-hand seat, is impressed with the professionalism of Steamer and Gibbo. Rescue crews like sailors to collapse the roofs of their rafts and sit on top during the rescue. Usually sailors have to be asked. But those two guys have already done it.

Pashley gets wet. He kicks slowly to the raft, fighting a strong westerly current. The wind doesn't blow steadily now, but gusts. The waves are still surprisingly aggressive and large. He grabs the rings on the edge and pulls himself up and over into the raft. He expects to land on a hard rubber floor, but instead he's back in the water. It doesn't register that the raft has no floor. Shane kicks back to the surface and looks at the two guys. These two blokes, he'll tell the crew later, were hanging on the edges, using their arms and legs as if they were sitting in a bathtub. Though Gibbo has full wet-weather gear on, Steamer is wearing just shorts and a spray jacket. Shane can tell that both men are in shock.

"G'day," Pashley says casually.

"We're right happy to see you, mate," Steamer says just as calmly as if they'd seen Shane only moments before. He'd actually like to show more emotion, but he hasn't got the strength. Shane thinks both men look like death warmed over as he untangles Gibbo's safety harness from the raft and affixes the rescue collar.

Gibbo and Shane begin the ride up. But the weather bomb's unholy alliance isn't finished toying with the fleet. A last-gasp jet stream gust slams into the Sea Hawk. Trimmer can't hold position as the helicopter is literally shoved sideways for two hundred meters. At the end of the cable, Shane and Gibbo are dragged across the sea. Gibbo's tongue is swollen too big for his mouth from swallowing seawater for twenty-eight hours. Even more water is shoved down his throat as he and Pashley are dragged, and Gibbo begins to choke. He wishes he could vomit as the salt water distends his stomach, but he cannot, and the water simply sits there.

Shane rotates their position quickly, so that Gibbo is above the water—above Shane. After what seems an eternity of confusion and indecision, the cable ride begins. Gibbo finally makes the chopper and is immediately wrapped in a thermal blanket and fed fresh water. His hand will need microsurgery, and word comes back that he's to be transported all the way to Canberra as soon as Steamer is pulled out.

KNOCKDOWN

Shane slips the rescue strop over his shoulders again and steps to the door's edge. He nods to Abbott for the cable to be lowered, but Trimmer's voice comes over Abbott's headset. The command is simple and logical, but its ramifications could be severe: the auto-hover is ineffective because of winds. If Pashley rides back down in the darkness and somehow loses his way back to the strop, there's no guarantee they'll be able to bring him back up. So he's to stay aboard. The strop will be lowered without a rescue swimmer.

So as good as Shane Pashley is, and after all this time waiting for the stars of Australian search and rescue to come to his aid, Steamer is now responsible for his own rescue swim. His destiny is in no one's hands but his own. It is an appropriate twist for a blue-water sailor.

The strop is tossed down. But Steamer's too weak to even dangle his arms over the strop. As the winch begins lifting, he slips out. Trying a second time, he rises twenty feet in the air before realizing he's tied a rope from the boat to his leg and the raft is trying to ride the wire with him. Broken ankle, darkness, and all, Steamer voluntarily drops himself back into the water. He's discouraged. It takes several more tries before he's lifted from the surface of the water. Finally, Steamer's hooked up and climbing to the chopper. For every moment of his ride, Shane and Aaron watch with bated breath—will he fall or won't he? When Steamer's close enough, both men lunge out and reel him in. The crew inside the Sea Hawk look at his waterlogged body incredulously—bare legs, arms, fingertips, and toes. Steamer is the most wrinkled thing they've ever seen in their lives.

"Where are the others?" Shane asks.

"Gone."

Tanzi Lea, the RAAF helicopter pilot who also flew over the Irish Sea as part of the 1979 Fastnet rescue, is part of the team that finds the bodies of Jim Lawler and Mike Bannister the following morning. The men are still in their life jackets. The body of John Dean has never been found.

"I let that man be the man he was," Shirley Bannister says when the news is broken. The champagne is put away, and she leans on their son Stephen for support. "And I would never have had it any different."

Bill Psaltis, given the news of lifelong friend Jim Lawler's death, is crushed. A brief flicker of an image—a phone call saying the same has happened to Ed and Arthur. He banishes the thought. His boys, Bill Psaltis hopes and prays, will pull through all right.

■ ■ ■

Media Release
17 November 1998

Festive Finish Planned for 1998 Telstra Sydney to Hobart
Cannons firing, spectacular night and day pyrotechnics, jazz
bands, a champagne celebration, and a special trophy presentation at historic Constitution Dock will mark the arrival of the
first three yachts to finish the 1998 Telstra Sydney to Hobart
Yacht Race.

The Cruising Yacht Club of Australia and the Royal Yacht Club
of Tasmania believe the finish of the 54th annual blue-water classic should have a festival of sail atmosphere similar to the finish
of the recent Whitbread Round the World Race and Gran Prix
motor racing events.

The Army will fire a cannon as the winning yacht crosses the
line off Battery Point on the Derwent River. Then, as she motors
to her berth outside Constitution Dock, the yacht will cut a rib-
bon across the new Kings Pier marina complex in Sullivans
Cove—heralded by jazz band and fireworks—and thousands of
Tasmanians and visitors.

The line honors winner, together with the second and third
yachts to finish, will berth alongside a large barge moored outside
Constitution Dock where, for the first time in the 54-year history of
the ocean classic, the line honors trophy, the JH Illingworth Trophy, will be presented immediately after the yacht has berthed.

Specially struck Telstra medallions will also be presented to
each crew member of the winning yacht—the first time the efforts of the crew have been recognized other than in the 50th
race in 1994.

Another first will be the presentation of trophies to the second
and third yachts to finish the 630-nautical-mile course.

The winning skippers and the crews, in between their celebrations, will be able to tell the public and the media through a public address system of their experiences during the race.

SEVENTEEN

HOBART

A single cannon round announces *Sayonara*'s arrival in Hobart. Fireworks and other celebrations have been scrapped as inappropriate. Instead of bands, a bagpiper plays a recessional, the piercing wail echoing along Constitution Dock. *Sayonara*'s crew are in shock as she butts up against the mooring. Due to the loss of their single-band radio, the crew received no news of storm fatalities until an hour ago, when Channel 10 sent a press launch to pull alongside for comment. The news hasn't sunk in yet. Distraught, fumbling for words, they step ashore. Some of their wives have flown down to wait for them, and as those men step ashore, they are enveloped in sudden screams of joy and loving arms. The words "I thought I'd never see you again" are repeated over and over as couples revel in each other's form, touch, smell; kisses and caresses.

Bill Woods watches from afar. The Channel 10 newscaster is finally wrapping up his three fateful days of coverage from Hobart. What was intended to be a jolly, chatty waterfront show had taken on the air of a funeral as the final numbers rolled in: fifty-five men rescued, six men dead. Two bodies—those of Glyn

Charles and John Dean—lost at sea. Normally, Woods is the hard-core journalist leading the pack in search of interviews. Now, as Larry Ellison steps ashore and is besieged by a mob of cameras and tape recorders, Woods maintains his distance. "I just didn't want to be a part of it," he will say later. "I'd just done a live feed and had sixty minutes until the next feed. I didn't go down to the boats. I just wanted to give those men breathing space."

Lachlan Murdoch steps onto Constitution Dock. Having passed muster, he will be selected over his siblings within the next month to take the reins of his father's media empire.

Sayonara didn't beat *Morning Glory*'s record, missing by five hours. And though they hit just the southern portion of the front, the wind and waves almost broke *Sayonara* in two. Ploughing straight over waves, she would free-fall into the trough. Weight-lessness would see men on deck seem to levitate five feet from the watch position during the five-second drops. Phil Kiely, head of Oracle Australia, broke his ankle during one such drop. The boat suffered damage, as well, with fittings seeming to disintegrate and the hull showing spots of delamination. An Oracle spokesman later downplayed the damage, saying it was just a matter of a few blown spinnakers and mainsail luff track pulling away from the mast. Nothing as severe as the rumored need to replace the deck, nothing that made the boat unseaworthy. But Ellison was panicked enough to issue a premature order to tack toward the Tasmanian coastline, away from the storm. Navigator Mark Rudiger cautioned that the move was wholly noncompetitive, and *Sayonara* risked letting the fading *Brindabella* catch up. But Ellison insisted, noting that they couldn't win the race if the boat sank. "Tack the fucking boat," he ordered Rudiger.

Now Ellison faces reporters, fighting back tears. "Sailing is supposed to be difficult, yes. Dangerous, no. Life-threatening, definitely not. If I live to be a thousand years old, I'll never do that again. Never."

Another *Sayonara* crewman, twenty-five-time Hobart veteran

Graeme Freeman, showed typical Aussie nonchalance. "The 1984 race was tougher," he said simply. But then added that this was his last Syd-Hob.

• • •

Earlier Tuesday morning, five hours before *Sayonara* will finish, Ed Psaltis was noticing kelp farther back along the Tasmanian coast. This is a good thing. Kelp means shore is near. Though Bob is a great navigator, Ed has been worried about their true position. When the GPS stopped working, and then the portable backup GPS failed, too, Bob resorted to dead reckoning. This involves keeping a close check on the helmsman's course, with the helmsman updating Bob on average bearing. Given the due-south nature of their attack, that angle is typically between 175 and 180 degrees.

The next step is for Bob to assess leeway, or amount of slippage to the east due to waves and current pushing *Midnight Rambler* sideways. This is difficult, as Bob has no instrumentation anymore to judge wind and current. He's also minus a boat-speed indicator, though he can approximate, as speed before the indicator broke averaged 7.5 knots. Ed flew a storm jib through the entire storm, never lowering to bare poles, so the type of sail isn't a variable affecting speed.

Then Bob puts all the information together, corrects for magnetic variation, and plots estimated position on his chart. Once that's done, Bob double-checks all the dubious information, then goes with his gut instinct about true location. Ed likes to say that a good navigator has a sixth sense that enables him to assess how all the factors are interplaying. Bob is one of these navigators. So it's with confidence that Bob passes along *MR*'s estimated position as the real thing during skeds. They're not in the top ten on Monday afternoon's sked, but they learn with disappointment that Bruce Taylor turned *Chutzpah* around. If nothing else, Ed wanted to beat *Chutzpah*. He wanted *Chutzpah* to finish well behind them, as ample confirmation of victory. But that's a moot point with *Chutzpah* out.

It's pitch-black on deck as Bob lies below, listening to the 3:05 A.M. sked and plotting positions. It's clear that *Sayonara* will win, with *Brindabella* two hours back. The storm has moved south with Ed, so he's still sailing in forty-knot winds. He's feeling aggressive though, and the mainsail is up. Suddenly, Bob comes running up on deck, screaming for Ed to get the mainsail down.

Ed, alarmed, gives the order immediately. Bob wouldn't make such a proclamation easily, so Ed is sure Bob saw the boat breaking up below.

"What is it? What's wrong?"

"It's our sked!"

"What about it?"

"It's really good."

"How good?"

"Ed, mate . . . we're winning."

Ed can't speak. He's overwhelmed with joy and disbelief. Bob continues, "The sked is so good, Ed, and we're leading by so much, that we would have to do something incredibly stupid like blow out the mainsail for us to lose this race."

The two partners look at each other, not knowing whether to laugh or cry. In all their years sailing, this is the most memorable sked they've known. Ed quickly passes the word to the deck crew, while Bob goes below to wake the rest. The jubilant crew crowds the cockpit, howling at the moon. They're doing it. One hundred miles from Hobart, taking the shortcut through the worst storm in Sydney to Hobart history. Is this a group of great sailors or what, they yell at each other. This . . . is . . . our . . . year.

No one sleeps for the next twenty-four hours. They learn that *Ausmaid* is behind. *Sayonara* finishes Tuesday morning, then *Brindabella*, then *Ragamuffin*. *Midnight Rambler* rounds Storm Point and angles up the Derwent River. This is the moment Ed dreamed of as a child—standing at the helm of his own boat, guiding her the last few miles to the finish. The radio crackles with congratulations, as the fleet learns that *Midnight Rambler* is the likely winner. The wind dies in the Derwent, and Ed is becalmed for a while. But they get the gust that propels them toward Constitution Dock. It's 5 A.M. Wednesday morning, with the sun barely lining the sky. Yet the dock is crowded with restrained well-wishers and media.

The maxis are all to one side, tied off. Just five have finished. No one on board has a cell phone, so Ed can't make a call as he angles toward the dock. If Ed had one, he'd call two people in a specific order. The first would be Sue. She's stuck by him, motivated him, believed in him. He'd call her and tell her what's happened and they'd share a laugh. Maybe—no, definitely—he'd have her wake the kids and let them know that Dad's okay and he's won the Sydney to Hobart. He'd tell Sue how much he loves her, and how he wishes she were here to share this great moment.

Then he'd call his dad. Bill would be restrained, of course. There would be congratulations, and maybe a reminiscence of the year *Meltemi* came close. Bill would give instructions for Ed to say hello to a few of the mates. Then Arthur would get on the phone to hear the same thing.

But no one has a phone. So Ed listens to the crew's jokes about taking a victory lap and guides his thirty-five-foot beauty into the dock. He aims her close; Arthur throws out a line. And just before *Midnight Rambler* is nudging against the dock—dry land, safety, the real world again—someone in the crowd catches his eye. So many people. Must be a mistake. It can't possibly be . . .

Sue.

She stands before him, beaming. At her feet is a celebratory case of Cascade lager. Ed can't get off the boat fast enough. He falls into her arms. This woman . . . this remarkable woman . . . "Congratulations," she says, pressing her face against his for this one private moment.

"I love you," he says. "I'm so glad to see you. So glad."

And they stand there, just the two of them. The crew is thrilled to have won, but their celebration is muted. Arthur steps in, presses a mobile phone into Ed's hands: "It's Dad."

And Ed Psaltis hears a sound he's never heard before: his father crying. Bill just wants Ed to know how happy he is that his boys are safe. That's really all that matters. The Psaltis boys are safe, and Bill wants them to know that he couldn't be happier.

"There's one other thing you should know, Ed," Bill says after they've gone over the details of the storm. Ed hasn't come down to earth yet (this is our year!), but the realization that his men survived a debacle is never far from his thoughts. If just one more wave had hit them those two times they were knocked down, they would have been rolled and dismasted. You could call it great sailing that pulled *Midnight Rambler* through, but you could also say it was a bit of luck.

"What's that, Dad?"

And now Bill's voice is emotional again. "Jim Lawler was lost at sea."

Ed deflates. Jim Lawler was as good as they come. Good sailors aren't supposed to die. This bit of mythology can carry a crew through an entire race, sure that their expertise will see them to safety. See them to home and family and all that really matters. But Jimmy Lawler's death gives lie to that myth. As time passes, and Ed learns about the other fatalities, it will become clear that all the dead were incredibly talented sailors. In the months to come, in those private moments where bravado is absent, Ed will reflect on that. And he knows he will never feel truly safe on a boat in the Bass Strait again.

At 5 P.M. Wednesday afternoon, the AusSAR War Room officially announces the end of the fifty-hour Sydney to Hobart search-and-rescue effort. The two missing bodies will never be found.

Life is not listed as a safe occupation. Life is full of danger.
—*Sayonara* helmsman Chris Dickson

PORTSMOUTH

Hugo van Kretschmar clears his throat. He speaks calmly, but clearly. "We will miss you; we will remember you always; we will learn from the tragic circumstances of your passing. May the everlasting voyage you have now embarked on be blessed with calm seas and gentle breezes. May you never have to reef or change a headsail in the night. May your bunk be always warm and dry."

On a hot summer afternoon, five thousand sailors, fishermen, rescue swimmers, helicopter pilots, and Hobart residents line Constitution Dock on New Year's Day. They've come to say good-bye to the six dead sailors of Sydney to Hobart. Flags are at half-mast on boats throughout the harbor, fingered by a small sea breeze drifting up the Derwent.

Karen Guy speaks next, telling of a father whose passion made Christmas synonymous with sailing. "Years of happy memories will now come back at this time of the year and are now more precious to me than ever."

Steve Kulmar eulogizes Glyn Charles, praising his sailing skills and fellowship. "He was a good bloke," a distraught Kulmar says simply. The mavericks of *Sword of Orion* stand at his side, all bruised and battered. They wear black suits, appear devastated.

Finally, Richard Winning, wearing a simple white sailing shirt, talks of three lifelong friends vanished. "A sea so vast and our boats so small" is how he describes their loss. Winning is not his composed self, but a man in flux. He has no plans to sail again, ever. He's lost, Winning says, "three terrific mates" and recounts the years of sailing with Mike Bannister, John Dean, and Jim Lawler. Paul Lumtin stands, feeling lost. The nightmares of being in that raft at night will not leave him, and he has begun drinking himself to sleep at night. It seems the only way.

The muted bells of St. David Cathedral toll as rosettes are cast into the water. The sailors of Sydney to Hobart weep openly, missing their comrades and remembering their own panic and fear as the waves tried to break their boats. Richard Winning and Rob Kothe shake hands warmly, just glad to be there. Sue Psaltis grabs hold of Ed and refuses to let go. How can she ever let him go to sea again?

The thrill of winning has left Ed, replaced by an emptiness. Friends have died, his dream is realized, and his once-focused existence needs a new direction. Now that he's won Sydney to Hobart, what's next? The notion troubles him, depresses him, makes him feel aimless for the first time since he climbed Barrenjoey Head at twenty-nine.

"This is necessary," van Kretschmar says of the memorial as it ends softly. "Every sailor here needs this opportunity to be with each other and put this in its proper place."

The feeling of necessity is shared by the people of Portsmouth. And so Glyn Charles is memorialized a month later by those who knew and loved him. The mavericks of *Sword of Orion* fly to England to say good-bye properly. Darren Senogles tells Margaret Charles of his great sorrow, and how hard he tried to save her son, and that there was absolutely nothing he could do to save him. The waves were so big. His guilt is enormous, and he can't stop telling Margaret how desperately he wanted to save her son.

KNOCKDOWN

And Margaret Charles, who knows a thing or two about loss, comforts the young man. As the mother of a sailor, she somehow knows more about the ways of the sea than her son, his friends, and men like them.

The church bells of Portsmouth toll for Glyn Charles, as they have tolled for sailors over the centuries. And from Portsmouth to Australia, the words of Margaret Charles to Darren Senogles are repeated in one way or another by the families of every missing sailor. "He died," she consoles Dags, looking him straight in the eye so his guilt will somehow diminish, "doing something he loved. That's the kind of man he was. He wouldn't have done it any other way."

In the end, this issue of motivation, and the nature of adventure and men who chase it, is best answered by Hugo van Kretschmar later that month in Sydney. A reporter asks if the tragedy will see the Sydney to Hobart field shrink. "Quite the opposite," Kretschmar chuckles grimly. "I expect the problems we experienced will make the race all the more attractive."